TRADING WITH
CROWD PSYCHOLOGY

WILEY TRADING ADVANTAGE

TRADING WITH CROWD PSYCHOLOGY

Carl Gyllenram

John Wiley & Sons, Inc.

New York • Chichester • Weinheim • Brisbane • Singapore • Toronto

To Ann-Charlotte, my wife, who is a very
special woman and the spark in my life.

This book is printed on acid-free paper. (∞)

Copyright © 2001 by Carl Gyllenram. All rights reserved.

Published by John Wiley & Sons, Inc.

Published simultaneously in Canada.

This publication is designed to provide accurate and authoritative information in regard to the subject matter covered. It is sold with the understanding
that the publisher is not engaged in rendering professional services. If
professional advice or other expert assistance is required, the services of a
competent professional person should be sought.

Library of Congress Cataloging-in-Publication Data:

Gyllenram, Carl.
    Trading with crowd psychology / Carl Gyllenram.
      p. cm.—(Wiley trading advantage)
    Includes bibliographical references and index.
    ISBN 0-471-38774-6 (cloth : alk. paper)
    1. Stock price forecasting.   2. Collective behavior.   3. Capital market.
    I. Series.

    HG4637 G95 2000
    332.63'222—dc21

00-039276

Printed in the United States of America.

10 9 8 7 6 5 4 3 2 1

PREFACE

David Fuller grew up in the United States, but has lived in London for more than 30 years. He is an internationally renowned analyst of the world's financial markets whose first official appearance in Sweden was in 1985, when he conducted his well-known "The Chart Seminar."

Chart Analysis Limited is David Fuller's base of operations. It has been one of the leading companies in the business for over 30 years, offering advice, seminars, and training in financial analysis and producing many publications. As an independent firm undertaking neither brokerage nor portfolio management, it is quite objective with regard to analysis, opinions, and recommendations.

Newly employed in the financial business in the United States, David was responsible for updating a large number of technical indicators that are intended to show the direction of the stock market. At a morning meeting, when the senior partners could not agree on the most likely development of the market, David was asked to explain what the indicators revealed. He replied that a third of them indicated a positive trend, a third showed a negative trend, and the remaining third was neutral.

Finally, David was asked to offer his personal opinion on the direction that the market would take. Fuller looked very surprised at the question and answered that he had no personal view. He knew only what the indicators showed.

Fuller realized that he had been too focused on studying indicators, and that he needed to expand his knowledge. Soon after, he was asked to teach an evening class in technical analysis at the New York Institute of Finance. He accepted the offer, but asked how, with his limited experience, he would manage. He was given a reassuring answer. All he had to do was to read a chapter in the textbook in advance and then repeat it in front of the class. Everything went according to plan until one evening, after David had explained that at a certain kind of signal the market moved in a positive direction, a student asked, "Why?" David had no answer. He did not know why. He had simply taught what he had read in the textbook.

David Fuller set about expanding his knowledge, reading all the literature available on technical analysis. His efforts nearly caused him to change careers. He knew too many rules, drew too many lines on the charts, and used too many conflicting indicators to be able to develop his analytical skills. Instead of observing with an open mind the drama that was unfolding on every chart, David was looking for stereotyped patterns.

Like most people, he reacted too late to changes in the market because he acted on facts that were obvious to everyone. Fortunately, he did not reject technical analysis at this stage, if only because he realized that a price chart was the easiest and smoothest tool for studying the market psychology. David realized that he had to understand why the markets reacted as they did. Once he concentrated on the fact that the chart formations he studied were "people patterns," created by you and me and everyone else buying and selling in the markets, his success as an analyst began. From his studies in psychology, he knew that people in a crowd quite easily lose their individuality and conform to their environment, making it considerably easier to predict the direction in which the crowd would move.

David Fuller has profound insight into traditional economic/fundamental analysis, but he is convinced that the study of the financial markets is essentially a behavioral science. Naturally it is important to understand specific economic factors, expectations of inflation and company profits, growth in gross national product (GNP), the direction of the economic cycle, and so forth, all of which affect the financial markets.

But it is difficult to come to any deeper understanding of the up- and downturns in the markets when taking only such hard facts into consideration and ignoring psychological mechanisms. Obviously, significant fundamental changes produce larger up- and downturns. But when do they start, and from what level? How quickly do they move? How high is too high, and how low is too low? These are some of the questions traditional economic analysis cannot answer; figures alone cannot explain market movements. A study of crowd psychology is essential to a better understanding of the markets.

As a young man with only a year of experience, it was very rewarding for me to participate in the seminar mentioned earlier and to hear how David Fuller had begun his successful career. This was especially so because, as a new employee of one of the larger commercial banks, I had presented my view on the most likely direction of the stock market with something less than success just before the seminar. When the most seasoned broker present asked condescendingly, "What the heck did the kid actually tell us? Will it go up or down?" it was abundantly clear that I had failed to get my message across.

David Fuller has an extraordinarily wide knowledge of when markets will move and why markets do what they do. Like so many others all over the world, I have been inspired by his behavioral approach to understanding and predicting how various markets are going to move. I thank him not only for the enjoyment and the knowledge I have gained listening to him and reading his discerning analyses, but also for his willing permission to make use in this book of the insights I have acquired from him.

CARL GYLLENRAM

Göteborg, Sweden
September 2000

ACKNOWLEDGMENTS

My thanks to Jan Ekström, my old and dear friend, whose help has been invaluable; David Fuller, who so willingly allowed me to make use of his profound insights; Tony Plummer, for his deep knowledge about crowd psychology; John Bollinger, who believed this book was worth translating; Pamela van Giessen and all her talented colleagues at John Wiley & Sons, whose efforts made this book possible; Joan Tate, who took the time and effort to translate this book; and Sigrid MacRae, who gave this book the American touch.

C.G.

CONTENTS

INTRODUCTION

This book is not intended to be a textbook on economic theory, the history of economics, investment analysis, or psychology. Nor does it claim to be a scholarly, academically accurate thesis. Instead, it was inspired by David Fuller's behavioral approach to the markets and is intended to describe my personal understanding of the importance of psychology in the stock market.

After more than 15 years at or near a trading desk, after discussing markets and stocks with thousands of clients, carrying out tens of thousands of trades and investments, and studying hundreds of thousands of charts on price and volume of individual stocks and different markets, I have come to a clearer understanding of how psychology influences stock markets.

My aim is to explain the various psychological mechanisms that play a role in the stock markets. A great deal has been said and written about psychology in connection with analyses and commentaries on the stock exchange. The following could be an example:

> When it became clear that the interest rate would not drop as anticipated, investors all rushed in the same direction, like a herd. Yet most profit lies in ignoring the experts and going against the tide. The stock exchange is ruled by young, nervous, savvy, and overpaid button pushers. Brokers dump shares in panic after an unexpected profit warning. Optimism about the year's market trend is obvious among the major market players. Trading today is

1

marked by uneasy and sporadic movements. Many investors, euphoric after a rapid rise, cannot imagine that anything might threaten this positive trend.

In spite of this, psychology is rarely considered an important
factor in explaining the behavior of the stock market. For years,
it was maintained, primarily in academic quarters, that the investor should make use of all available information in order to
create a "rational expectation" with regard to not only the future value of the company in which he or she is considering
investing, but also the general health of the economy. The stock
market is supposed to accurately reflect the value of the company; movements occur only when unexpected information is
presented. According to this view, financial markets are rational, stable, and effective; and it is impossible to predict when
there will be any movement.

But how can markets be consistently rational and effective
when it is human beings who are buying and selling stock?
Human beings are often noticeably irrational, not least in their
relation to money. Chapter 1 contains a study of one of the old-
est and most well known financial bubbles—the Dutch tulipomania, an excellent example of people behaving extraordinarily
irrationally in an economic context. Chapter 7 is an in-depth
analysis of economic theory versus the psychology of the markets. The following section is simply a taste of irrational economic behavior.

Abstract and Real Money

It is not unusual for an investor to be fairly unconcerned about
whether the stock market has gone up or down a percentage point
during any one day, even though it might mean that his net worth
had gone up or down by tens of thousands of dollars. Yet on the
same day, this same person may be noticeably irritated or pleased
to see that an item in a grocery store costs a dollar more or less
than expected. The owner of a major food store once told me
that, to his amazement, he sometimes saw some of the country's

major stockholders browsing through the cut-price special offers, pleased to pick up extra canned tomatoes or a package of candles because the price had been reduced by a few cents. Meanwhile, the increase in the value of their stocks in the course of that day might have been enough to purchase the entire store.

This is irrational but typical human behavior. Capital invested in the stock market is abstract—just figures on paper that cannot be physically touched. Until it is realized and the profit is in hand, or a loss has become fact, a change in value is perceived as relatively unreal.

On the other hand, the dollar bill taken out of your wallet is tangible, concrete. It is absolutely real. You see what it looks like, you can hear it rustle. Profit or loss is realized the instant the dollar is handed over and goods received in exchange.

But my approach to understanding and analyzing the markets is not based primarily on the irrational behavior of individuals because a single individual's behavior can be very hard to predict. Instead, I am interested in human beings in a crowd, as it is in crowds that people easily lose their individuality and adapt to their environment. In crowds, their behavior becomes much more predictable.

In this book, it is primarily the psychology relating to a long trading range that will be under scrutiny. Both the stock market as a whole and individual stocks are apt to spend a lot of time in phases during which they move laterally, with very little in the way of price movement up or down. When there is a powerful breakout—a rapid, major price change from the trading range with expanding volume—the psychological dynamic that plays out creates conditions for conspicuous crowd behavior.

Crowd psychology is a critical factor in explaining the stock market's behavior, and this book will take an in-depth look at the phenomenon of crowd psychology. Some statements and conclusions may be repetitious, but this is no oversight; it is a conscious decision. The same event will be seen through the eyes of different people in order to establish certain important psychological reactions that are shared by many people, despite different backgrounds, experience, and values. The aim is to give the reader insight into the way crowd psychology operates in the

marketplace and, I hope, to help readers to recognize and to identify with some of the characters in the book.

Cast of Characters and Companies Involved

Except for the real examples in Chapters 11, 14, and 15 and in
the glossary, all characters and companies in this book are entirely fictional; any similarities to real people or companies are
purely coincidental.

Principal Characters

Intersystems is a high-tech growth company with major opportunities for expansion within its niche because of its unique,
cutting-edge products. Listed on the stock exchange relatively
recently, the company was the winner of the year—the stock went
up several hundred percent. Then company management announced what amounted to a profit warning: owing to lack of
capacity and the acute shortage of qualified technicians, they were
unable to meet the great demand. During the coming year their
expansion and profit potential would be considerably inhibited.
These lower profits, but mostly the market's skepticism about
management, have caused a considerable drop in the share price.
As this story opens, the price of Intersystems stock has fallen by
more than 30 percent from its all time high.

Max Bork is an ambitious young man with a couple of years
experience as a broker. He works for Wilson & Partners as a
stockbroker for private clients. This entails keeping in touch with
these clients, suggesting trades, and making stock recommendations. Bork has very high expectations and hopes to be one of the
best in his profession.

Ian Benson is an engineer and a department head in an engi-
neering company listed on the stock exchange. Recently, he sold
his bonus options, making a handsome profit, and used the money
to open an account at Wilson & Partners. Ian Benson is very
pleased to have made what he regards as easy money. He now

wants to make even more money from "real" trading, figuring it cannot be particularly difficult to buy at a low and sell at a high. Ian is Max's latest client.

Other Characters

Lena Bergwall is not usually active in the stock market; but when she had an opportunity to participate in an initial public offering (IPO) that she was told was as good as risk free, she used part of her savings for a chance to test the water in the stock market, buying shares in Intersystems at the time of its IPO.

Kenneth Erland has never owned stock in an individual company and did not have the opportunity to buy Intersystems at the IPO. Apart from some savings in mutual funds, he has his money invested in high-grade bonds. When he sees a television program on this successful company, the temptation to put money into Intersystems overcomes him.

Samuel Rosenberg is a stockbroker with Berlin and Levander. He prefers long-term investments, and he has been happy to recommend that his clients follow the upward trend. He was pleased to see Intersystems constantly hitting new highs. Now, the sharp drop in price after the profit warning seems brutal and unexpected.

Peter Ericson has inherited a small portfolio from his mother. He is not particularly interested in the stock market, allowing his holdings to follow the market swings—up and down. Peter has noticed that even when he makes no changes to the portfolio, the value tends to go up from year to year. The bank's trust department looks after it, so he is active in the market only rarely. But now he has to do something; one of the companies in which he held stock has been taken over, and Peter has cash he wants to invest.

John Stennis thinks trading is fun, even though he has trouble understanding how the market works. Because he works nights, he can follow the market during the day. Several times a day he surfs the Internet to see if there have been any major movements. When he sees any rise or a fall that he thinks is unusual, he usually calls a broker at the local brokerage. The brokerage thinks John Stennis is a nuisance.

Karen Thurston manages individual portfolios for high-net-worth individuals for Credit One. She discusses various factors such as asset allocation, time horizon, risk level, and so on, with her clients and then makes investment decisions independently, without discussing them further with the client. Karen has not had any Intersystems in her clients' portfolios, and now she feels under pressure for not having invested in the winner of the year. Some of her clients have pointed this "mistake" out to her.

Chapter 1

TULIPOMANIA

One of the basic themes of this book is that people are just people—with all the irrationality and emotional behavior that entails. It is why people so often think more with their "gut" rather than with their heads. After experiencing a powerful, dynamic rise in the market followed by an apparently bottomless fall, it is easy to see this as something unique, something that will never happen again. So people feel they have learned a lesson, until the next time.

Yet financial bubbles and their collapse have been a constant element in the recent history and will be in the future as well. People are emotional creatures, not soulless, rational robots. Once a number of years have gone by after a major financial crash, there will be a significant number of investors who did not experience it, and the willingness of those "not involved" to listen to warnings from people who had expensive experiences is minimal. Just listen: "The situation is very different now." "You can't evaluate companies the same way anymore." "Different value norms apply now." "Market patterns have changed." "Recessions will never be that long or deep again." "The market is so liquid, you can always get out if it starts to drop." "We have much more sophisticated financial instruments to work with now than we had before." "You have to take big risks to earn big money." "High leverage is for everyone nowadays." "This is no game for weaklings." "High risks produce high profits."

It is true that norms and principles change. New financial

products will certainly be marketed, and the course of one business cycle is never quite like the one before.

Although both the desire for money and the fear of losing it have not changed—at least not in recent centuries—taking big risks has an unpleasant tendency to end in economic setbacks. Knowledge and technology have made huge advances in recent centuries, and presumably people have become more civilized. Otherwise, the only real difference between twentieth-century financial bubbles and the seventeenth-century "tulipomania" in Holland is that the objects of speculation now are securities, property, commodities, and currencies instead of tulip bulbs. What happened during the "tulipomania" was described by Charles MacKay in his 1841 book, *Extraordinary Popular Demand and the Madness of Crowds.* The story, presented in the rest of this chapter, clearly demonstrates that in spite of technical developments, behavior in the markets is essentially the same now as it was in Holland more than 350 years ago.

The Tulip

The *tulip*—its name said to stem from a Turkish word describing a turban—first appeared in Western Europe around 1550. Conrad Gesner, a Swiss naturalist who wrote extensively on botanical matters, said he first saw one in the garden of a lawyer named Herwart in Augsburg in 1559. Herwart had obtained the bulbs from a friend in Constantinople, where tulips had long been popular. Within 10 years, tulips were much sought after by the well-to-do, particularly in Holland and Germany. Wealthy Dutchmen brought bulbs home from Turkey, paying considerable prices for them.

Tulips increased in popularity; and by 1634 it was unthinkable for a man of position in society not to have his own collection. Soon the middle class caught the tulip fever; and despite the unreasonable prices they fetched, even merchants and shopkeepers of modest means began to compete with each other to acquire these strange flowers.

A Haarlem businessman was said to have been willing to pay

half his fortune for a single bulb, not intending to resell it, but simply to keep and admire it. It would be reasonable to assume that some special quality made the tulip so valuable and desirable, but it was neither as beautiful nor as sweet-smelling as the rose or the sweet pea, nor did it have their hardiness.

Charles MacKay made reference to *The History of Inventions*, a book by a poet named Beckman, for the following description of the tulip:

> Few plants—whether by accident, weakness, or disease—acquire such a variety of colors as the tulip. When growing in the wild, it is nearly always one color, has large leaves and an unnaturally long stem. When it has been weakened by cultivation, it becomes more attractive in the eyes of the florist. The petals are paler, smaller, and with more nuances, while the leaves are a softer green. The more beautiful this cultivated masterpiece becomes, however, the weaker it is likely to be. Even with great skill and care, both replanting and survival are rare.

To understand the irrational fascination with these delicate flowers, it is important to understand that subconsciously, people are often attracted precisely to those things that can create problems for them. In 1634, the Dutch passion for tulips was responsible for a serious neglect of traditional industry, for all levels of society threw themselves into the trading of tulip bulbs. As the tulip hysteria mounted, prices rose. In 1635, just one year later, 40 tulip bulbs could bring the fantastic price of 100,000 florins. Bulbs began to be sold by weight, in "perits"—a measure of weight even smaller than "a grain," the equivalent of 0.06 gram.

A tulip named *Admiral Liefken*, weighing 400 perits, was valued at 4,400 florins; an *Admiral van der Eyck* (446 perits) cost 1,260 florins; and a *Semper Augustus*, the most desirable of all, weighing only 200 perits was valued at 5,500 florins. The species was so sought after that even damaged specimens could fetch 2,000 florins. In 1636 it was announced that there were only two perfect bulbs of this kind to be found in all of Holland, one in Amsterdam and the other in Haarlem. Speculators were so eager to own these that one offered a nine-acre site with all rights of occupation for the Haarlem bulb. The Amsterdam specimen was bought for 4,600 florins plus a new carriage and two gray horses, with complete harness.

The following list gives some idea of relative costs of the period. One *Viceroy* tulip bulb, with a purchase price of 2,500 florins, would equal the total value of the following goods:

Two loads wheat	448 florins
Four loads rye	558
Four fat oxen	480
Eight fat pigs	240
Twelve fat sheep	120
500 liters wine	70
Four barrels beer	32
Two kegs butter	192
450 kilos cheese	120
A complete bed	100
A suit	80
A silver cup	60
Total	2,500 florins

A Hungry Seaman and an Enquiring Botanist

People who had been away from Holland and returned when this lunacy was at its height sometimes ended up in difficult situations because they were ignorant of the state of the nation. Two stories illustrate this.

The Seaman

One well-to-do merchant who was fiercely proud of his tulip collection was expecting a very valuable consignment from the eastern Mediterranean when a seaman came to his warehouse to inform him that the eagerly awaited goods had arrived in the harbor. To reward the seaman for his good news, the merchant gave him a tasty smoked herring for his breakfast. But the seaman was also very fond of onions and glimpsed a single onion, apparently abandoned, among the silks and velvets in the warehouse. He put it in his pocket to add zest to his herring and went on his way, untroubled, to enjoy his breakfast.

Hardly was he through the door when the merchant noticed that his valuable *Semper Augustus* worth 3,000 florins was missing. The entire trading house was in turmoil; everyone looked high and low for the precious little bulb, but in vain. Finally, the merchant brought all the curses of heaven down on whoever had stolen his valuable bulb. The search was taken up again, but again it was fruitless. At last, someone recalled the seaman. The unhappy merchant rushed to the harbor, his entire retinue behind him, to catch the wretched thief.

Unaware of the seriousness of his crime, the seaman was sitting peacefully on a heap of ropes, enjoying the remains of the "onion." He made no effort to hide; he could not have imagined, even in his wildest dreams, that he had just consumed a breakfast costing as much as the wages of his entire ship's crew for 12 months. Or, as the merchant who had been "robbed" put it: "Anthony had pearls dissolved in wine to drink the health of Cleopatra. Dick Whittington was just as foolishly wasteful when he was to entertain King Henry V; Sir Thomas Gresham drank a diamond dissolved in wine in praise of Queen Elizabeth; but the breakfast this villainous Dutchman has just eaten surpasses them all."

Because the price the poor ignorant seaman had to pay was spending a number of months in an Amsterdam jail, it is to be hoped that the costly bulb provided a memorable experience for his taste buds.

The Botanist

An amateur English botanist also came to grief on a Dutch sojourn when he happened to see a tulip bulb in a wealthy banker's greenhouse. Unaware of the value of the bulb, he took out his pocket knife and began peeling it, intending to carry out an experiment. He cut the bulb up into smaller parts, all the while making insightful comments on his findings. Suddenly the owner of the bulb was behind him, furiously demanding whether the botanist was aware of what he had done.

"I have peeled a highly unusual bulb," was the answer.

"A hundred thousand cursed demons," the banker swore. "That's an *Admiral Van der Eyck!*"

"Thank you," replied the Englishman, jotting the name down in his notebook. "Are these admirals common in your country?"

"Death and blast and bloody hell," roared the now nearly apoplectic Dutchman, picking the surprised botanist up by his collar. "Just you come with me to the magistrate. You'll find out."

Despite his protests, the English botanist was dragged through the streets, followed closely by a mob. Before the magistrate, he found to his dismay that the bulb on which he had experimented was worth four thousand florins. Despite the extenuating circumstances that the poor man enumerated, he was held in prison until he managed to arrange for the necessary guarantees of payment.

Hysteria

The demand for rare tulips increased so enormously in 1636 that regular markets for trading in bulbs were established on the stock exchanges in Amsterdam, Rotterdam, Haarlem, Leyden, Alkmar, Hoorn, and other large towns in Holland. Gambling cropped up for the first time. Speculators, always to be found when new business opportunities surface, did great trades in tulip bulbs, using the skills in which they were so adept to manipulate prices. At first, just as in similar instances, they were all delighted because they were making money.

Tulip brokers speculated on the rise and fall of tulip prices. Buying when the price fell and selling when it rose, they made huge profits. A golden carrot was dangled in front of people's noses, and one after another, like bees to honey, they rushed to the tulip markets to get rich.

Everyone thought tulip mania would last forever—that wealthy people from all over the world would buy tulips from Holland and pay whatever prices were demanded. The wealth of Europe would be concentrated in the towns by the Zuider Zee, and poverty would be banished from Holland's favored climes.

Noblemen, the bourgeoisie, peasants, engineers, seamen, soldiers, maidservants, chimney sweeps, and washerwomen— were all trading in tulips. People from all levels of society turned their property into cash and invested the money in flower bulbs. Land was sold for a song or assigned as security against the purchase of tulips.

Foreigners too were infected by the Dutch hysteria, and money poured into the country from all directions. Prices of both everyday goods and luxury items soared. For a few months, Holland looked like the antechamber of Pluto, the god of wealth in Greek mythology.

The trade gradually became so enormous and so complex that regulations for running it had to be instituted; public notaries and bookkeepers were given the sole task of ensuring that the tulip trade functioned satisfactorily. In smaller towns, where there was no regulated market for tulips, public notaries were replaced by "tulip notaries," and the largest inn usually served as a market. All social classes traded in tulips there, often confirming their deals with extravagant parties, sometimes with 200 or 300 people, and with great vases of tulips in full bloom on the tables for all to enjoy.

In the end, however, a few people with slightly more insight began to realize that this hysteria could not last forever. Rich people no longer bought tulips for their gardens, but only to sell. Clearly, someone was bound to lose in the end. As this realization spread, prices fell—and never recovered. Confidence vanished, and panic broke out.

The Sick Pallor of Hindsight

A and *B* signed a contract that stated that, six weeks after the contract was signed, *A* would buy from *B* 10 *Semper Augustine* bulbs at a price of 4,000 florins each. At the agreed time, B had the bulbs ready for delivery; but by then the price had fallen to 300 florins, so A refused to live up to the contract.

Day after day, there were reports of more and more broken contracts all across Holland. A great many people, who only a few months earlier had questioned whether there was such a thing as poverty in the country, now found themselves with stocks of bulbs that no one wanted to buy, even at a quarter of the price they themselves had paid.

Cries of anger, frustration, anguish, and desperation went up everywhere; anyone who had been your friend was now your enemy. The few people who had managed to get rich in the tulip trade were careful to hide the fact and invested their money abroad. Many of modest means who had risen to wealth, however briefly, were now thrown back to their earlier obscurity. Rich merchants became beggars, and many members of the nobility saw their family fortunes drained away so dramatically that they could never hope to recover them.

After the first alarm had subsided, the owners of tulips held public meetings to discuss measures to restore confidence. They decided that representatives from all corners of the country should go to Amsterdam to negotiate with the government. At first, the government refused to deal with the matter and advised the victims to find suitable solutions themselves. Meetings were held, but no solutions that satisfied the disillusioned or that even addressed some of their troubles were found.

These meetings were singularly stormy, with noisy complaints and reproaches. In the end, after much quarreling and many harsh words, the delegates assembled in Amsterdam decided that all contracts signed when the hysteria was at its peak— before November 1636—should be declared invalid. Contracts signed after this date could be dissolved by the buyer paying 10 percent of the agreed purchase price.

This decision was not greeted with much enthusiasm. The merchants who had tulips ready for delivery were not happy; and because the market price had fallen to about 8 percent of its original value, buyers who had to pay 10 percent were not happy either. Everyone tried to get the local courts to deliver judgments for breach of contract, but all the courts refused to deal with what they considered gambling debts.

The End

Eventually, the matter ended up at the provincial council in The Hague. Hopes that the wise men there would propose measures that would restore confidence and the reputation of the tulip trade ran high. As time passed, expectations rose, but no proposals were forthcoming. Week after week, members of the council continued their discussion. Three months later, when a statement was finally issued, it was nothing but a declaration that no decision could be reached without additional information.

The council did suggest, however, that the seller should invite his buyer—in the presence of witnesses—to keep the tulips in exchange for the agreed purchase price. If the buyer then refused to pay what he owed, the tulips were to be sold at public auction, the buyer to pay the seller the difference between the contract price and the price obtained at auction.

This proposal offered nothing that had not already been tried unsuccessfully. No court in Holland was willing to deal with the matter. A last attempt at arriving at a definitive judgment was made in Amsterdam, but the judges merely concluded—unanimously—that gambling debts were not debts in the eyes of the law.

After this, the matter was laid to rest. The government was unable to find a cure for the consequences of tulip hysteria. Those who had made money were allowed to keep it. Those stuck with nearly worthless tulip bulbs had to bear their loss as philosophically as possible. The Dutch economy suffered considerably, and it was many years before it recovered—but that is another story.

Chapter 2

THE FORMATION OF
A TRADING RANGE

When trying to predict price and market fluctuations, people generally rely on a number of commonly accepted standard patterns and formations. These can be identified by using such traditional technical analysis tools as *bar charts* or *point and figure charts* (see glossary). Each pattern then has a shifting certainty of prognosis. The problem with this is that each pattern in a chart is unique. No single pattern is exactly like any other when it comes to both price and volume swings. Even if two formations look identical, the likelihood of other market conditions being identical is low. What is the general trend in which the formation is found? Is the market on its way up or down? Or is it standing still? What is the prevailing mood on the floor—euphoric, panic-stricken, abandoned, or guarded? What are the other important factors—bonds, currencies, and overseas stock markets, to mention only a few—doing?

If it were possible to produce a foolproof template of standard market patterns in charts, you could use them to become a successful and wealthy investor, calling in buy and sell orders from poolside. Traditional *technical analysis* (see glossary) has tremendous value, but technical knowledge without a real understanding of why so-called buy/sell signals develop will not make market swings comprehensible. Unless the psychology behind up movements and down movements is understood, it is easy to miss what is truly critical in the analysis—crowd psychology. And what is studied there is not chart patterns but people patterns. It is people who buy and people who sell; predictions should focus primarily on the most probable behavior of a crowd.

Most of the formations and patterns found in charts are variations of a trading range—the difference between two relatively stable price levels between which a stock price moves for a certain length of time. Markets and individual stocks usually stay still most of the time regarding price, regardless of trends up or down. Actual up-or-down fluctuations tend to be relatively swift, with longer or shorter periods needed for the market to gather strength before the next price move.

This chapter will use three hypothetical trades to show how trading ranges are formed. But first meet Ian Benson and his broker, Max Bork, the two main characters in the "drama" of Intersystems.

The First Trade

Buying Opportunity—Max Bork at Wilson & Partners, Stockbrokers

Max is an ambitious young man with a couple of years of experience as a stockbroker for private clients. He very much wants to show Wilson & Partners what he can do, but he sometimes feels that trades recommended to the firm's clients should be researched more thoroughly. Max wants his clients to feel they can really trust him. So in situations where he and the firm's analysts have differing views, he dutifully presents the analysts' conclusion to the client, with no exaggerated enthusiasm.

When it comes to Intersystems, however, the situation is to be different—and more fun. There is good chemistry between Bork and the pharmaceutical analyst. She is not status conscious and has no need to be overly assertive. Both her manner and her method of analysis are straightforward and clear. If she thinks one of the companies she is tracking is worth buying, she says so. When she has to explain her conclusions, she explains herself simply and clearly, without getting tangled up in theoretical valuation models.

When at the beginning of November, she presents her buy recommendation for Intersystems, Max is infected by her enthusiasm. In this instance, she also has a little more to add. This story is such a good one, it might even work for his latest client, Ian Benson. Max doesn't think there is anything really wrong with Ian Benson; it's just that he made some money very easily and now thinks he is unusually smart. It's just a question of buying low and selling high, Ian told Max the first time they talked. When Max delivered the standard response that if it were that easy, all brokers would be as rich as Croesus, Benson hadn't answered. He sounded a bit condescending, as if Max were too dim to be rich, and he, Benson, could quickly show him how to beat the market.

As expected, when Max calls to suggest that he buy Intersystems, Benson is reluctant. How can it be worth buying, he asks, when it is valued four times higher than the company he works for? Max is not annoyed; he's mentally prepared for Ian's reaction. Calmly and carefully, he explains the difference in value between growth companies and companies sensitive to the business cycle. When Benson still hesitates—in spite of Max's efforts to explain that this is a really good opportunity—Max puts extra pressure on his client's tenderest spot. The price has actually fallen more than 30 percent from its high of 162. It's really cheap now, says Max.

Almost immediately, Benson changes his attitude. Why didn't I say those magic words, "It's really cheap now," in the first place? Max wonders, surprised at the reaction. Now, instead of pushing, he has to stop Ian and ask him to consider the risk. Putting more than 25 percent of your money in any one individual stock is definitely not advisable. (See Figure 2.1.)

But Max is satisfied with the deal. He has acquired a new client by selling him a stock in which he truly believes. Now the time has come to call his other clients. If he could get Benson to buy, he should be able to get his other clients to buy, too.

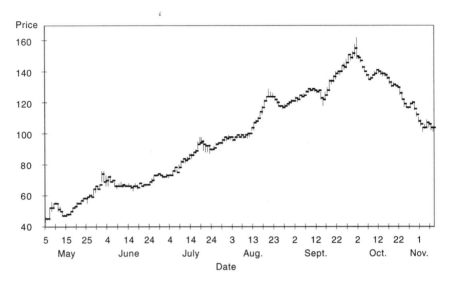

Figure 2.1.   Intersystems price chart. First trade—Ian Benson buys at 105.

Buy Order—Ian Benson

Ian Benson is an engineer and a department head at a company listed on the stock exchange. He has recently opened an account with the profits he made from selling the options he acquired as an employee. Delighted with what he sees as easy money, he now wants to devote himself to "real trading." However, he has heard from a colleague that many brokers like to make trades just to earn commissions. So when the eager, fast-talking young broker calls to suggest buying stock in a company that Ian knows nothing about, he is a bit suspicious. The broker is keen to close the deal, but Ian thinks that the recommendation to buy seems to have been carefully thought through. The broker's pharmaceutical analyst visited the company and concluded that the drop in share price after a profit warning was an overreaction. She feels that, considering the company's long-term potential for growth, the current price is clearly attractive.

Still, Ian is not willing to buy shares in a company that he does not really understand and that does not seem to be significantly undervalued. But when the broker tells him that the price has fallen more than 30 percent from its high, Ian immediately decides to buy. (See Figure 2.1.) If the shares have already fallen that much, the risk of future price declines must be very small, Ian figures. He buys a thousand shares of Intersystems at the beginning of November. He would really like to buy twice that much; but because the broker is emphatic about the risk being too high, Ian contents himself with a thousand shares.

Now that he owns stock, Ian realizes that he is much more interested in reading his morning newspaper's business pages than he was before. Trading is really fun. He hasn't seen any big profits yet, but up 2 percent after a week is actually not a bad annual rate. Then, about two weeks later, he reads at breakfast that the financial paper feels that Intersystems stock is undervalued and feels an almost physical pleasure.

He knew he had done the right thing. He knew he was clever. Trading isn't all that difficult; buy low and sell high. Ian's only regret is that he didn't start trading the stock market sooner.

When the stock market opens, he calls his broker. Up 4.5 percent. He knew it, he knew it! This'll be a good deal! If he had listened to himself instead of Bork and had bought more shares instead of keeping the rest of the money in his account, it would have been even better.

Next day, he calls the broker to check the price and is told that Intersystems has dropped more than 1 percent. Oh well, Ian sighs to himself. The young man actually said he was looking at an investment horizon of several months.

During the next weeks, Ian delights in following the price trend. The Intersystem's managing director is interviewed on the television's *Economy Facts* program and talks captivatingly about the great opportunities for expansion in the company's niche. The company is analyzed by a well-known business journal and given a positive rating, although the analyst does see some risk of a correction if the expectations of major growth are not met. They have to carp about something, Ian thinks, now feeling very pleased with himself. It is the second week in December and the price is 125, the same return a decent bank interest would have provided—over four or five years, not five weeks.

First Selling Opportunity—Max Bork

At the morning meeting, the pharmaceutical analyst gives a presentation on Intersystems. She thinks the stock is not yet really fully valued; but it has begun to approach her estimated target price, so she wants to post a "heads up." She is contemplating changing her recommendation from buy to hold. She emphasizes that this is not a recommendation to sell but feels that for clients with short-term investment horizons, there are reasons to consider profit taking.

Max Bork's attitude is more that of a trader than of an investor, and he finds the situation unambiguous. This is an excellent opportunity to sell. If he doesn't advise his clients to sell now and make a good profit, and the analyst really downgrades her recommendation, there is a real risk that all Wilson & Partners' other clients will push the sell button at the same time. Besides, most of his clients snapped up Intersystems below 107, and he knows that many of them like making quick profits.

Max thinks it will be exciting to see how Benson reacts. I won't be all that surprised if he is sulky and suspicious. He's sure to think I'm just trying to make commissions. He seems to think trading is as easy as learning to ride a bike, he thinks to himself. (See Figure 2.2.)

Sell Order—Ian Benson

Ian Benson is surprised when his broker calls to suggest he should sell his shares of Intersystems at 125. Ian is attuned to hearing good news about the company. Everything seems to be going swimmingly at the moment. Why shouldn't the share price go up again to its previous high of around 160? If the price has gone up almost 20 percent in just six weeks, Ian thinks, it could well go up by 50 percent in a year.

But the broker sticks to his guns; their pharmaceutical analyst feels the shares are now fully valued. It was to be a trade, not an investment, and one shouldn't be too greedy. A profit is al-

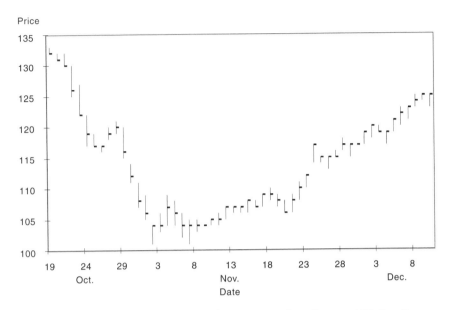

Figure 2.2. First trade—Max Bork recommends selling at 125. Ian Benson says no.

ways a profit, he says. Still, it is Ian's money, and of course, he can do as he likes. No one can force him to sell.

Ian Benson is surprised. The company fully valued! The managing director had talked about expansion over the next 10 years, hadn't he? The problem was that he hadn't bought enough shares. No, he should have done what the big boys do: pushed the boat out—not listened to advice about diversifying, like a cautious clerk contenting himself with a mere thousand shares. Still, he has to admit that it was the broker, not he, who had made the recommendation: their analyst ought to know the company better than he does. Apart from what Max told him, he knows no more about Intersystems than the little he has read in the newspapers and heard on television. He doesn't like this pressure to make a decision when he feels so uncertain, and he doesn't like his indecision either. His stomach clenches slightly. Suppose he sells and the stock doubles, as he suggested to the broker? Or suppose the price goes down? Then he would lose his profit. In anguish, Ian decides not to sell, but he follows the stock price very closely over the next few days. (See Figure 2.2.)

The next day, he has no desire to call to ask about the price. If he is advised to sell again, he doesn't want to appear to be shilly-shallying, so he can't decide. Instead, he goes into the board room and studies the Reuters screen. Intersystems has gone up to 127! Well, he wasn't really worried. It's a good company. Trading isn't so hard.

Now all he has to do is wait until the shares reach their high, then sell. How disconcerted that young whippersnapper in the big city will be when he, Ian Benson, calls and firmly asks him to sell—but at a price considerably higher than the price at which he had been recommended to sell.

Over the next few days, Ian follows the quotations on the Internet. Nothing much happens. The market doesn't go up or down, but just remains static. All he has to do now is wait for the next jump, then the broker will see just who was right. On December 17, Ian looks at the opening price and gets a minor shock. The screen says Intersystems is down 7. That must be a mistake. A stock can't go down that much so quickly. Some nervous young broker must have pushed the wrong button. Tensely, he waits in front of the screen for the next quotations, annoyed that the prices are not updated in real time. His head is swimming, but he feels better when he remembers that he hasn't actually invested any more than 25 percent of his money. His profit—even if the quote is true—is still a decent one.

Second Selling Opportunity—Max Bork

What happens is exactly what he had been afraid of. That clever Benson didn't want to sell, did he? Instead he, Max, was almost reprimanded. Although Benson didn't actually say so in so many words, there was no mistaking his annoyance when he said his holding could have been bigger. If Benson really thinks the shares are sure to go up 50 percent, there's no point in banging my head against a wall, Max decides. It's Benson's money, after all, and you actually do have to be humble. Persuading a client to sell and then watching the price soar is a pretty effective way of undermining the relationship.

A week or two later, when Intersystems falls 7 points in one day, Max feels a certain malicious pleasure, but he quickly shakes it off. Work isn't about triumphing over a client, it's about suggesting good trades. Still, Max thinks, Benson can just sweat it out for a while. He actually hurt his pride the last time they talked, with those innuendoes about inexperienced brokers. I wonder if he's still so cocky, Max thinks, as he picks up the phone to call Benson. (See Figure 2.3.)

Sell Order—Ian Benson

Later that day, when Ian gets the call from his broker, he feels almost grateful. He hadn't been able to bring himself to pick up the phone. As expected, the broker again recommends that he sell, even though he says there's not much to worry about. The

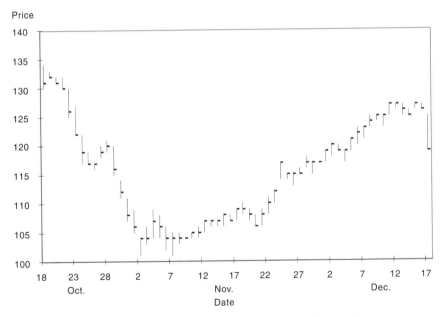

Figure 2.3. First trade—Ian Benson sells at 119.

market seems to be overreacting. A competitor has published an earnings report that was lower than expected, so Intersystems has fallen, too. The other company, however, is in a niche with different requirements, and their poor results shouldn't affect Intersystems' share price. It's only profit taking; unfounded nervousness has lowered the price, the broker says.

Again Ian is indecisive. Yesterday, everything was so obvious and easy, but now he doesn't know which leg to stand on. Should he sell now or wait until tomorrow? Or maybe he should just look at the whole thing as a long-term investment? At the same time, he doesn't want to look like a dithering beginner in Bork's eyes. He thinks for a minute or two; then, going along with the dictum "it's never wrong to take a profit," he sells his shares. (See Figure 2.3.) Thirteen percent really isn't bad at all. Still, he's not sure he has done the right thing. He tells himself that the next time he makes a trade, he will be surer—more decisive. A few days after closing, Ian takes off for the Christmas holidays. In spite of himself, he can't seem to stay away from the tape. The first thing he does every morning after the market opens is to see if the price of Intersystems has changed. He is glad the market is closed on weekends because then at least he doesn't have to worry about whether he has done the right thing.

In the first week of the new year, he notices that after a failed attempt to go up, the shares fall below his selling price. He feels calm, pleased with himself. It's just as he had said from the start: Buy low and sell high. It simply isn't all that difficult. Gone is the humiliation he felt in the days just after he sold. In his next trade, he will be tougher and play for higher stakes. Then he can build up some capital quickly.

The Second Trade

Buying Opportunity—Max Bork

Max Bork is enjoying life. His clients have congratulated him for the way he handled Intersystems. That is just the kind of business his clients love—a quick, profitable trade that makes everyone happy. And his timing was almost perfect. Still, if Intersystems falls to an attractive level again, his rationale to buy will be a bit more aggressive, and he will also try to persuade the clients who had refused to buy last time. He is sure to get more orders from those clients who made a handsome profit. They are positively inclined toward the stock now because they have made money on it.

Max feels impatient. After the sharp drop of 7 points in one day, Intersystems climbs for more than two weeks. Then in the first week of January, the price declines sharply. When the power behind the drop fades, the price inches slowly downward. His fingers itch to do something. It would be fun to call his clients to tell them that the time had come for a sure-thing trade. When he talks to the pharmaceutical analyst, she insists that her fundamentally positive assessment of Intersystems is unchanged. There are no definite signs that the company's market has been affected by reduced demand. Actually, it just seems that one segment, in which the competitor is active, is a bit weak. But she wants to be surer of this before she upgrades her recommendation to a buy.

Max thinks he knows what will happen. All the analysts are being guarded now, and no one is willing to make a buy recommmendation until Intersystems next report is published. If things go well, the crowd behavior will no doubt be as it always is, with everyone saying buy at the same time, and then it is too late to act. No, this time he will be tougher than usual. This time he will follow his own instincts. As he picks up the phone, Max wonders what Ian Benson's reaction is going to be. (See Figure 2.4.)

Buy Order—Ian Benson

Back at work, Ian is ready for some new trades. He is tempted to buy back the shares he sold earlier, now at a lower price. He certainly does not want to buy at a higher price than last time. But the price is not behaving as he would like. It has not moved

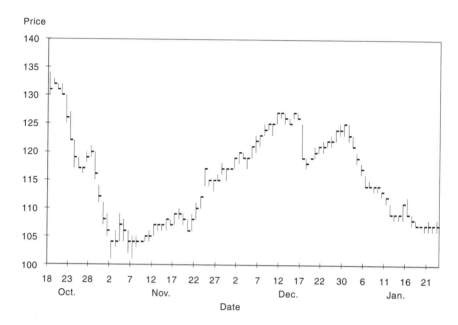

Figure 2.4. Second trade—Ian Benson buys at 107.

from a point or two above his previous purchase price for several days. His impatience mounts. He would like to call the broker and leave a buy order twice as big as the last one.

When the young man calls to say that their pharmaceutical analyst is considering a renewed buy recommendation for Intersystems, he is rather annoyed. It goes against the grain to buy so soon; still, he doesn't want to miss such a good opportunity. Well, greed wins. Though he does have some doubts, Ian buys twice as much as before—two thousand shares. (See Figure 2.4.)

A Sweaty Forehead—Max Bork

Phew, says Max, wiping his forehead. Things get anxious when Intersystems suddenly starts to drop, just as he was busy pushing it to his clients. He has decided to be logical and follow his own line; but clearly, you have to wonder whether someone out there knows something you don't know. Intersystems drops several percentage points in one day at the end of January. Soon Benson will be on the phone wondering what happened. He seems to think that all market moves are logical, and that you can always explain everything.

Max understands that sometimes you don't actually know why a stock goes up or down. It could be because of some new analysis that has just been published or because a major investor has decided to dispose of a large holding. He has to admit he's uncertain, and it is unpleasant now that Intersystems has fallen below the level at which his clients bought the last time. Though he still thinks he has done the right thing, it seems best to take it easy. If he keeps pushing and the report is bad, he will have trouble justifying his actions. He decides to advise those clients who have already bought to hold on to their shares. He will wait before recommending Intersystems to other clients until the report is published.

A Burst Balloon—Ian Benson

Nothing happens to the share price over the next few days. Ian is more and more convinced that he has actually done the right thing. For someone as clever as he is, he thinks, making good trades is really not a problem. But the next day, somebody has burst his balloon. Unexpectedly, incomprehensibly, Intersystems stock drops several points.

This is a new situation for Ian: he is now trading at a loss. But after a day or two of anguish, he's used to the new situation. No panic here, no sir! A professional would never sell at a loss, he argues. All you have to do is keep cool and wait for it to go up. When Intersystems slowly starts to climb upwards just as he had hoped, it is a very satisfied Ian Benson who reads the tape. That's the way things should be done, he thinks. If things go awry, just wait it out. It always goes back up as long as you keep your nerve.

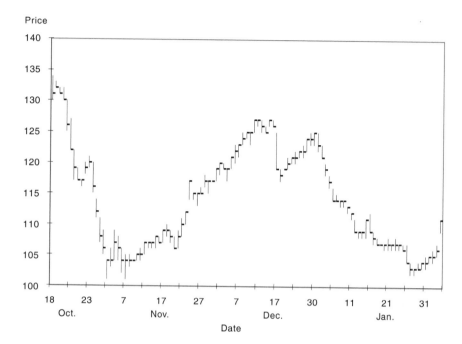

Figure 2.5. After a positive report, Intersystems goes up.

Joy and Frustration—Max Bork

The morning after the report is published, when Max sees that an important daily financial paper has put Intersystems' report in large, fat headlines on the front page, he is both pleased and frustrated. (See Figure 2.5.) It feels good to have been right and to know that many of his most important clients already have a stake. On the other hand, it is horribly annoying that he had not dared to be really consistent and to act on his idea. If only he hadn't worried about there being an unusually large number of shares on the market at the point where he wanted to buy and had just had faith in himself, he would be in an ideal situation now. All his clients bought, or had at least been asked whether they wanted to buy Intersystems at a very good price. He would have been king of the market. What timing—just before the coming bonus negotiations!

Once he has cooled down, Max turns rational again. The price may well spike up sharply today, he thinks, but this rise will very probably hold steady for more than a day. The price has actually fallen off a little since his last recommendation, so clients buying today should still be able to buy at a decent level, he reasons. He decides to follow up his original idea and push Intersystems.

A Swelled Head—Ian Benson

Now that Intersystems has gone up again, Ian is feeling fine. (See Figure 2.5.) He thinks of himself as having acted very professionally; the time has come for his colleagues at work to be made aware of his abilities. Benson remembers that his colleagues in purchasing used to say that people don't understand the market. When the talk during the afternoon break drifts toward the current trend in the stock market, Ian sees an excellent opportunity to show what he can do.

"No," he tells Johnson from purchasing. "You're wrong. You shouldn't just buy 10 different shares as a long-term investment. You should do what the professionals do: buy low and sell high." He can't understand why everyone thinks it's so hard, and he tells them about his recent advantageous trade in Intersystems.

"But what do you do if things go wrong?" asks Johnson.

"Just what the professionals do," Ian replies. "If you've bought shares in a good company, all you have to do is to keep cool and wait until the price goes up again. Only amateurs sell at a loss," he says with confidence. "Not only that, but Intersystems is a growth company. It can increase its profits over 10 years. Companies like that never have anything more than a correction on the exchange."

Nearly all his colleagues in the lounge have made money on their option programs, and several of them are influenced by Ian Benson's self-confidence. Greed and envy are a powerful combination. It's very irritating when Benson just sits there smugly, making easy money. Some of them decide to ask their broker the next day what the thinking on Intersystems is.

Bork and Benson—Symbiosis I

The next few weeks are good ones for both broker and client. Intersystems puts in a stronger performance than either of them had dared hope for. It is clear that investors really do appreciate a growth company that meets its projections—and with interest to boot. The rise to 127, which previously took about six weeks, is now accomplished in little more than three weeks.

Selling Opportunity—Max Bork

From the beginning, Max had decided to recommend that his clients sell when Intersystems reached the level at which it had previously turned downward. Now he has begun to wonder what to do next. For the first time in ages, he is actually considering looking at the long term.

The pharmaceutical analyst is more positive than she was the last time the shares were at this level. That isn't surprising; the situation at the company seems more stable now. If he recommends that his clients sell and the price continues to go up, some of them will be upset. But if he doesn't suggest taking a good profit, now that the price has reached the level he had planned and hoped for, and Intersystems starts falling, he risks being exposed to even worse criticism. Max also figures that there are several good reasons why his clients should sell right now. Later, he takes great personal pleasure in calling around to his clients, pointing out what a handsome profit they made in just a few weeks by following his advice. That makes him feel even better. This year he ought to get even better Christmas presents than last year, he concludes with some satisfaction. (See Figure 2.6.)

Sell Order—Ian Benson

Ian Benson thinks the recent weeks have been some of the best he has experienced in a long time. It has felt good to make money,

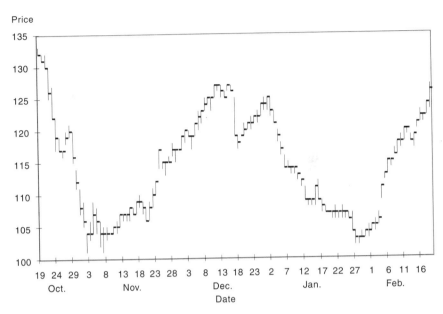

Figure 2.6. Second trade—Ian Benson makes another profitable trade and sells at 127.

and his colleagues in purchasing are treating him with much more respect than before. True, he has heard in a roundabout way that some of them think he goes on a bit much and acts too big for his britches; but then, everyone knows all that stuff about not thinking you are a hotshot. There is so much jealousy, Ian thinks philosophically. Making money on the lottery, pools, bingo, the horses, and so on, is perfectly all right, even acceptable. But if you're a clever investor, such as he is, envy soon rears its ugly head. Still, maybe he ought to tone it down a bit. Making copies of all the positive articles in the recent weeks' *Financial News*, putting Wilson & Partners name at the top, and then distributing the copies in the lounge may have been asking for it.

Though Ian Benson should have realized that Max Bork would be likely to call, now that stock has gone up 18 percent since the buy recommendation, he is still surprised when the broker phones with all his reasons why Ian should sell Intersystems. Just like the last time, Benson is attuned to hearing good news—not that there is any real reason for renewed nervousness about the company's growth possibilities, which could result in a sharp drop. He has to agree with Bork that the trade has gone well. It has gone up more quickly than expected. After some talk, Max asks Ian Benson what his trading strategy really is.

Suddenly, Ian has a "wake up" experience; this is exactly how he shouldn't behave: shilly-shallying. The last time it had cost him some of his profits and a great deal of torment. Now, when he thinks about how much money he has already made, the thought of taking the profit is suddenly an unalloyed pleasure. He is really happy to hear the broker close the trade while he's on the line. (See Figure 2.6.)

Bork and Benson—Symbiosis II

At this point, both broker and client experience a certain anxiety. It's strange, Max thinks, that you're almost always more worried about the market reaction after you've sold than before. It's hard for him to tear his eyes away from the screen. His colleagues have taken to calling him a "screenaholic" these days. Head in his hands, elbows on the table, he intensely studies every little movement of Intersystems on the screen, barely aware of his surroundings.

Business has actually been excellent, but he wants the stock to go down. It doesn't matter if it doesn't go down as much as last time, as long as it doesn't start flying. Now that everything is swimming along nicely, he doesn't want Intersystems to turn into a winner, jeering at him as it soars like a hot air balloon. If that were to happen, Max is afraid his clients would think he had been overconfident in recommending so unhesitatingly that they sell. But he has to admit that Benson really was making sense this time. After some thought, he had made a quick decision, telling Max that he had given his colleagues Max's telephone number, in case they were looking for a good broker.

Ian Benson is also feeling a little nervous after the deal. Now that his colleagues know that he has sold and made a tidy profit, there are some, with Johnson in the lead, who would be more than happy to see Intersystems turn into a high flyer. Ian actually feels quite pleased with his profit and lets his satisfaction show. But, of course, it would really hurt if some major investor decided that the stock was a bargain and started buying in a big way. It is hard not to keep looking at the quotes on the Internet now and again. Anxiety gnaws at him; perhaps he did the wrong thing after all.

One morning, someone has covered up the Board Room sign with a sign saying "Stock Exchange." Benson is not amused. He is very annoyed. The thought that he may have sold too soon becomes even more troubling and insistent.

The Third Trade

Waiting Time—Max Bork

Intersystems stubbornly remains just above the level at which the great majority of Max's clients disposed of their holdings. It would have been wonderful if the shares had taken a nosedive after all the sell orders were in, instead of hovering just a point or two above the selling price. Max thinks it looks more and more likely that someone, or some major operator, decided to buy a large stake in the company. He ought to have had a few more reservations and not been quite so emphatic in recommending that his clients sell.

He decides that greed is a serious affliction. If the stock continues to go up now, which he is beginning to fear it will, there will always be some clients who'll start whining. Instead of being pleased with a good profit, they will start grumbling about how much more money they could have made. Sometimes, he actually gets quite fed up with his job. If a trade has gone well, it was the client who made the decision. But if it ended in a loss, then it was always Max's recommendation that was bad. Oh well, most of his clients are actually very nice, Max says to himself. He'll just have to take it easy now and not get stressed. After all, his clients have actually made money.

If Intersystems keeps going up, he'll simply have to swallow that bitter pill. Even if he personally doesn't think it's wrong to buy the shares back at a higher price if demand turns out to be considerably greater than expected, he knows that it would be extremely difficult to handle his clients' psychological attitudes. How could he explain that selling at 127 turned out to be a mistake when he feels it is right to buy it back at a higher price? He doesn't even have any new information to back up his opinion, nothing but an intuitive feeling that it would be right. If the stock keeps going up, everything will be rosy. If he is wrong, he will really be opening himself up to criticism.

He doesn't dare take that risk. After all, if things don't develop as he had hoped, there are other stocks on the market besides Intersystems. Max feels that the situation is actually under control, if only he could stop looking at the quotes every five minutes.

Waiting Time—Ian Benson

Ian knows he is being irrational. He has made a really good trade and actually did what he had planned, but he doesn't want Intersystems to keep going up. He wants the stock to fall, quickly, dramatically, so that he won't have to wonder whether he was right to sell. He really ought to be walking around beaming instead of feeling disgruntled. If only Intersystems had gone down since he had sold, instead of going up a point or two, he would be really happy.

Ian is aware that this kind of thinking is irrational and absurd. But it is tormenting him, and he is having a very hard time giving up the idea that Intersystems might actually be a winner. He is so uneasy when he imagines Intersystems' stock soaring without his being in on it that the temptation to buy back his shares is very strong. But of course, Benson thinks, if Johnson in the purchasing department gets wind of his buying back at a price higher than that at which he had sold, he would laugh out loud. He would know that, in Johnson's eyes, he was an amateur and a braggart who had made a fool of himself on the market. As long as Intersystems keeps going up, Johnson will just go on grinning,

Benson says to himself. But if the price began to drop after he bought them back at a higher price, then Johnson would positively gloat. He feels tortured but decides not to do anything. If the stock goes up any more though, he will have to ask Max Bork for advice. Presumably that's what a broker is for.

What a Relief!—Max Bork

Great . . . great! The whole market keeps going down and Intersystems with it, after the major drop occurring late the day before. (See Figure 2.7.) Of course, his clients have other holdings besides Intersystems stock. It would actually be better if the market went up, but it is in Intersystems that he has invested his prestige. Wonderful! At last he can relax. Still, Max has to admit he really was lucky. If he hadn't been at a seminar yesterday when Intersystems at the opening jumped to reach the year's

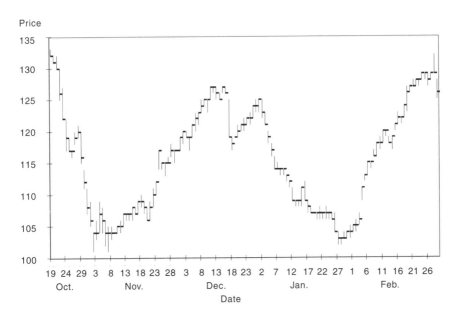

Figure 2.7.   After the major drop on the stock market the day before, Intersystems keeps going down and Max and Ian heave a sigh of relief.

high at 132, he doubts whether he could have kept his fingers under control and stopped himself from recommending that his clients buy back at least some of their previous holdings.

Now let's just hope that the downturn gets really serious, he thinks, so that Intersystems keeps dropping. It is actually one of the stocks that has done best on the exchange recently, which should mean that many investors will want to take profits.

Exhaling—Ian Benson

Ian breathes a sigh of relief. At last, Intersystems is falling. (See Figure 2.7.) When the price started spiking up at the opening the day before, he thought he'd get an ulcer. Now it feels good not to have to prepare any responses to Johnson's sarcasms when he goes to the snack bar today. True, he has been lucky, but he doesn't have to admit that in public. If the sharp downturn hadn't come after profit warnings from two major companies, Intersystems would certainly have kept on going up. What he would have done then he doesn't know.

Now he will see how the price develops. Benson figures that if the headlines about a crash on the front page of the newspaper turn out to be true, there may actually be a chance to buy Intersystems at a lower price for a third time. Should that possibility arise, he will invest a lot, he tells himself. The stock has shown that it always goes up again after a drop. Imagine the profit he would have made if he had put all his money into the two previous deals! That, he thinks with some frustration, would have been a return to brag about.

Buying Opportunity—Max Bork

The mood of the market is not exactly cheerful, Max decides. The downturn was sharper than both he and his colleagues had feared. It is really quite natural, considering the significant upturn on the exchange. His conclusion, however, is that this is a question not of a crash, but just of a sharp correction in an other-

wise positive trend. The anxiety over earnings doesn't seem justified, and he feels intuitively that now should be a great buying
opportunity—except that it's so difficult to counteract the pessimism prevailing among his clients and on the trading desk, not
to mention in the media.

Max knows from experience how quickly sentiment can
change, but he needs to summon up more mental energy before
tackling this situation. If he thinks about it, things aren't actually too bad. True, he ought to have suggested that his clients
sell some of their other holdings—not just Intersystems. But
Intersystems was by far the biggest position most of his clients
were holding. Most of them actually have respectable cash positions in their portfolios and can use them for bargain hunting.
That is how Max sums up the situation.

Inspired by his analysis, Max slowly but surely feels his ability to act returning. Now Intersystems has actually fallen back
to the purchase price. If there is an opportunity he ought to
exploit, then this must be it. Why hasn't he pulled himself up by
the bootstraps yet? When they sold Intersystems last time, he
even joked with his clients, saying that there might be a third
chance to buy the stock. Suddenly he is bursting with energy
and impatience. He simply must act now! If the third trade also
hits the bull's eye, his clients, colleagues, and, not least, his boss
will all realize that he has the right stuff to be a great broker. Ian
Benson is the ideal client for the first call, Max decides. Because
Intersystems was his only holding, he is in cash, isn't he? He
doesn't have a single stock. (See Figure 2.8.)

Buy Order—Ian Benson

Trading is just as he had imagined it: not hard at all—in fact,
quite simple. You buy stock in a good company that has gone
down for no apparent good reason and sell when the price has
bounced back up again. Then it's just a matter of waiting until
the price drops again and buying it back before the next rise.

Ian is nearly lyrical when he calculates the annual return on
his capital if he succeeds in a third trade in Intersystems, this

Price

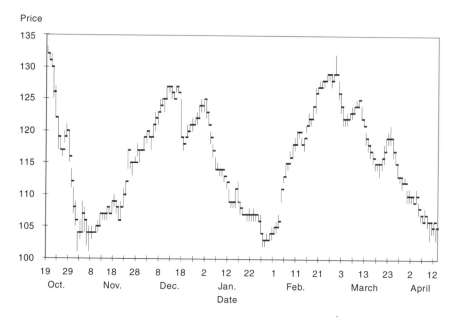

Figure 2.8.   Third trade—Ian Benson buys at 106.

time investing all his cash. Then, if he can continue making around a 15 percent return every time he trades, he should be a millionaire within two years, starting from the time he made his first trade. What a wonderful thought! Ian happily paints a mental picture of how he will handle his future trading profits. He imagines a Christmas cruise in the West Indies that would make Johnson green with envy.

When the phone call from Max Bork finally comes, he begins by expressing his annoyance with Bork for having waited so long to call. As a broker, he should understand that Ian is obviously interested in buying Intersystems again. It's really a silly question. No, this time he wants to put all his capital into one single trade. He had wanted to do that on the first and the second trades, but he hadn't had the nerve then. Yes, it may seem risky, but Intersystems always goes up again after a downturn. The company has an enormous market to penetrate with its high-tech products, and it is not sensitive to the business cycle. Ian has decided to do what the "big boys" do and get cracking. He feels pleased and very successful when Max Bork closes the trade while he is still on the line. (See Figure 2.8.)

Bork and Benson—Catching the Wave

Both Bork and Benson are surfing the waves of success. Inspired by how quickly Benson jumped on board, Bork frantically calls his other clients. It is a wonderful experience, feeling that he has them in the palm of his hand. He thinks they should buy, and they do as he says. But his colleagues are not going to allow Max to shine in solitary splendor; soon the entire trading desk at Wilson & Partners is wildly busy, touting Intersystems to their clients.

Ian has totally repressed how sweaty and stressed he felt on some of the previous occasions when he was wrong about Intersystems. The humiliation he felt then is nothing but a memory now. He knows how to make money trading, and anyone who cares to can listen to his advice on how to get rich. It amuses him that his colleagues think he is cocky. Most of all, he likes seeing Johnson's sullen expression.

Johnson isn't the only one who is jealous of Benson's successful trading and finds his self-confidence irritating. No one in the snack bar has escaped receiving bits of Benson's market wisdom. Even if few of them would care to admit it, many of his colleagues are pretty impressed, and they are tempted by the possibility of profits. As Benson puts it, it actually seems amazingly simple to make almost risk-free money in the market. If he can make money trading, they can, too, can't they? That is the growing body of opinion among Ian's colleagues when he is not around. If Benson risks investing his money in one single stock, then he must really be sure that it will go up. If he's been right before, he may well be right this time, too. If you're envious, but don't dare take the chance of speculating a little, you have only yourself to blame. This kind of thinking has taken root among Benson's fellow employees, and, over the next few days, the local brokerage notices that there seems to be an unusual amount of interest in Intersystems.

Bork and Benson—Symbiosis III

Bork and Benson are extremely pleased with the way things are going. They were right for the third time (Figure 2.9). When the Federal Reserve announces a lowering of the Federal funds rate rather than the opposite, which many people had feared, the entire market, including Intersystems, starts going up sharply.

Ian has invested all his capital in Intersystems and is enjoying contemplating the considerable fortune he will make, if only he can keep up the present tempo in his trading for a few years. It is almost incredible how quickly capital grows once you have a decent platform, he thinks. When he has gradually put together $2 million, one single deal bringing a 15 percent return means he makes $300,000. And when he realizes that he will make a very good annual salary in one single, successful trade, the thought is almost dizzying. If he goes on at this rate, he could actually become a full-time speculator. Ian smiles broadly.

The change in attitude in the snack bar also seems very

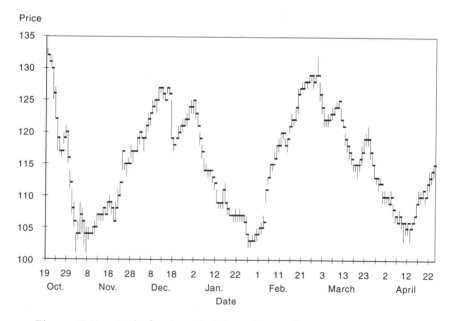

Figure 2.9. Right for the third time, Max and Ian are enjoying life.

positive. Suddenly, a number of people are unusually friendly and interested in whether he has any news on Intersystems. Does he have any opinion on how high the price might rise, and how quickly?

For his part, Max Bork feels he is on his way to taking the next step up to a higher level. His clients shower him with praise. Even his older colleagues show him more respect than before. If he continues to be as successful as he has been to date, there is no doubt whatsoever that he will soon have many more clients, all recommended by his present clients.

His ability to make money will increase geometrically and so will his value to the firm. Serious bonus discussions will be in order soon. It's been a long time since going to work was as much fun as it is now. He can't understand why he ever even considered any profession other than that of a broker. The pressure and the stress of clients complaining about poor recommendations and the stomachaches when the market moves in the direction opposite from what he predicts are now all forgotten. He is on his way to greater heights.

It is very difficult to predict how long a trading range will last. But one thing is certain—it never goes on forever. Whatever causes the breakout, either down or up, from the range—a strong or a poor report, a positive or a negative evaluation of the company's prospects, a rise or a fall in the dollar, strong buying or selling on the part of major operators, the launch or the discontinuation of a product, rising or falling bond prices—can never be known with any certainty before it happens.

Mental Preparedness?

Both Ian and Max assume that their third trade will also go well. They had been slightly unsure about the first and the second trades, but now there is no reason to worry. If it has gone well twice before, it must work a third time, too. They haven't even considered any other alternative. It simply can't go wrong. It mustn't go wrong. Ian has invested all his money in the deal, and Max has staked his career on being lucky the third time around.

Neither of them is mentally prepared for a price movement other than the one that happened with the two previous trades. Just as they are not mentally prepared for the unexpected, they naturally don't have a plan of action in the event that the outcome should be other than the positive one they anticipate. Their only preparation is what their previous experience has taught them: if things go wrong with Intersystems, just wait until the price rights itself again—since it always does!

The question is: What is their psychological reaction likely to be when the price takes an unexpected turn—up or down—from the established trading range? But before examining that question, the next chapter will touch on the psychological dynamic that takes place above and below a trading range.

Chapter 3

THE PSYCHOLOGICAL DYNAMIC ABOVE A TRADING RANGE

In Chapter 2, I described how psychology functions within a *trading range*, that is, how brokers and investors behave when a share price moves between two relatively stable price levels for a certain length of time. Those acting within the range are only a part of the market, however. Many people who own stock in a company are essentially passive when the stock is in a consolidation phase. In this particular time frame there may also be people who are not stockholders but who are watching the price with an eye to becoming buyers. All this is part of the constant "gamble" of the market.

Some try to exploit short, rapid price movements within a trading range. Others intend to sell or to reduce their holdings, but they feel the price within the range is too low and are waiting for the price to go up before they sell. Others may want to buy or to increase their holdings, but they feel the price within the range is too high and are waiting until the price is lower. Those who, for strategic or other reasons, have significant long-term holdings in the stock are not active in the market and so are not relevant here. However, this does not mean that major, carefully analyzed companies are not subject to crowd psychology in the marketplace.

Ericsson, one of the largest companies in the world and one that is quoted on the Nasdaq, is an excellent example of theory coinciding with reality. We will look at Ericsson later to see how stock prices may move when a long-term trading range is broken on the upside.

The Right Price

There is never a "right" price for a share. There are only perceptions, opinions, estimates, and calculations of what might be considered the right price. Then there is the price the market sets, though the fact that the market has set a price does not mean that an investor will accept that particular price. A market exists because there are buyers and sellers. The buyer naturally wants to buy at the lowest possible price, and, obviously, the seller wants to sell at the highest.

When a stock moves in a clear upward direction, the seller is in a positive situation. Often, if she is patient enough and has a realistic perception of prices, she can wait until the market has priced the particular stock at the price she considers the "right" price.

When a stock moves in a clear downward direction, the buyer is in a correspondingly agreeable situation. It is likely that the price will gradually approach his "right" price, if he is patient and his perception of an attractive price does not deviate too markedly from what might be considered reasonable. The investor also has the advantage of never *having* to buy. If the price does not go down to an attractive level, he can simply stay out of the market or forget about that stock and look for other opportunities. The seller, on the other hand, does not have that choice. If the price does not rise to the seller's "right" level, she has to either accept the prevailing price level or wait for the market to prove her right.

The psychological dynamic in price setting is usually set in motion when a trend—up or down—stops and the stock begins a longer consolidation period, that is, it moves laterally. Both markets as a whole and individual shares spend most of their time in consolidation phases. This is true regardless of whether the main trend is up or down. Actual movements in the market tend to be relatively quick; then consolidation phases are required for the market or the stocks to gather strength before the next real change in the situation. The longer the strength-gathering period lasts, the stronger the psychological dynamic will be. After a sufficiently long consolidation phase, a psychologically explosive situation has built up, which can result in powerful price movements, either up or down.

As mentioned earlier, most patterns and formations found in price charts are variations of lateral movements, consolidation phases, trading ranges, or whatever you care to call them. It is extremely important to be aware of the psychology that builds up in these phases if one is to gain any insight into the psychology of the markets. Understanding what happens here is essential to understanding how price movements—which many of those involved see as violent, unwarranted, and unexpected— are set in motion.

Of Course We Want to Sell—If the Price Is Right

Before studying the psychology of the seller—the psychological dynamic above a trading range—we begin with three short studies of individual investors that will provide a deeper understanding of the seller's situation and of how people with different experiences, backgrounds, and values behave similarly in a given situation.

Lena Bergwall

Lena Bergwall tells her friend that she is beginning to feel uneasy about the price fluctuation in Intersystems. She bought the shares at the IPO (initial public offering), and because the price is now considerably higher than at the IPO, she has made a very nice profit. Really, she ought to be extremely pleased, but she feels disappointed and increasingly uneasy. Originally, she had intended to use her savings to take a brief flyer on the stock market. Given the opportunity, it would have been stupid not to participate in the IPO when she was told that it was as good as risk free.

Lena's friend can't understand her disappointment. If she wants to use her money to renovate her house, all she has to do is sell and take the profit. Lena is inclined to agree with her, but she doesn't want to sell at a low price. For a week or two, Intersystems was around 150, and she now feels that it's beneath her to sell at more than 15 percent below that level. Why should she sell at a lower price now, just because the Intersystems price has suddenly begun to act like a roller coaster? She is certainly not going to let the market cheat her, even if she is impatient and it feels as if those wretched shares are never going to start to go up again. She doesn't really need the money yet.

About a month later when Lena sees her friend again, her friend asks whether she sold her shares. Lena is not exactly delighted by the question. She imagines that she sees a malicious smile on her friend's face. No, she hasn't sold them, she replies curtly, hoping to end the discussion, but her friend will not be brushed off so easily. Why not? the friend asks.

When Lena sees it is not malice but teasing in her friend's eyes, she admits that she hasn't sold her stock, mostly because she is greedy and feels tricked. Of course, Intersystems would have the effrontery to drop 30 percent since she first considered selling. She remembers that the last time she met her friend the price had actually been really good. At that time, she definitely did not want to sell below 150. On the other hand, now she would be more than pleased if she got that price. She has already planned how to spend the profit, but in recent weeks the price has dropped again. Now she is at once frustrated that she still doesn't have the money available to her and worried that the profit that had seemed guaranteed earlier is evaporating.

Yet Lena tells her friend quite definitely that she refuses to call the broker to ask him to sell at today's price. When her friend points out that the profit won't be enough for the planned renovation of the house if the price falls below 100, Lena feels like selling immediately. Her worry grows that the profit will slip away. She is tired of waiting for Intersystems to go up to its old high again, and she reluctantly resigns herself to selling at a price considerably lower than what she had really hoped for (Figure 3.1). If Lena is disappointed and tired of the market's sluggishness, she is still considerably better off than Ken Erland after he bought Intersystems.

Kenneth Erland

Kenneth Erland did not have the option of buying Intersystems at the IPO. Until he saw a program on television about several companies that would play a big role in the future, he had never heard of the company. Of the five companies mentioned in the program, Ken thought that Intersystems was the most exciting, with a unique product and the whole world for its market. He imagined how rich the company's founders must be. If you owned even a small piece of a company like that, he thought dreamily,

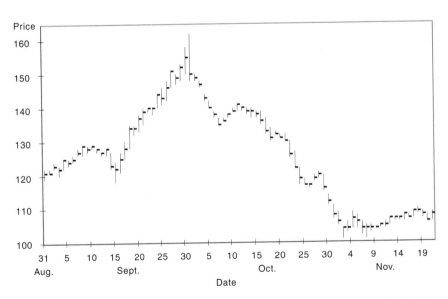

Figure 3.1. Lena gets worried that the price will drop below 100. She is also tired of wating for it to go back to its old highs and accepts a lower price than she had intended.

you'd be able to lean back in your armchair and just watch your money grow!

A few weeks later, Ken Erland is at his bank to discuss refinancing his mortgage. "If I were a part-owner of Intersystems, I wouldn't have to worry about a mortgage," Ken tells the banker.

"Why don't you become one then?" the fellow asks.

Ken is puzzled. "Are you kidding?" he asks, guardedly.

"Anyone can be a part-owner in Intersystems," the banker explains. "The company is listed on the stock exchange. All you have to do is put in a buy order with a broker."

Leaving the bank, Ken envisions himself lolling under a palm tree, sipping a rum punch, as the sun sets over Caribbean waters. He could actually sell his bonds and invest the money in Intersystems. That's the way to get rich: find a winner on the market and invest in it. He doesn't want to do what all the others do—play bingo, save in funds, and wait until he retires before he can enjoy life. But the idea seems to make him a little dizzy, and his stomach protests. He feels simultaneously exhilarated and slightly uneasy. The idea of doing something different, risking something, and having a little excitement in his life strikes a chord deep inside him, a chord he has hardly been aware of.

A few days later, he hears an item on the evening's business news about Intersystems winning a prestigious order against fierce competition. Now Ken Erland definitely decides to act. Next day, he is very pleased when the nice lady at the brokerage house puts through his order.

What Ken does not know is that since the IPO the stock has gone up several hundred percent. The price, especially these last few weeks, has been driven up sharply by all the news and positive reports published about the company. Like many others in the market, Ken has now been given the final and conclusive push he needed to dare to buy. He doesn't realize that his own actions are part of the final phase of the slight hysteria that has built up around Intersystems.

If Ken had studied the volume on the day he bought (around October 1), he would certainly have noticed that it was unusually high. And when a share is at its highest price, growing numbers of people think the rise is reliable and easily understandable. An investment in Intersystems is risk free, harmless, and a sure route to riches. The shares look like a wheel of fortune on which every invested dollar brings in a profit. There are only winners—no losers.

After scarcely six weeks, Ken is down 50 points on his investment, and he thinks life is damned unfair. It's typical that he's the only one with such bad luck. But he refuses to sell at this price. In his present frame of mind, he thinks a loss on that scale is unacceptable. Things were not supposed to go this way. He was to going to get rich, not lose money.

He ought to have known better. It is just like what that politician said on television—the stock market is a casino. Of course he'd been cheated. Some of those money men surely sold just as he was buying. In his agitated state, Ken decides that his purchase of Intersystems is the first and the last trade he will ever make. He ought to have known better than to play in that kind of game. Intersystems is probably just a new bubble some clever whiz kid created to cheat small savers like himself out of their money.

But almost two months later, when the price is approaching 125, Ken feels better and assesses the situation a little more soberly. Things actually seem to be going in the right direction. After another spell, when the price goes down again and touches its previous low, he feels his stomach churning. He seems to be a victim of market forces. When Intersystems swings up for the second time, he has a rosier view of life again, hoping things will still work out. When the price turns down for the third time since he bought, his new-found optimism turns to profound pessimism. He doesn't think this is much fun any more, and feels extremely frustrated.

After waiting for several months, he is exhausted. He impatiently waits for Intersystems to repeat its upward trend. When he switches on the TV every evening to get the day's quotes, his nervousness is getting to be unbearable. He doesn't like losing money. Even though he has begun to get used to the idea and is closer to accepting the situation, he is increasingly concerned that he not lose any more money. He doesn't even want to think about what his stomach will feel like if the price drops below 100.

Now that he is in the red again for the third time for 50 dollars,

Ken no longer counts on retrieving his money intact. But if he manages to sell at about the price the shares hit on two earlier occasions before going down again, he will have come out of it without losing too much money. He decides to wait a little longer and hope for the price to go up.

Over the next few days, the price stays just above 100, and Kenneth feels he can't cope with this constant anxiety, worry, and impatience. Even though he knows he will lose money when he sells at the price limit on which he and the broker have just agreed, he feels as if a burden has been taken off his shoulders. (See Figure 3.2.)

At last, he has made a decision. The constant, nagging worry has subsided. Kenneth Erland leaves the brokerage, his head held high, his shoulders straight, and he is surprised that he does not feel dissatisfied. His decision means that an illusory profit has turned into a real, substantial loss. After thinking it over for a

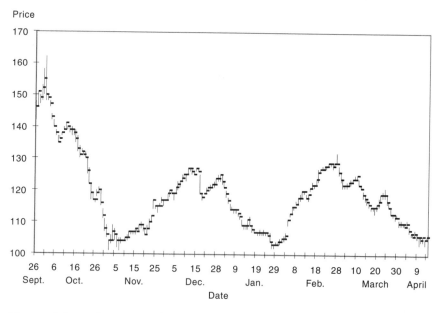

Figure 3.2.   When Ken is down 50 points for the third time, he is so anxious and impatient that he decides to sell even though the price is at the bottom of the range.

while, he sees it all quite clearly. He has in fact lost a lot of money, but in exchange he will get back what he has been missing for a long time: peace of mind and some sleep at night.

Samuel Rosenberg

Samuel Rosenberg is a stockbroker with Berlin & Levander. He is more and more annoyed and frustrated by Intersystems' price fluctuations. He thinks he has been very patient compared to many of his colleagues, who sometimes seem to be trying to exploit every move in a stock price to make a trade—even if only for a very small profit—just to show how smart they are.

A month or so ago, Sam was delighted with Intersystems. The shares were moving up in a clearly defined trend. It was a great feeling to watch the stock constantly reaching new highs. Both he and his clients were inspired by the force driving the price rise and by the company's enormous opportunities for expansion with its products. When Intersystems accelerated almost vertically in its latest upward thrust, apparently with enough strength to take off into the stratosphere, it brought on the euphoria of success.

Now his awakening is brutal. The apple of the entire market's eye, and its obvious favorite, disappoints them all when management issues a profit warning because of "growing pains." Company management has underestimated its production capacity. There is also an acute shortage of skilled technicians, which means that the strong demand cannot be met. These factors are obviously going to inhibit expansion and profits in the coming year. Shrinking profits, but, more important, skepticism about management of the company are making the price movements look like a wounded bird's efforts at staying aloft as it plummets irremediably earthward.

After the shock of the sharp drop of more than 30 percent in price has subsided, Sam begins to look at life more soberly. But when Intersystems dropped in the end of October from 121 to 101 a week before the price stabilized, he felt as if he had a lump of lead in his stomach. He was like a donkey standing between two piles of hay, vacillating. He was faced with a decision: whether to rush mindlessly for the exit like the rest of the crowd, or to relax and view the decline as simply an exaggerated panic reaction.

He opts for the latter and feels he has done the right thing; but he resents Intersystems' having caused this unpleasant emotional turmoil that he finds so hard to cope with. The company's fundamental conditions have actually not changed at all; its positive trend just had a glitch, albeit a considerable one, in the curve.

Of course it would have been wonderful to bail out at the top; but now that he hasn't done that, it's actually pointless to kick himself. It's just unfortunate that some clients are so unfair, he thinks. Instead of realizing that they have still made a considerable profit on their holdings, they choose to focus on how much they have lost compared with what they would have made if they had sold at the high. Oh well, people are only human, he thinks resignedly.

After about six weeks, as the price approaches 125 in the middle of December, Sam assesses the situation favorably. Obviously, he had been right to recommend that his clients not sell in panic. It looks as if the market is beginning to realize that Intersystems is a vigorous and expanding company despite the profit warning. Then, when more time has gone by and the price touches the earlier rock-bottom price in the end of January, Sam is worried.

His doubts begin to creep up on him. Has he really done the right thing? Shouldn't he have at least suggested that his clients reduce their holdings at the last upward correction? What if this so-called fantastic growth company is establishing a downward trend? If some major investor decides that this company of the future has no future, there could be some serious selling.

When Intersystems swings up for the second time, Sam has a strong impulse to recommend that his clients reduce their holdings by half. In spite of everything, the profit will be really good, and he won't have to worry or risk being criticized for doing nothing.

When he sees that Intersystems is going down again, Sam

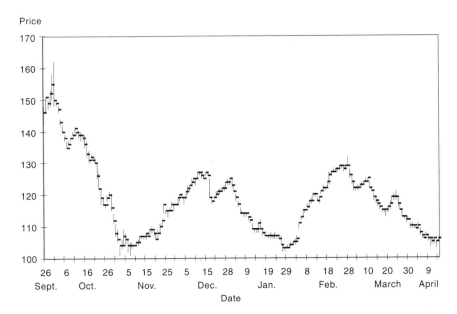

Figure 3.3.   Sam would be delighted to recommend that his clients sell their remaining Intersystems holdings, as long as the price goes above 125 for the third time.

Rosenberg is satisfied with the steps he has taken, though maybe he should have been more emphatic about his recommendation to sell. It would be really good if his clients got right out. Then he could forget Intersystems until the air cleared and concentrate on finding other promising investments. Now that the price is creeping ever closer to its previous low, he is forced into anxiety and uncertainty again. He questions whether he really did what he ought to have done.

Sam is now heartily sick of Intersystems, and his discomfort with the situation intensifies. The stock simply doesn't seem to be reliable any more. He thinks the price fluctuation—swinging back and forth like a weather vane—has made it quite impossible to predict anything. If only Intersystems could correct to up over 125 for a third time, he would recommend, with no reservations whatsoever, that his clients sell the remainder of their holdings. (See Figure 3.3.)

Chapter 4

THE PSYCHOLOGY OF SELLERS: A SURVEY

Sometimes stepping back a bit allows us to get a broader perspective on what has happened. In Chapter 3, three people, shareholders in Intersystems, all experienced their situation quite differently. Because each individual is unique, the individual's reaction and behavior in a specific situation may be difficult to predict. People may actually judge similar situations quite differently, depending on their background, experience, and values, among other things. Although Lena, Ken, and Sam are individuals, and each one's experience of the fluctuations in Intersystems is different, it is nevertheless extremely likely that there are common features in the way they see their predicament.

All three perceive the situation negatively. To varying degrees, they are disappointed, anxious, troubled, uncertain, and frustrated. To varying degrees, they all wish they had sold their holding close to the top so that they didn't now have the feeling that they are stuck in an investment whose price seems to be swinging mindlessly within a certain range, going neither up nor down but only sideways.

An Abstract Phenomenon

In many respects, a *share* is an abstract phenomenon that cannot be touched physically. It is evidence of a person's ownership of capital in a company in the form of an entry in the company's owners' share register and in a report from the bank's trust department or a stock brokerage. The shares are numbers on a computer screen or in the financial pages of the newspapers or on television. A share is simply a legal term: it has no emotions, no will of its own, nor does it care whether the price goes up or down or just stands still.

Nonetheless, Lena, Ken, and Sam feel ill-disposed toward Intersystems because owning its stock has brought unpleasantness with it. Instead of realizing that they themselves bear the responsibility for their actions and reactions, they see the stock in particular, and the feebleminded market in general, as the reason for this unpleasantness.

It is not unusual for rapidly growing and high-value growth companies to suffer reverses. Lena, Ken, and Sam could have sold while the price was soaring or, in Ken's case, not bought when the rise in price translated into a nearly vertical line. Everyone in the market knew about the "profit warning" at the same time; they could have sold Intersystems the next day, instead of behaving as if they were incapable of action. But it is easier to blame company management, the market, or headline-hungry journalists than it is to admit that maybe you should have thought, analyzed, acted, and reacted differently.

Regardless of whether Lena, Ken, and Sam blame others or analyze what has happened and learn from their mistakes, not one of them is happy with the situation. The longer Intersystems stays in its present phase, the more alike their individual assessments of the situation are. Although they are increasingly reluctant to wait, much less to hope that the price will start to go up again, they realize that it is unlikely that they will be able to sell at the same price as the earlier high at any time in the foreseeable future. If they want to get out of their holding without having to wait too long, they will be more and more willing—even tempted—to sell somewhere between the prices that represent the bottom and the top of the trading range. Because a greater or a lesser part of their own or their clients' money is locked up in an investment that is simply standing still, their aversion to Intersystems gradually turns into frustrated resignation.

If the market as a whole moves up while Intersystems vacillates, the investors' despondency and their inclination to sell will increase. It is annoying to have lost money on a price drop and to be left holding shares that do not move, even when the market as a whole goes up. If the market in general is down and Intersystems goes sideways, the opposite applies. Just as in the previous case, it is annoying to have lost money on Intersystems. But if other investors in the market are also losing money, it doesn't feel as bad, even if other securities are involved. Furthermore, there is less of a sense of being locked in because, after all, there are not too many attractive alternative investments.

At the core of this reasoning is the fact that in certain market situations individual investors with widely differing backgrounds, experiences, values, wealth, and so forth, without knowing each other, begin to behave with greater conformity and in increasingly similar and more predictable ways. But the time element is critical if this behavioral pattern is to appear within a trading range. If Intersystems had fallen from 150 to 110, stayed still and consolidated for a week, and then started to go up at the same rate as before, it would have been very unlikely for the stockholders to experience the depression and the frustration over the price movements that Lena, Ken, and Sam felt. Initially the stockholders would have felt the same reluctance toward and aversion to Intersystems. Some would have found the sharp drop more painful than others. More-experienced investors with more capital might have felt that what happened was disagreeable and troubling, but they know that in the end, when investing in stocks, you have to live with that kind of thing. Any combined sense of growing pressure and increasing weariness due to the situation would certainly not have crystallized within a week. Instead, the first feelings of animosity toward Intersystems would have blown away quickly when the stock resumed its previous upward climb.

Intersystems Stockholders as a Crowd

Naturally, Lena, Ken, and Sam are not the only ones in the market to find themselves in the situation we've just described; a great many people are in similar circumstances. These three represent only a few of the different types of investors, and they will have to stand in for the anonymous group of people who hold shares of Intersystems.

We've looked at the psychology on the individual level and drawn some important conclusions from our observations. Now it's time to leave the individual investor for a while and to look at Intersystems stockholders collectively—as a crowd.

Three Possible Choices

In the situation previously described, an Intersystems stockholder basically has three possible choices: (1) Do nothing at all. (2) Regard the drop as an overreaction, and decide not to sell at the prevailing price within the range but to wait until the price has risen to a level at which selling seems reasonable. (3) Accept the prevailing price, and sell at the market price—the price prevailing within the range.

Choice 1—The Stubborn Ones

One common method of dealing with such a situation is to do nothing. Investors who make this choice think that the price in the range is wrong, so they decide to wait for the price to go up. Investors who do this are stubborn—they feel that sooner or later the market will discover that the stock is undervalued and that eventually it will go up. Frequently, a rise to the previous high is what these investors are after. They see no reason to sell at a price any lower than the earlier high. Sometimes this view is rational and considered, but just as often it is emotional and illogical. The investors simply may not want to feel cheated by the market—if others have been able to sell at 150 or higher, there is no reason why they or anyone else should accept a lower price.

Or it is possible that investors in this group are so farsighted that they are not overly concerned by the drop. They figure that it is nothing but a hiccough in a upward trend, so they wait a few years before selling.

Choice 2—The Less Stubborn Ones

Just as the stubborn investors did, the less stubborn ones think that even the highest price in the trading range is unacceptably low. But selling at a price below the previous high might be a possibility for them. These investors often feel that the market overreacted when the stock went up and that now, when the price fell, it overreacted again. These investors usually think more rationally and less emotionally than the previous group; they are likely to admit that they ought to have behaved differently, but they now hope for, and count on, a second chance in order to correct their previous mistake, which was not selling in time.

Choice 3—Adjusters to the Market

The adjusters feel that the market's assessment of Intersystems is essentially correct. Naturally, the adjusters have various opinions on which price within the range is the right one, but they hold the common view that, considering the profit warning, a substantial downward price adjustment for Intersystems was actually justified. They understand that, even if it isn't much fun, there is always the possibility that the stock might go down. The fact that these investors think that there was some justification for a price drop does not mean they are correct; but they tend to be more rational in their assessment of the situation and more inclined to adapt to prevailing price levels.

Mental Adaptation

As discussed earlier, when the situation does not develop as they had hoped, the stockholders feel growing annoyance. Those wanting to sell are more and more inclined to accept the prevailing market price. However, this is a gradual mental process. Immediately after Intersystems' price drop, most investors fall into the first two categories; the last group is a minority. But with every passing day, the number in the third group grows.

Instead of being locked into the idea of necessarily having to sell at about the same level as the old high—150 or better—the stubborn stockholders might begin to think about disposing of their shares if they can get at least 140. The less stubborn investors are also more willing to adjust their selling price downward. Many of the adjusters surely missed selling at the first or the second upward correction because they thought it would go higher than it did. Some of them, perhaps being afraid of a further drop in price or thinking they could accept a price that although low is still slightly higher than the most recent low, now "step" down into the price range to dispose of their shares. Some will always sell at the bottom price in the range. It is entirely human to feel tortured by a drop in price and, in a moment of anxiety and stress, to sell at a price essentially perceived as too low. It is a way of escaping all the negative things connected with any eventual further decline in price. Figure 4.1 is based on David Fuller's illustration of the mental process described in *The Chart Seminar Workbook.**

Gradually, more and more investors tire of waiting for a rising trend in Intersystems. At first, many just lower their selling limits. They are not prepared to accept the price the market is offering, namely, a price within the trading range. But after lowering their limit once or even twice, even the most stubborn investors have an insight: If they want to dispose of their shares, they must "come down." Naturally, not all of them are inclined to sell at the prevailing market price, but the longer the trading range lasts, the more supply is drawn into the range, since it is only within the range that a deal can be closed.

As pointed out earlier in this chapter, the time factor is critical. It takes time for an investor to come to acceptance of a price lower than previously anticipated. In the first two groups, resistance to selling is ground down only slowly. The longer the consolidation phase lasts, the more powerful the psychological dynamic is. After a sufficient length of time in this phase, a

---

*David Fuller, *The Chart Seminar Workbook*, London: Chart Analysis Ltd., 1985, p. 9.

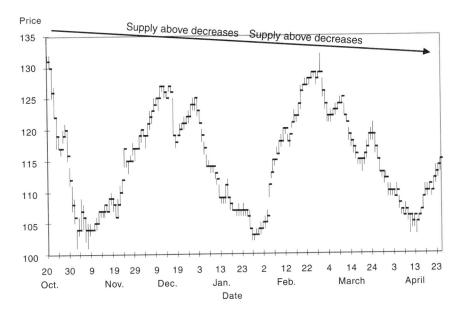

Figure 4.1. The number of shares for sale (latent supply) above the price range decreases with each passing day.

psychologically charged situation builds up that may result in powerful price movements—both up and down. But that situation has not yet come up. An important ingredient is still missing—the buyers. For every share sold, there must be a buyer. All supply that is "sucked in" within the range has been bought by other people. So before we arrive at a "breakout phase," it is important to study the psychology of buyers.

Chapter 5

THE PSYCHOLOGICAL DYNAMIC BELOW A TRADING RANGE

Of Course We Want to Buy If the Price Is Right

Before going into the psychology of the buyer—the psychological dynamic below a trading range—let's look briefly at three individual investors. To see how people with differing experiences, backgrounds, and values will behave similarly in a given situation, it is important to have a deeper understanding of their situation.

Peter Ericson

Peter Ericson has inherited a small portfolio from his mother. He is not particularly interested in the stock market and lets his holdings follow the market swings, both up and down. Peter has noticed that the value of his portfolio tends to go up from year to year, even though he has changed nothing in it. He has stayed in the background, and the bank's trust department has looked after it all. Now, however, a situation has come up in which he has to do something.

One of the companies in which he is a stockholder has been

bought by a competitor. Because of that sale, Peter realized some cash that he wants to invest in some other stock. At a dinner with some old friends, he is pleased when he finds a recent issue of *Business Today*. It might contain some useful tips. His host is rather surprised to see Peter reading a business publication and asks whether he has finally begun to take an interest in the stock market.

"Not at all," says Peter. He just wants to find some stock he can buy and then not to have to bother about.

"Then you definitely shouldn't read the article on Intersystems," says his friend. "That's a stock you should have bought long ago when it rocketed up. Now it is flapping down like a wounded crow."

Although Peter doesn't think Intersystems is the kind of company in which he wants to invest, his curiosity is aroused and he wants to know what the company does. He wants to own stock in old, big, and safe companies that can't —as he puts it— go bankrupt. There is no way he wants to have to worry that his money is about to "disappear."

After reading the article on Intersystems, Peter is a little ambivalent. He teaches technology and admires the people who built up the company. It is a pity he hadn't read about this before the price went up so much. At the present price, an investment in Intersystems is really riskier than what he finds acceptable. The paper's analysts think that the stock is an interesting long-term investment at a price below 120 but that an investor would have to be prepared for it to be a "journey," on which he might experience major swings.

Peter Ericson doesn't really know how to deal with this situation. Intuitively, he feels he would like to buy Intersystems, now that the price has fallen back sharply from the high, but he doesn't really dare. There must be something else he could do. He might be satisfied with putting just half of his disposable capital into Intersystems. Buying stock in Intersystems would give him the long-term investment for which he is looking, but then he would have to find another investment as well.

After mulling it all over for some time, he almost gives up the idea altogether. He just can't decide. Should he buy, or shouldn't he? It's seems silly that it is so hard to make a decision.

Over breakfast the next day, Peter can't understand why he didn't see the solution to the problem earlier. He'll escape that unpleasant feeling of not knowing which leg to stand on. *Business Today* recommended the stock as a long-term investment at a price below 120. But if the shares fluctuate a lot, there must be a chance that they will go even lower. If he could buy Intersystems as low as 100, he'd be in at such an attractive price that it would make up for the high level of risk. Peter is very pleased with this conclusion and decides to leave a limited bid with his portfolio manager that day.

Peter is very pleased when, just a few days later, Intersystems drops below 110. He's sure that it is only a matter of time before his bid will go through. In fact, maybe it wouldn't be a bad thing if he were slightly more active in regard to his other stocks. Buying at a low and selling at a high doesn't actually seem all that difficult.

When Intersystems falls to 103 in the beginning of November, Peter is convinced that the deal will soon be done and thinks how easily the money was made. Supposing he'd bought at 110! He would have been really mortified.

A week or two later, he's not quite so sure that he made the right decision. The stock never went below 101, and now it has started going up again. He should never have left a limited buy order with the portfolio manager, he says to himself with annoyance. If he had paid attention to the price, he would surely have realized that 101 was a low. When it was first quoted at 101, then corrected upward, then fell back again without going below 101, it was actually fairly obvious that this was the low, he says to himself rather confidently. Now that it's quoted at 111, buying is inconceivable. The price is a whole 10 points up from the low. If he's going to buy Intersystems, he tells himself firmly, then he's going to buy at a low or not at all.

Shortly after this, Intersystems goes up another 10 points. Peter thinks he's just been unlucky, missing the purchase by one miserable point. Though he's never really been particularly interested in the stock market, he now surfs the Internet every evening to see what Intersystems is doing. Every time he looks, he is hoping for a good minus sign next to the quote. If the price happens to have gone down, it's only by a point or two; and then, just a few days later, it starts going up again. Peter finds it hard to accept that he was so close to making a really good trade. When he calculates how much money he has missed out on, he is very annoyed. His earlier philosophy of not making any changes in his portfolio seems to suit him best after all. He should have followed the bank's advice, invested his money in a mutual fund, and not tried to play at being a financial wizard. He had been stupid to try gambling on the stock market. He might as well forget Intersystems. He tells himself that putting his money in that kind of company is actually against all his principles.

Although Peter has decided not to bother with Intersystems and to listen to what the bank suggests instead, he can't help following the price movements. After a while, to his surprise, he sees that Intersystems has dropped several points in a single day— December 17. Suddenly he is exhilarated. He knew he had been right on principle, not "chasing" after the stock as it went up. Perhaps now, he'll have another chance to buy at a low price. In spite of everything, he thinks investing in stocks is really a lot of fun.

After an upward turn that makes Peter uneasy, he is delighted to see that Intersystems is going down. Within two weeks, when the price is down to 113, he begins to be unsure of the deal. Should he be less greedy and buy now that the price has fallen back significantly? He remembers how quickly it turned up the last time—at 101—and how annoyed he had been for not buying in time. Greed wins, and Peter decides to buy at least a few points below the day's price. It looks as if his tactic will succeed. When the price is down to 108 (January 13), he feels like a professional. A few more days, he thinks, and then I'll bid quickly and efficiently.

Now he is absolutely counting on another downturn and is caught napping when Intersystems suddenly and unexpectedly goes up a few points. He certainly does not want to miss out on the deal, but again, he is forced to watch the price racing away from him as he stands there watching. When he calls the manager the next day and is told that the price is up another point, Peter feels he must act *now*. But torn between greed and the fear of losing money, he asks him to buy, at the best possible price, only half as many shares as when he tried to buy at 100. (See Figure 5.1.)

A week or two later, Intersystems is down, and touches 102. Peter is extremely angry with himself. He had been so close to buying at a low twice, and he had to go and buy at 112. Well, what's done is done, he thinks resignedly. He will stop following the stock market every day now. He has actually considered keeping his shares for a few years; then he wouldn't have to look at the price every single evening. It does not occur to Peter to buy in the "remaining" block, now that the price has fallen by 10. The thought that he might then "lose" even more money is entirely too painful. The leftover money can stay in his account, or it can end up in the mutual fund that the portfolio manager had recommended earlier.

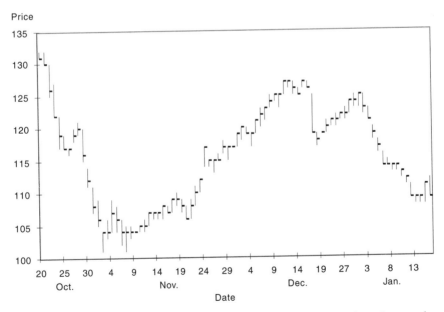

Figure 5.1.   Peter Ericson doesn't want the price to get away from him, so he buys at a price considerably higher than what he had intended to pay.

John Stennis

John thinks trading is fun, even if it is hard to understand exactly how the market works. Because he works at night, he can track the stock market during the day. Several times a day he surfs through the quotations to see if there have been any major moves. When he sees what he thinks is an unusual rise or decline on the market, he usually calls his local brokerage office.

The broker thinks John Stennis is a nuisance. He always wants explanations for why stocks are going up or down, but he rarely does any business. The young broker tries to get Stennis to understand that it's often impossible to know why a share price changes by a few points. It doesn't necessarily mean that anything special has happened. The reason for price fluctuations could be profit taking, general nervousness, a positive mood, an unconfirmed rumor, an article in a newspaper, a recommendation from an analyst—any one of a hundred things. John doesn't realize he is a trying, time-consuming, and unprofitable client; but the young broker is so interested in the stock market himself that he hasn't the heart to ask John Stennis to stop calling him.

In late October, John notices that the price of Intersystems has been dropping steadily for over a week. He actually hasn't called the broker for a while. He had been noticeably irritated the last time he called just to chat for five minutes before the market closed. But now John feels he has to call. He's really curious about why Intersystems has gone down so much, when earlier, it just went up, day after day. This time there must be some obvious reason for the drop in price.

The broker isn't at all annoyed when John Stennis's call comes in. For once, John has really thought through his question. John listens with interest while the broker explains that the high profit expectations built into the price have not been met. Because John's knowledge of economics is limited, he is not sure he really understands the explanation. But he understands that many people were disappointed in the company's results and are now selling because they are afraid that Intersystems will drop even further.

John is surprised when the broker asks whether he shouldn't take the opportunity to buy, now that the price has fallen so far.

He just thinks it's fun to follow the market; he hadn't really thought of jumping in. As a way of buying time, he says the first thing that comes into his head: Why?

The broker really does think it is time John Stennis did some business. He tells John that Intersystems is a high-tech company that makes excellent products and that it has simply been undergoing a temporary downturn due to "growing pains." The firm's pharmaceutical analyst feels that the stock is an obvious "buy" at around 100.

"That'd be something for you to keep your eye on," the adviser tells John. "You'll never learn how the market works if you never dare to do anything. You might also make some money if you manage to buy at 100. What you should do," he continues, "is to find a sound company with a good product, whose price is at an unwarranted low, and try to buy."

At first, John is nervous at the thought of actually buying shares in Intersystems, but then he is suddenly exhilarated. The guy is right; he has been looking long enough now. The time has come to do something. He also realizes the broker's patience is running out. He has actually called them quite a lot recently.

The next day, as he studies the price for Intersystems, he does so with greater attention than before. He has decided to buy as soon as the right situation comes up. The broker said that 100 was a good level, and he ought to know, John thinks to himself.

A week or two later the price is at 104, and John Stennis's earlier decisiveness begins to waver. Before, the price never seemed to stop going up, but now it never seems to stop falling. He begins to feel uncomfortable. Even firms on the stock exchange have been known to go bankrupt. The more John thinks about it, the more he begins to question his earlier decision to buy if the price dropped to 100.

He doesn't want to lose money. If he buys stock, he wants to make money on it, otherwise he might just as well leave his money safely in the account. He figures it might have been different if he had been given that advice just as the price began going up. Then he wouldn't have had all these doubts. But now he is torn between contradictory emotions. He doesn't like being made to decide, and he is afraid of losing money. Still, he knows this might be a good deal; he has to have the courage to act when a good opportunity comes up.

John finds that he thinks best while wandering around his apartment. After a spell of pacing back and forth, he finally hits on the solution to his problem. No one is making him buy at 100. He doesn't have to if he doesn't want to. Why not compromise? I'll stand by my decision to buy Intersystems, but not at 100. I'll buy when the price goes to 95, or lower. Pleased with his decision, he feels the tension ease. He looks forward to watching Intersystems continue to fall.

John did not take much pleasure in following the price movements, and he ended up profoundly disappointed. He had actually had the chance to buy just above 100 but hadn't dared. Anyhow, one consolation is that he wouldn't have been able to buy even if he had stood by his original decision to buy at 100, not when the price has gone to 115.

John calls the broker. He needs cheering up. Even though there had been no deal, at least he had tried. The broker realizes that Stennis is a little depressed. Those are the rules of the game, he explains. John is not the only one in the market who wants to buy at the low. A hundred is also the level at which people like to put in bids for psychological reasons. When a stock has been up around 150, 100 seems pretty low. And if the broker has a clear buy recommendation for Intersystems at 100, it is natural that a lot of clients put in their bids a few points above that level because they know they probably won't be able buy as low as 100. At that level, there ought to be plenty of other buyers. Now the broker thinks the stock has already gone up too much; John should either look for another investment or wait and see if the price falls again.

But John finds it hard to accept that he has missed a good deal. He no longer gets a kick out of following the tape during the day. If he had behaved differently, he would have made a really good trade. Still, after a while, he accepts the situation. There really are other stocks on the market, he thinks. His broker had suggested some alternatives.

He has just decided to forget Intersystems when to his surprise, he finds the shares have slumped by several points that very day. He starts hoping for a second chance, but hardly dares to believe that he could be that lucky. When Intersystems is down to 115 he watches the price with delight. About a week later, Intersystems is listed at 108, and John begins to feel pleased with life.

The quick, steep decline suddenly begins to torture John. His earlier decisiveness crumbles. The stock had turned at 101 the first time, and he had thought of trying to buy at 104. Now he doesn't know what to do. Suppose that there is a crash or that foreign investors get nervous and start selling Intersystems? He remembers reading somewhere that a mutual fund had large holdings in the company. John feels indecisive; he knows the price level is attractive, but what if it drops even further? He really can't afford to lose money. After some more pacing, he feels more decisive. The next day, he phones in a limited bid at 99, thinking that is actually just 4 points higher than the last time, and just below the 100-point level.

At first, he appears to have made the right decision. After some consolidation, Intersystems quickly drops to 102 in the end of January, and John is very pleased to have lowered his limit to 99. But two days later, the price starts cautiously moving up again, and then rises almost explosively when the company issues a positive report.

If John was frustrated when he missed buying Intersystems the last time, things are much worse now. (See Figure 5.2.) This time he definitely feels that trading is no fun anymore. He certainly doesn't want to look at the quotes in the future; he has absolutely no desire to be reminded of his mistakes. Instead he will try for an allocation in an initial public offering (IPO). Then he won't have to worry about what to do. Either he is given an opportunity to buy some shares, or he isn't. He can't do anything about that.

Karen Thurston

Karen Thurston manages individual portfolios for wealthy private clients on behalf of Credit One. She discusses asset alloca-

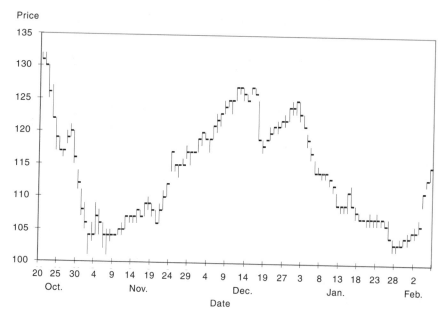

Figure 5.2. When John Stennis fails for the second time to buy Intersystems, he is frustrated and looks for an IPO allocation.

tion, time horizon, risk level, and similar aspects of the portfolio with her clients and then makes investment decisions independently, without discussing them further with her clients, who expect her to look after their money in the best possible way.

Although she herself decides what she will buy and sell, it is not unusual for a client to comment. If she has bought stock that subsequently went down or sold stock that later went up, she knows that she will be in for some critical remarks, often from the same people. Karen then tries to explain to the clients that neither she nor the firm's analysts and economists know which way a stock will move. She has no crystal ball; all decisions are made with varying degrees of uncertainty. All she can do is act in the best interests of the client. She usually tells a client who is being unnecessarily critical that if it were easy to know which way the market would go, every manager and stockbroker in the country would be as rich as George Soros.

Karen Thurston likes her job, but undeserved criticism is apt to get her down. If she makes a good trade, some clients take it entirely for granted. If a trade goes badly, clients imply that she is being unprofessional. "Sitting there by the screens, you should know how things are going" is one of the most ridiculous comments she has heard.

Karen has not had any Intersystems in her clients' portfolios. Most of her clients' portfolios have done well this year, even without Intersystems stock; but if they had had Intersystems, things would have gone really well. Now that everyone, results in hand, can see that Intersystems is the winner of the year, several of her clients tell her that they had actually thought of calling her to suggest buying Intersystems but hadn't got around to it. Karen is aware that neither she nor the firm's analysts had realized Intersystem's potential. She tries to explain to the complainers that the explosive price movement was impossible to predict and that, given the current situation, she thinks the stock is too high to buy.

Now, Karen notes the drop in Intersystems with some satisfaction. At the same time, she thanks her lucky stars she didn't buy the stock when it was at the high. Then she would certainly have been raked over the coals and told that even a beginner should have known that, after such a dramatic upswing, there has to be a sharp downturn.

Had she bought at the high, the clients to criticize her would almost certainly have been the same clients who, only a week ago, pointed out that *Stock News* had suggested that Intersystems had the potential to go up 100 points within a year.

Karen is enjoying her work again now. Instead of worrying about the price of Intersystems going up, she is on the lookout for the best level at which to buy. The firm has finally completed a major analysis of the company, and their conclusion is that it may take longer than most people expect to overcome the "growing pains" and that the stock is worth buying at about 85 to 90.

When the price stabilizes at just over 100 in the first half of November, Karen gets a number of calls from clients asking whether she shouldn't buy Intersystems. The common view is that now that the price has fallen so far, the stock must be cheap. Karen says she is thinking of buying, but not at this level; she will act once the price approaches 90, she says firmly, and goes on to explain her conclusion on the basis of the analysis.

When Intersystems does not go below 100, but starts climbing instead, Karen is not worried. She feels that an upward correction must come after such a sharp decline, and is convinced the stock will soon continue its downward trend. But when the price goes above 110, she is not happy with the situation. She knows she was very clear when she advised against buying when the stock was down and touching the 100 level. However, she is not particularly concerned. In spite of everything, the recent upturn is fairly modest.

Barely two weeks later, when the price approaches 120 at the end of November, Karen is no longer quite so sure she has done the right thing. She knows that the firm's analyst of medical companies is very smart but that his recommendations also tend to be cautious. Now it actually looks as if she has missed an excellent opportunity to get into Intersystems at a low price. Her difficult clients will probably be calling in soon. Most of her clients are really very nice and feel she does a good job, but Karen figures some clients were probably given to her to make her atone for her sins. With 20/20 hindsight, they like to point out that she ought to have done things differently, though when she points out that they are free to handle their portfolios themselves if they like, their tone of voice usually softens somewhat.

When Intersystems goes up over 120, Karen begins to feel stressed. More and more she wonders whether she was right not to have acted. Even if she had bought at 110, that would still have been excellent in today's market. Supposing *Stock News* is right? Maybe she should buy a small lot just to be on the safe side. Her fingers itch to buy, but intuitively, she feels it would be wrong. After struggling with herself for a while, she refrains from rushing in to buy.

Good God, what luck she hadn't got carried away, Karen thinks as Intersystems falls several points on December 17. After an upward correction, which she thinks goes on for a painfully long time, the price finally turns down again, and for Karen, the air seems easier to breathe. She is glad that she trusted her instincts and did not act like the rest of the crowd. She decides to wait for the right opportunity and then act decisively.

When the price drops below 110, she intensifies her watch. She thinks that in all likelihood, the price will fall below the previous low, figuring that if it doesn't turn at that point, many stockholders will presumably start worrying nervously. When they sell out of fear of another price decline, she plans to be on the other side buying.

Karen is very disappointed when Intersystems trades somewhere near the previous low but does not fall any further. In her estimation, the stock must make another small upturn, then gather strength for the downturn. When she has established that this is actually natural, with an upward correction after a downturn of more then 20 points, she feels better.

But a week or two later, when Intersystems passes 110 at express speed, painful uncertainty enters the scene again. What if she has missed buying at a low for a second time? Then, on top of that, at the monthly business meeting the analyst says that although he still stands by his recommended buying price of 85 to 90, after studying the latest report, he has probably exaggerated the Intersystems problems.

Karen feels her stomach tighten. This is certainly not what she wanted to hear. Now that Intersystems is up over 120 again, she notices that she simply can't bring herself to buy. After two fine opportunities to buy at a low near 100, she just cannot jump in at almost 20 percent higher. She can almost hear sour comments from her troublesome clients, and that thought alone is enough to cause her not to do anything in the prevailing market situation.

A few days later (February 21), she regrets she hadn't given in to her impulse to make a grab for the stock. Now that the price is at 128, it would have been just fine to buy at 120. Life is hard, she thinks. Every time the telephone rings, she wonders whether it is someone calling to criticize. She is well aware that in some clients' eyes, she has made a mistake, even though she always had her clients' best interests in mind. She knows she is the one who makes the decisions on buying and selling for her clients' portfolios independently, but she does think the analyst gave the wrong signals.

At first he was quite sure Intersystems had serious problems. Then, when he noticed that his analysis was the most pessimistic on the market, he was suddenly less negative. It's strange the way analysts sometimes exhibit crowd behavior, too, Karen thinks, though she knows that it is an enormous mental strain to deviate too much from the prevailing view of the market.

Karen feels paralyzed. She just can't buy at the prevailing price. If the price should start to decline, she would be wide open to criticism. She decides to do nothing and hope the analyst's view is actually correct.

When, contrary to all expectations, Intersystems begins to fall again, Karen feels great. The tension that had recently been tormenting her begins to subside, and she is greatly relieved, if not entirely relaxed. Suppose she makes a mistake for the third time? She certainly does not want to go through all that stress and unpleasantness again—thinking as soon as the telephone rings that it may be a complaining client about to reprimand her.

After another visit to the management of Intersystems, the analyst's earlier negative assessment has changed to one of cautious optimism. The management of the company has a better grasp of their situation than he had anticipated, and they have taken quick, effective steps to increase their production capacity. When Karen hears this news, she feels relieved rather than annoyed. Now she can start buying as soon as she deems the present correction at an end. When Intersystems falls 10 points, she is ready to buy. The new analysis indicates that the shares are a buy at 110 or 115. She is not going to miss the opportunity this time. When it reaches 115 on March 17, her nervousness increases. Should she buy or does she dare to wait a few more days and try to buy even lower? Two days later it is still at about 115, and Karen sees the volume increasing as more and more people buy. Which is worse, she wonders, buying slightly too early and watching the price go down even further, or waiting a little longer and perhaps missing a good opportunity for the third time?

After weighing the arguments, she sees the choice as clear:

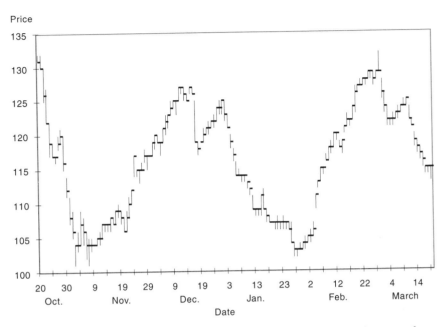

Figure 5.3.   Karen Thurston is not going to let Intersystems slip away from her again. She buys when the price turns down from its high the second time.

Compared with the high around 160 back in October, the day's price is considerably lower; and with the firm's analysis behind her, it would just be stupid to hope for a lower price. Once she has carried out the transaction, she is pleased and satisfied. Again, she thinks how truly stimulating her work is. (See Figure 5.3.)

Chapter 6

THE PSYCHOLOGY OF
BUYERS: A SURVEY

Let's survey the situation: we have three people wanting to buy shares in Intersystems, all of whom size up the situation differently. As mentioned earlier, everyone is unique, and an individual's reaction and behavior in a given situation may be hard to predict. Similar situations are often perceived differently depending on background, experience, and values. Although the three main characters here are individuals and Peter's, John's, and Karen's personal impressions of the buying situation of Intersystems vary, it is very likely that their interpretations share some clear, common features.

To some degree, all three are interested in doing good business. All three wish they had bought shares in Intersystems before the steep rise in price began. But now they have been given another chance; and even though they are unsure and slightly hesitant about how best to exploit the situation, they all view it in a positive light.

An Abstract Phenomenon

As we've seen, a stock is an abstract phenomenon. It is numbers on a screen, in the financial pages of newspapers, or on television. A share of stock is a legal concept with no will of its own and no interest in whether the price goes up or down or just stays still.

Peter, John, and Karen, however, are kindly disposed toward Intersystems because buying stock in the company gives them an opportunity to make money. But the psychology of buyers is not the same as that of sellers. The unpleasantness of losing money is much greater than the pleasure of making it; and the delight and satisfaction of a good trade has far less impact than the anguish, uneasiness, and anxiety that a bad one may bring. Panic is a stronger, more intense emotional experience than euphoria. A seller is more likely to behave emotionally than a buyer is; a drop in price is often much more dramatic than a rise.

A buyer always has greater freedom of choice. A buyer does not have to invest if he or she does not want to. It may be very frustrating to miss a good buying opportunity, but the capital remains intact and there will be other possibilities the next day. But once a decision is made and money is invested, freedom of choice is immediately and drastically curtailed. In principle, the investor then has only two alternatives: either keep the holding or sell. Unlike the potential buyer, the investor can no longer just step aside and see how the situation develops if the price drops. He or she must make a decision—hold on or sell? A decision to sell at a loss is stressful; a decision to wait yet another day to see if it is possible to buy even more cheaply is less so.

Clearly, it is not true that people are rational when they buy and emotional when they sell. It is easy to think that you must be there when the market or the price of a certain share moves off. The desire to "make a killing," to do a big trade, and to find a real winner is very common. When a stock price rises quickly and unexpectedly, it is entirely human to feel that other players in the market seem to have discovered an opportunity that escaped you. You think you are missing the boat and quickly throw in a buy order.

In most cases, it feels less unpleasant to have behaved emotionally, having rushed to buy—perhaps unnecessarily high—than to have been caught in a collapse and lost money simply because you were unable to act rationally and sell at a smaller loss, when it was still possible to get out in time.

Gradually, Peter, John, and Karen begin to feel less positive about the situation they're in. The longer Intersystems stays in its present phase, the more Peter's, John's, and Karen's assessments of the situation coincide. Even while they feel tired by the protracted wait, and their hope that the shares will sink to the level at which they want to buy fades, they gradually begin to realize that if they want to be Intersystems stockholders, they will probably have to buy at a higher price than they had originally planned. If they want to invest without waiting too long and not risk having the opportunity evaporate, they gradually resign themselves to buying somewhere between the bottom and the top levels of the price range. Slowly, as more or less of their or their customers' capital waits for an investment opportunity that never seems to materialize, their good feelings and positive attitude toward Intersystems turns into dislike and impatience. If the market as a whole moves up while Intersystems fluctuates within its range, this contributes to their impatience and the inclination to buy. Being out of the market and in cash, which yields only interest while the market is going up, naturally increases the pressure.

If the market in general is on the way down, while Intersystems only moves laterally, the opposite is true. In this instance, too, it is tempting to try to enter the market, but the feeling is not as strong when the market is going up. Being in cash while the market is going down is an agreeable situation and brings a feeling of freedom. You do not have to invest in the stock market if you do not want to; you can simply wait to buy until the time is right.

In certain market conditions, the behavior of individual investors with very different backgrounds, experience, values, and net worth who do not know each other becomes much more predictable and begins to conform more and more. However, the time element is very important for such common behavior to emerge within a trading range. Had Intersystems fallen from 150 to 110, stabilized and consolidated for a week, and then begun to go up again rapidly, it is very unlikely that buyers would have felt the same stress and irritation over the development as Peter, John, and Karen did. At first, the buyers felt just as positive as

Peter, John, and Karen did about the chance to buy Intersystems at a low price. Some buyers saw the strong downturn as a favorable opportunity. Others felt uneasy because the company had real problems—the downturn was so steep—and they wanted to wait before buying. Then there are the investors who almost always want to buy at a price lower than the prevailing one, even if it has already fallen sharply. They want to be absolutely convinced that they are buying at a truly low price. Certainly, in such a situation, no common feeling of unease and aversion would have crystallized within such a time frame as short as one week. Most likely, only a small number of potential buyers were decisive enough to manage to buy at a low price. Many potential buyers surely grumbled about missing the chance to buy at a low level. Some rushed in and bought at the prevailing market price, while others decided that the price was too high and began to look for other investment opportunities.

Reduced Output and Increased Dynamic

Of course, Peter, John, and Karen are not the only ones who find themselves in the situation just described; there are many others in similar circumstances. These three investors represent only a few investment categories and merely serve as examples of all the anonymous people interested in becoming Intersystems stockholders.

Having looked at the psychology on a more individual level and drawn some important conclusions from our observations, let's leave the individual investor for a moment and devote ourselves to studying potential buyers of Intersystems as a group or crowd.

Four Possible Choices

For a potential buyer of Intersystems, there are essentially four possible choices in the situation described: (1) Decide that the prevailing price is attractive, and then buy at the market price that is the price prevailing in the range. (2) View the downturn as an overreaction, but wait until the situation is clarified before making a decision. (3) Decide to buy if the price falls to a level so low that a trade could be considered almost risk free. (4) Simply not concern yourself with whether Intersystems has gone down; after all, just because a stock has gone down sharply does not necessarily mean you have to consider buying it.

Choice 1—Those Inclined to Buy

The buyers see the market's valuation of Intersystems as faulty. Of course, there are different views as to what price in the range is the right one. But a common view is that, considering the future prospects of the firm, the steep downturn is exaggerated and this strong overreaction ought to be exploited by buying shares in a sound company at a low price. Although these investors think that the downturn is exaggerated, their view is not necessarily correct. Some of them are making a highly rational judgment, whereas others assume that because the shares in Intersystems have gone down so much, they must be cheap. Naturally this group also wants to buy at as low a price as possible, at the lower end of the price range.

Choice 2—Those Who Wait

The waiters feel that because the stock went down so dramatically in such a short time, the market has probably overreacted. Yet they do have some questions about how much of the downturn is the result of a strictly economic assessment and how much is due to psychological factors. Their reasoning is usually more rational and less emotional than that of the other groups. Just because the stock has gone down a great deal does not mean that Intersystems is valued low. They do know, though, that because people very often behave irrationally in pressured situations it is very probable that unless the reason for the downturn is very serious, the considerable decline in price is essentially unwarranted. So before they decide whether to buy, they often want to know more about the company's situation. Even though the market price may have dropped sharply in percentage terms, they do not want to fall into the trap of paying too much. If they buy, the waiters want to pay as low a price as possible. They prefer to buy stock at the lower end of the range.

Choice 3—Bargain Hunters

One common tactic is to wait for the price to drop even farther. These potential investors think the price is too high, even at the lower end of the trading range. They decide to wait out a continued downturn, thinking—or hoping—that the market will continue in a downturn, whether for rational or emotional reasons. The investors often look for a price to decline to a level at which the valuation is unquestionably low. To invest money in Intersystems, they want to buy at what could be regarded as a bargain basement price. This attitude may be both sensible and rationally motivated. The market may well exaggerate a company's problems, forcing the price down to an unreasonably low level for psychological reasons. But just as often, it is subjective and illogical. Many potential buyers simply want an almost-risk-free trade that will also give them a chance to make a killing. They hope that some stockholders will be so nervous and worried as to sell at bargain prices.

Choice 4—The Disinterested

A sharp drop in price does not automatically stir up buying interest in all investors. There may be any number of reasons why a downturn in Intersystems received little attention. You may see the entire market sector as too risky for investing in a company with Intersystems' profile. Your knowledge of the company is far too limited for you to be able to decide whether the stock is cheap or overpriced, for example. You may have insufficient disposable capital for more investments. You may not want to sell any present holdings to buy Intersystems.

Potential buyers have an advantage over potential sellers. Buyers can simply ignore the fact that a slump in Intersystems' price might place it at an interesting buying level. Shareholders in a company, on the other hand, cannot ignore the situation; they must decide whether to hold or to sell all or part of their holdings.

Mental Adjustment

In the period just after the drop in the Intersystems' price, the group described first, the buyers, is in the minority, the others in the majority. But with each passing day, the number in the first group grows. When the price does not develop as these potential buyers had hoped, they feel growing impatience, even despondency. They are more and more inclined to accept the prevailing market price. However, this is a mental adjustment that takes place over time. Investors in the second category, those who wait, become increasingly inclined to act when they notice that there seems to be considerable demand for Intersystems shares just above the 100 level.

Instead of locking onto the idea of just buying at a price considerably lower than the prevailing price in the range, the bargain hunters, the third group, begin to think about buying if they can buy at about 90, or lower. Potential buyers are now noticing that the price seems to swing within a range. Because they thought the price would fall further than it did, many in the first two groups have probably missed buying at the first or the second bottom level. Some of them now "climb" up in the price range in order to be able to buy. Because they are afraid of missing a good trade, they are prepared to accept a price that is in fact higher than the one they had hoped for but still considerably lower than the top price. Some will always buy at the upper level of the range. It is all too human to feel stressed during an upturn and to buy, in an anxious moment, at a price that is really thought to be too high. No matter what, it avoids the grinding remorse that you know will gnaw at you if the upturn continues.

Figure 6.1 is based on David Fuller's illustration of this mental adjustment process in *The Chart Seminar Workbook*.

Gradually, more and more investors get tired of waiting for Intersystems' continued downturn. At first, many just raise their buying limits; they are not prepared to buy at the market price—the price within the range. After they have raised their limit once or twice, however, there is a growing awareness, even among the most persistent investors, that if they want to buy, they will have to climb up in the range. Naturally, not all potential buyers are inclined to pay prevailing market prices; but the longer the period within the trading range lasts, the more demand is drawn into the range because that is where deals can be made.

As I pointed out at the beginning of Chapter 3, the time factor is important. It takes time to accept the idea of paying a higher price than planned. In groups two and three, resistance to buying

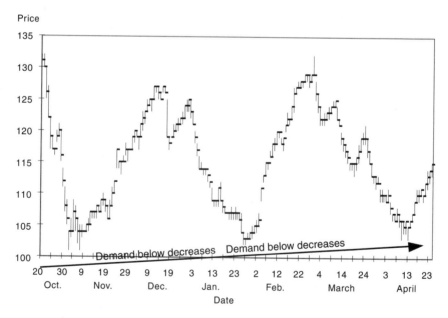

Figure 6.1. The number of shares in demand (latent demand) below the range decreases with every passing day.

is worn down slowly. The longer the consolidation phase lasts, the stronger the psychological dynamic becomes. After a sufficient period in this phase, a psychologically charged situation has built up, which can result in forceful movements, either up or down. The psychological base is now complete. The previously missing ingredients—the buyers—have fallen into place. We have arrived at the "breakout phase."

The Vacuum Effect

David Fuller calls this situation the "vacuum effect" (Figure 6.2). Most of the latent supply above the trading range has vanished because most potential sellers have sold their shares at the price prevailing within the range. Similarly, most of the latent demand that existed below the trading range has also vanished because most potential buyers have bought at the price prevailing within the range.

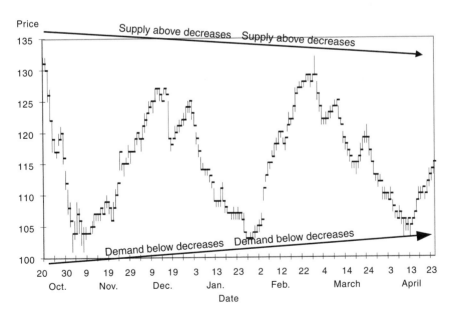

Figure 6.2.   The vacuum effect.

It is impossible to know in advance how long a trading range will hold; but one thing is certain: it never goes on forever. What will trigger a break either up or down from a range—a good or a bad earnings report, a positive or a negative investment analysis, buying or selling interest on the part of major market players, the launch or the withdrawal of a product, and so forth—is never known in advance. When, after moving within a given range for a protracted period, a stock breaks out of that range, either up or down, it is not unusual for price movements to become powerful. Because the latent volume has been withdrawn from the market by shares being absorbed within the range, there is a vacuum of sellers and buyers both above and below the range.

A clear break from the range's top and bottom levels means that there is an obvious imbalance in the market. As long as the stock price moves within its range, the number of people who have been "right" or "wrong" are about equal. Certain sellers have sold at the upper end of the price range and are pleased. Some buyers have bought at the lower end of the range and are satisfied. Of course, the opposite happens just as often. Some sellers think they have sold too low and are dissatisfied, and a number of buyers think they have bought too high and are also discontented.

When the price breaks upward, everyone who has already sold will think that they have done the wrong thing. All the shares they sold within the range have been disposed of at a price lower than the present one. If the price breaks downward, everyone who has already bought will kick themselves for paying too much. The shares they bought within the range have been acquired at a price higher than the present one.

Now the psychological reactions of the buyers and respective sellers may be considerable, and it is in situations like these that crowd behavior manifests itself very clearly in the market. But before studying the psychology connected with a breakout from the Intersystems range, it is essential to talk a bit more about the reasons for crowd behavior on the stock market.

Chapter 7

CROWD BEHAVIOR: A STUDY

Humans have banded together in groups since time immemorial. The support and protection of others greatly increased a person's chances of surviving the struggle against predatory animals and the elements. Being thrown out of one's own tribe and not taken into another was often the equivalent of a death sentence.

Originally, belonging to a group or a tribe was essential for the survival of the individual; but banding together also meant the survival of the species. A lone hunter attempting to bring down large prey with only a primitive weapon had very limited chances of success, and the hunter risked being injured or killed. Hunting in a group was not without its dangers, but hunters working together had much better chances of bringing down large animals and ensuring the survival of the tribe.

A person's desire to belong in a group of like-minded individuals is as old as humanity's existence on the planet. So it is hardly surprising that people like to gather together, even in modern society. Feeling accepted as a valued member of a community contributes to a feeling of security and well-being. If, for instance, a person does not feel accepted by his family, his friends, his fellow workers, or society, perhaps his physical survival is not threatened, but certainly his psychic well-being is. The degree of alienation depends on the form that the rejection and distancing takes.

The Individual and the Crowd

Each human being is unique and, to a greater or lesser degree, attuned to his or her own thoughts and actions. Predictions of individual behavior in certain situations can be difficult or at least marked by considerable uncertainty. On the other hand, predictions of group behavior can be made with relative certainty. In all likelihood, if a building full of people catches fire, a panicky situation will develop. It does not require any extraordinary insight into human behavior to realize that the majority will try to get out as quickly as possible. But how any individual will behave cannot be known. A person's instinct for self-preservation dictates that he or she get away from danger, but instinct does not determine the particular way in which this will be done. Some individuals might try to put the fire out before leaving the building. Others might attempt to organize an orderly retreat, so that the premises can be vacated calmly and methodically. Some people will probably make sure they get out first, regardless of whether anyone else is injured; others will be paralyzed by fear, passively allowing themselves to be swept out with the surging human herd. Individual behavior will vary, depending on relative egoism, ruthlessness, or an unselfish consideration for others that borders on heroism. One thing is certain: with varying levels of energy, most people will try to leave the premises.

A few people at a movie or on a dance floor can hardly be called a crowd. Rather, they are a collection of individuals who happen to be in the same place at the same time. If they are simultaneously exposed to some external danger or threat, a general feeling of insecurity and anxiety will result, making most of them act emotionally rather than rationally. As a result, they will behave more as members of a crowd than as independent individuals.

In his book *Forecasting Financial Markets,** Tony Plummer

---

*Tony Plummer, *Forecasting Financial Markets*, 2d. edition (London: Kogan Page, 1993).

makes the point that human beings can behave as independent individuals while simultaneously wanting to belong to a group. This explains why a person can veer between roles as a multifaceted individual and a conforming member of a group. The tendency to shift between these roles—from individual to group member who more or less accepts and adapts to the norms, rules, and point of view of the group—varies, depending on circumstances.

Figure 7.1 is based on a figure from Plummer's book. His main conclusion is that man's ability and tendency to shift from individual behavior and independent thinking to group behavior, using group values and rules as a yardstick, is very important to the understanding of market psychology. Predicting individual behavior is difficult, but predicting the likely behavior of a larger group is realtively easy.

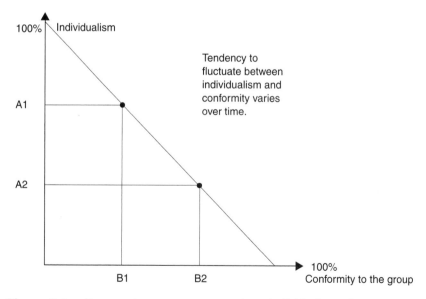

Figure 7.1. To a greater extent, a person is an individual, to a lesser extent a member of the group—(A1, B1) compared with (A2, B2). *Source:* Tony Plummer, *Forecasting Financial Markets* (London: Kogan Page, 1993), p. 22.

Economic Theory versus the Psychology of the Market

The economic models constructed in the academic world for the purpose of prognosticating how various markets—stocks, bonds, currencies, and commodities—move are based largely on the assumption that human beings make decisions on a strictly rational basis.

Three main reasons are put forward to explain why that assumption is correct:

The first is that individuals do not behave irrationally—for example, they will not put their hand in a fire (unless, of course, they get pleasure from doing so). Second, individuals learn from their mistakes—that is, if they burn themselves by putting their hand in the fire, then they will not willingly put their hand in again. And third, individuals arrive at their decisions independently of one another—that is, they do not put their hands in the fire simply because someone else does so or tells them to do so.*

But this analysis of behavior does not take crowd psychology into account. The psychology within the group or crowd is viewed as merely the sum total of individual rational decisions. There are several objections to be made to this point of view.

Obviously people do not think and act only rationally—they are often highly irrational and emotional in their decision making. The dangers of smoking, for example, are almost as obvious as the probability that you will be burned if you put your hand in the fire. Most smokers are aware that smoking increases the risk of lung cancer and that nicotine is a powerfully addictive poison. If the reason for smoking were merely that the individual finds it enjoyable, this notion would require considerable modification because coughing and nausea are the "enjoyment" a first-time smoker experiences. The fact that habitual smokers find a cigarette "good" is directly connected with the need to satisfy

---

*Plummer, *Forecasting Financial Markets*, p. 57.

the body's nicotine dependency, not with any carefully thought through, rational decision.

Because the first experience of smoking is negative and also because the smoker knows that the practice is unhealthy and addictive, the logical and rational decision would be to stop smoking (or not to start).

Regardless of the irrationality of many people's decisions, it is almost impossible to understand or to explain why so many people take up smoking. On the other hand, remembering that, to a large extent, people's behavior is driven by the behavior of others and that various states of mind influence their decisions makes it suddenly much easier to explain why people start smoking.

Peer pressure is a powerful factor that contributes to a person's starting to smoke. Suppose that a nonsmoker joins a group. The leader of the group smokes, and most members of the group think smoking is tough and cool. Then unless the nonsmoker has a remarkably strong sense of self-esteem, his or her need for acceptance and respect within the group will quickly demolish all rational reasons for not smoking—regardless of how well founded they may be. If there is also a prevailing attitude in the group that smoking is something positive, something that confers respect and status, the nonsmoker's resistance to accepting irrational behavior is further reduced.

It might be easy to discount objections to the statement "Human beings always make rational decisions" simply by establishing that it is mostly young people who start smoking. Presumably, their lack of intellectual maturity and self-esteem limits their ability to make rational decisions. But dismissing objections so casually lacks seriousness and is insulting to young people.

When markets soar sky high in hysterical frenzy or plummet in panic and crash in chaos, the irrational behavior of individual investors is readily recognizable. It would be hard to explain how so many ostensibly rational individuals can simultaneously and unanimously hold opinions that, in the end, turn out to be economically catastrophic.

This book began with a description of the tulip mania in seventeenth-century Holland. That chapter was intended to demonstrate the tremendous impact that crowd behavior can have on a market. People's readiness to sell off houses and estates at rock bottom prices simply to buy tulip bulbs that they thought would make them rich hardly seems indicative of rational behavior. When individuals became so involved in hysterical speculation in tulip bulbs that a whole country's prosperity was threatened, their behavior could not be seen as based on carefully considered, rational decisions.

It would be easy to disregard this example of crowd behavior and of humanity's tendency to make emotional decisions by arguing that people in the seventeenth century were not as educated and knowledgeable as we are today, and that this naturally impaired their ability to make rational decisions. But dismissing objections on such flimsy grounds is not only flippant but also condescending to our forefathers.

The tulipomania is only one of a number of major financial crises in history. In his highly regarded book on financial crises, *Manias, Panics, and Crashes,** Charles P. Kindleberger lists more than 40 financial crises, starting in 1618 with the currency devaluation in the Holy Roman Empire and ending with the Japanese bubble in 1989. The first crisis is not very familiar, compared with the second on Kindleberger's list—the Dutch tulipomania. The third crisis occurred about 75 years later, when many British citizens lost their savings in the notorious South Sea Bubble,† in which the South Sea Company took over a part of the national debt in return for a monopoly on trade to the South Seas. When King George I bought shares in the company, a frenzy broke out, and the shares soared to many times their original value. Speculative fever gripped British society; investors unable to buy shares in the South Sea Company were offered shares in a wide range of other ventures. Many of them, like the "wheel of perpetual motion," "a company for carrying on an undertaking of great advantage though nobody was to know

---

*Charles P. Kindleberger, *Manias, Panics, and Crashes* (New York: John Wiley & Sons, Inc., 1996).

†Jonas Bernhardsson, *Tradingguiden* (Stockholm, Sweden: Fischer & Co., 1996), 26.

what it is," and "for importing a number of jackasses from Spain" were dubious. When the South Sea Bubble finally burst, the famous scientist Isaac Newton, who had lost most of his savings in the crash, wrote, "I can calculate the motions of heavenly bodies, but not the madness of people."

At about the same time, on the other side of the English Channel, the Scottish economist, John Law, implemented what would be known as the Mississippi Scheme, crisis number four on Kindleberger's list. He wanted to expand economic growth by means of paper currency not backed by gold. After arousing little interest in other European countries, the French regent, Philippe Duke of Orléans, permitted John Law to carry out his plan in France. About two years after setting up his private bank, Law had built a gigantic conglomerate, fully backed by the state, the Compagnie des Indes, or The Mississippi Company. Blinded by the company's potential profitability, Paris was engulfed in mania; the Mississippi shares rose from 100 to 2,000 in two years. It is said that the word *millionaire* came into existence during that period, and there is an abundance of stories about the riches created during that very short time span. The Mississippi Scheme came to an end in 1720, when a decree was issued, reducing the value of shares and bank notes by almost 50 percent. Panic broke out.

In his book *Crashes*, Robert Beckman wrote: "The reason crashes happen is because we learn nothing, which is why they will continue in the future just as they have in the past." He referred to John Kenneth Galbraith, who observed that for as long as reliable records have been kept, "the suicidal tendencies of the economic system" have been repeated approximately every 50 or 60 years. This time frame is "perhaps roughly the time it takes for men to forget what happened before."*

The crashes on Kindleberger's list make the point that because people are "just" people, ruled to a large extent by emotions and often irrational when making decisions, manias, panics, and crashes are natural elements in human history. There is no reason to believe that the future will be different.

---

*Robert Beckman. *Crashes* (London: Sidgwick & Jackson, 1988), 213, 229.

Despite a history of 350 years with frequent manias in the financial markets, psychology was not accepted as an important factor in the panic of 1987. Tony Plummer points out that the academic community put great energy into explaining the crash of 1987 with a hypothesis about rational expectations. One of the principal arguments was that the "bubble" was based on faulty and irrelevant economic information.

Apparently no one thought of asking why most participants did not realize that their information was irrelevant. The fact is, according to Tony Plummer, that the investors were given relevant information. They could have studied the market's euphoric behavior and drawn rational conclusions instead of responding emotionally and engaging in crowd behavior. Clearly, as we discussed in the Preface, it is significant financial facts that trigger major upturns or downturns in the market. But taking only such facts into account, and ignoring psychological mechanisms, makes it very difficult to come to any deeper understanding of market ups and downs. When does a major market move begin, and at what level? How quickly does it move? How high is too high, and how low is too low?

Of course there are reasons why financial markets diverge from economic reality at certain times, but the reasons are of a psychological nature, not an economic one. This is an area in which traditional economic theory is inadequate; figures alone cannot explain the movements. A study of crowd psychology is essential in gaining a better understanding of and insight into patterns of market behavior. Though economists have begun to pay more attention to psychology, prevalent thinking still maintains that people are essentially rational. This thinking does not give psychology sufficient weight when an attempt is made to explain market fluctuations, and a brief analysis of crowd psychology as a phenomenon is useful.

A Brief Analysis of Crowd Psychology

Even an investor who has been active in the stock market for only a short time has probably felt ambivalent when faced with certain decisions. On the one hand, it makes sense to buy when everyone else is selling; on the other hand, it is hard to go against prevailing pessimism and crowd psychology. However disciplined and professional an investor may be, he or she is easily carried away by the mood of the market, rushing in the same direction as everyone else. The investor who can say in all honesty that he or she has never bought at the top nor sold at a bottom is an extremely rare creature.

The reason for this ambivalence is the crowd behavior of human beings. Individuals have the ability to act independently, but they also have a desire to belong and to be accepted within the group. And people in a group, pack, or crowd often behave very differently than they would as individuals.

Gustave Le Bon was interested in several different areas of science, such as archeology, physics, and the biology of race, but he is best known for his pioneering analysis of crowd psychology. His 1895 book *Psychologie des Foules*, better known under the title *The Crowd*, is considered a classic in the field, influencing, among others, Sigmund Freud, who confirmed many of his conclusions.

Le Bon argued that in certain contexts, and assuming a common objective, individuals were capable of constituting a crowd. The implication is that crowd behavior can be found in various contexts, such as companies, military units, political parties, sports teams, gangs, lynch mobs, and religious sects. Le Bon saw a crowd primarily as a psychological rather than a physical phenomenon, arguing that crowds were influenced more by unconscious feelings than by intelligence. As he put it: "We are now aware that by the mere fact that men form part of a crowd engaged in action, their collective psychology differs essentially from their individual psychology, and their intelligence is affected by this differentiation."[*]

---

[*]Gustave Le Bon, *The Crowd* (1895; reprint, Marietta, GA: Cherokee Publishing, 1982), p. 159.

The most striking peculiarity presented by a psychological crowd is the following: whoever be the individuals that compose it, however like or unlike their mode of life, their occupations, their character, or their intelligence, the fact that they have been transformed into a crowd puts them in possession of a sort collective mind which makes them feel, think, and act in a manner quite different from that in which each individual of them would feel, think, and act were he in a state of isolation. There are certain ideas and feelings which do not come into being, or do not transform themselves into acts, except in the case of individuals forming a crowd."*

This fundamental insight into the nature of crowd behavior is based on two important conclusions that now constitute the central tenets of crowd psychology: (1) a crowd is not merely the mathematical sum of its parts; and (2) an individual's behavior is changed by belonging to a crowd. Financial markets are seedbeds of crowd behavior, something we will study later in this chapter.

A human being's inclination to belong to a group presupposes the adaptation of individual behavior as a condition of acceptance by the majority. Referring to Arthur Koestler's book, *Janus: A Summing Up*, Tony Plummer states that three prerequisites must be met before an individual can join a group. The first is that the person in question identifies with the group. The second is that the person accepts the group's rules and norms. The third condition is acceptance of the group's leader. Several scientifically substantiated examples illustrate that individuals exhibit a tendency to reject people in other groups, to accept the view prevailing among the majority of the group to which they belong, and to accept instructions from a leader.

A series of experiments carried out by Henri Tejfel[†] at Bristol University demonstrated that schoolboys aged 14 and 15 changed

---

*Le Bon, *The Crowd*, p. 5.
[†]Plummer, *Forecasting Financial Markets*, p. 32.

their behavior when they were told that they belonged to a certain group—even though the group was unknown to them. It is remarkable that these boys automatically associated themselves with other members in the same group and expressed their open support for this group, while responding negatively toward members of other groups.

Researchers at Harvard University* found that the ability of experiment participants to carry out a task changed markedly under group pressure. When individual participants were asked to decide the length of a line in relation to three other lines, they made mistakes in only 1 percent of cases. When the same individuals were put into a group that had been given instructions previously, their rate of errors increased from 1 percent to 33 percent, even though the actual difference between the three lines was significant.

The best-known experiment demonstrating how far people are willing to go to satisfy the demands of a leader/authority figure was carried out by Dr. Stanley Milgram† at Yale University. In this experiment, the participants were invited to expose an innocent victim to repeated pain, with the understanding that it was for the good of the nation. The leader/authority figure was represented by a scientist in a white coat who repeatedly urged the participants to give the victim electric shocks. In fact, no electric shocks were administered, but the participants were not aware of this, and the victim behaved as if responding to pain. During the entire experiment, the participants knew what they were doing—not only did they see a meter registering how much electric current was being used and how dangerous this was for the victim, but they heard the screams and protests of the subject, who was tied to a chair. Milgram established that more than 60 percent of the participants were prepared to administer the highest, most lethal dose of electricity, even after the victim had stopped screaming and pretended to be unconscious.

Again, based on Tony Plummer's book *Forecasting Financial*

---

*Plummer, *Forecasting Financial Markets*, p. 32.

†Plummer, *Forecasting Financial Markets*, p. 34.

Markets, we can reach the following conclusions: These scientific experiments illustrate that a group, or crowd, led by a person of great authority can be a terrifying force. People within a group can develop such fierce idealism toward other members of the group that in extreme cases the idealism can lead to suicide. In striving to achieve a common goal, a group may use methods that individuals would consider unacceptable. To some extent, belonging to a group entails the suspension of personal responsibility, and people behave differently as group members than they do as individuals. In striving to achieve its purpose, a crowd tends to behave irrationally and emotionally, and its members are influenced to behave the same way—more so when the survival of the group is somehow threatened. Thus conflict and stress are excellent catalysts for crowd behavior.

To some extent, these observations explain some of the less attractive characteristics of human nature and make it easier to understand why otherwise peaceful and sensible individuals can march to war against their neighbors when inflamed and excited— to the applause of the masses. They help to explain, for example, why members of certain religious groups murder and torture others simply because they are of another faith. The list of examples can be frighteningly long. However, the purpose of this book is not to bemoan certain regrettable aspects of human nature, but rather to illuminate the significance of crowd psychology in behavior on the stock markets. Obviously, crowd psychology may generate negative behavior, mostly in times of crisis, stress, and conflict; but in normal circumstances people see group activity as a positive element in life. Joining various societies, camaraderie with colleagues at work, religious fellowship, and team spirit in athletics are all viewed as pluses in everyday life.

Crowd Behavior in Electronic Markets

Functional and enduring financial markets are relatively new in history. Even in the seventeenth century, during the mad days of tulip hysteria in Holland, there were transactions for future delivery, but that market collapsed after only a few years. The New York Stock Exchange was formed in 1792 as a club with a dozen or so members. On sunny days, they used to carry out their business under a large buttonwood tree; if it rained, Fraunces Tavern became their meeting place.

The structure of individual markets and the rules that regulate business vary from market to market. Today there are floor brokers who make eye contact only on exchanges that do not have electronic trading. In many countries the traditional stockbroker has disappeared, and orders are executed electronically or by telephone.

Although markets are structured differently and have differing regulations, they still have a number of features in common. The first is that it may be difficult to identify the people who actually constitute the market. A financial market is very much larger than just the people appearing on the exchange floor or doing business via computer or telephone at a given moment. Anyone owning shares, or selling short, or thinking about selling short, or buying now or later is a part of the actual market. Modern high-tech communication means that the same crowd behavior that used to develop in a group whose members were physically present can now develop just as easily among people who are not in the same place. Newspapers, television, computers, and telephones replace direct personal contact between group members. Players in financial markets all have the same aim: to make money. Even though they may not meet personally, they feel a kinship and identify easily with others who share their views on the direction that a particular stock or the market in general will take. Long before today's means of communication, Gustave Le Bon argued: "The disappearance of conscious personality and the turning of feelings and thoughts in a definite direction which are the primary characteristics of a crowd . . . do not always involve the simultaneous presence of individuals on one spot. Thousands of isolated individuals may acquire at a certain moment, and under the influence of certain violent emotions, the characteristics of a psychological crowd."*

---

*Le Bon, The Crowd, p. 2.

Naturally, crowd psychology exists in a purely physical sense in the electronic market of today as well. Just observe, for instance, the behavior in a major trading room when an unexpected economic event, such as an unexpected increase or lowering of an important interest rate, occurs. The mood change is palpable, and you can study the way the opinions of different individuals merge until the entire group accepts a similar view.

It is extremely important that you study crowd psychology in the market without being a part of it yourself, to observe what really happens—staying alert and clear-sighted. Otherwise it would be easy to be carried away and to allow your feelings to color the analysis of the markets or of an individual stock.

From Independent Investor to Crowd Member

Tony Plummer notes that this process can be described as follows: Whenever someone buys or sells stock, he or she is emotionally involved. The decision to buy or to sell may well be rational, but the actual action entails financial involvement, and an investor wants to feel that he or she has done the right thing. Now the investor has a holding with a value that may fluctuate. These fluctuations are beyond the investor's control. If the price goes in the right direction, the investor is delighted; but if it goes wrong, he or she is dissatisfied and unhappy.

These feelings of delight or anxiety are intensified when the investor mixes with other people. If the investor is correctly positioned in the market, the positive feelings are strengthened when he or she communicates with other investors who are also correctly positioned, reinforcing the correctness of both his or her position and the decision-making process before the purchase or sale. If newspaper articles or company analyses confirm this, the investor's satisfaction is even greater. People who made similar decisions seek support from each other and tend to belittle arguments produced by groups with a different opinion.

The more the price goes in favor of the correctly positioned investors, the stronger their arguments for being right are. The focus is more on the short-term than long-term price development. The group holding the opposite opinion naturally feels inferior and has an obvious need to communicate with and to seek support from like-minded people. They focus on the missing elements in the other group's argument and concentrate on the long-term perspective, where their view will turn out to be correct.

Although the decision was made on rational grounds, once the investment has been made, it is easy and very human to become less rational and more emotional. The individual is then more disposed to slide into crowd behavior. The more significant the differences of opinion, the greater the need to seek support and to join a group of like-minded investors. The herd instinct is very deep-rooted.

Price Is the Leader

When the price moves in the right direction, an investor can feel elation, expectantly awaiting the market's next move. When things go in the wrong direction, the investor can be angry, depressed, and nervous, anxiously waiting to see what the market will do to him or her next. The more emotional the investor becomes—excited and enthusiastic, or stressed and pressured—the easier it is for him or her to lose independence and to do as everyone else does, following the leader of the pack.

Tony Plummer points out that there may be an individual on the market who functions as the leader. An individual who is very successful on the stock market and who claims that his or her opinion is most often correct may directly influence price. Time and time again, someone appears with a reputation for predicting the market with great accuracy. A reputation of that kind is usually made when someone has predicted a move in direct opposition to general opinion and has subsequently turned out to be correct or when someone has succeeded in following a trend farther than anyone else.

But it is very rare for individuals to function as crowd leaders for very long. A position based on a high profile and significant media exposure is easily lost. Retrieving it, and renewing credibility, is rarely possible.

The true market leader is the price itself. Crowd behavior in the financial markets, unlike that in other groups, can be studied through two simple variables: (1) price development and (2) volume development. These two demonstrate the strength and the force of the crowd. Thousands of investors follow the price index or an individual stock constantly. Plummer makes the critical observation that a price development, moving clearly in a given direction, fulfills the function of the crowd leader. In a strong bull market, a price rise is the flag around which the majority of investors rally, declaring their respect, loyalty, and allegiance. In a bear market, a drop in price assumes the role of a severe, punishing ruler, before whom his subdued subjects kneel.

Crowd behavior develops in emotionally charged situations in financial markets, as is the case when large price movements make people either excited or panicky. A final accelerating movement in the last phase of a long-term trend and a powerful upward or downward break from a long-term range are effective catalysts for crowd behavior.

We have established the three fundamental prerequisites for crowd behavior in financial markets. (1) All investors have one single and common purpose—to make money. They identify easily with other participants on the market. (2) A decision to buy or to sell has a certain emotional effect on the investor. Anxiety and panic or joy and jubilation may develop quickly in the markets, making it easy to adapt to and accept the prevailing view of the price development. (3) A price moving clearly in a given direction fulfills the function of the crowd leader.

Now it is time to return to Max and Ian, to see how they and others behave, think, and feel when the price of Intersystems breaks up sharply and unexpectedly down from its lengthy interval.

Chapter 8

FACED WITH THE BREAKOUT

Ian Benson—Born Trader?

The last time we saw Max and Ian, Ian had just done his third trade in Intersystems. Both men were feeling very pleased with life. Ian has invested all his capital in the company and is now savoring the thought that he might be a millionaire in the relatively near future. After two successful trades, he figures trading is pretty straightforward. He calculates that if he could do two successful deals in a row, there would be nothing to stop him from making 10 killings in succession. He might actually become a full-time trader, if he just goes on with what he has been doing.

The thought that he might lose money in stocks has hardly occurred to Ian, though occasionally he feels a little twinge of anxiety. It really is a little risky, putting all your money into one stock. Oh well; he doesn't have a problem dealing with this vague uneasiness. He feels he has proved that he has what it takes to trade successfully. In the snack bar at work, they call him a "Little Soros" and a speculator. Those of his colleagues who have now also invested money in Intersystems treat him very respectfully, almost obsequiously. Ian is enjoying the situation. He feels he deserves his colleagues' admiration. It is because of him that they are now sitting there with their profits—though as yet unrealized—in Intersystems. It would really be only fair if they were to give him 10 percent when they have collected their profits. They would never have dared to make the investment if he hadn't shown them the way. He doesn't want to suggest it himself, but that is how he feels. He doesn't want to look greedy, but he might drop a few discreet hints; and maybe his colleagues would bite, now that he is enjoying such appreciation and respect.

Afternoon coffee is turning into a small ceremony; at a quarter to three, they assemble in the snack bar. Ian gets coffee first, then the others get theirs, in no particular order. Once they are all seated, Ian comments on the day's developments, then he repeats his daily conversation with Max Bork. Those of his colleagues who have invested in Intersystems usually sit together on one sofa, while those who haven't sit on the other one. The tone is good-natured, but there are clear undercurrents, a tendency to jealousy and maybe even to self-righteousness. After all, apart from Ian, no one has made major amounts of money; and of course, Ian is the only one who has booked any profits. There hasn't been any controversy, but it is normal for the two groups to bicker before Benson starts his run-through.

Ian's group is essentially united. They all want to make money, and they share the opinion that Intersystems has been a good investment; it is only a matter of time before profits start rolling in. Ian is the group's natural leader, given to downplaying fears and the critical opinions on the future of Intersystems that are aired occasionally. He usually announces loudly that he certainly wouldn't have put all his money into Intersystems if it hadn't been a pretty safe investment. They are all free to sell whenever they want to. It's never wrong to take a profit, however small, he says. But he emphasizes that he does not intend to worry. Just like the last time, he is going wait for the right moment to sell.

Max Bork—Born Broker?

After recommending Intersystems successfully, Max Bork has acquired a more secure position in Wilson & Partners. Of course he is not the only one in the firm who recommended the stock, but he was unquestionably the driving force and the most active one on his clients' behalf. Bork is finding that life is very good.

He has entirely forgotten those occasions when he made less successful recommendations, sometimes not even wanting to answer the phone for fear that the call might be yet another dissatisfied client. Now he gleefully picks up the phone on the very first ring. Of course, his clients don't only have shares in Intersystems; but for most of them, Intersystems is their largest holding. When Max recommended the stock for the third time, most of his clients, since they had already made two profitable trades in the stock, bought considerably larger lots than before.

Max's colleagues have nicknamed him "Ice," the kid who is so cool that frost forms in his footprints. Bork is too young to be a leader at work; but when it comes to Intersystems, he notices that even his more experienced colleagues are clearly following his movements very carefully. After all, he was the one who dared to trust his intuition and go his own way.

Although Max is enjoying his success, he does occasionally feel a slight twinge of anxiety. Supposing it all goes wrong? This third time he really did push Intersystems, and now everyone's eyes are on him. His older colleagues aren't usually inclined to listen to his opinion; but now, suddenly, he seems to be leading the pack. Max remembers a saying he read recently in some newspaper: "Success has a thousand fathers, but failure is fatherless." If the third trade in Intersystems goes well, his stock will go up considerably in their eyes. If it goes wrong, he'll be criticized for his cockiness. He knows how easy it is to become the target of other people's anger if you're wrong and you've stuck your chin out too far.

Yet when he has thoughts of this kind, Max disposes of them easily. There is nothing to indicate any risk of Intersystems breaking out of its range on the downside. His clients are also on the plus side on the third trade, and the fact is, his clients and his colleagues will have to take the responsibility for their own decisions. He is a broker, after all, not a portfolio manager. No, he'll live up to his nickname. Like the wolf leading the pack, he'll lead both his clients and colleagues to more hidden prey.

Chapter 9

UPWARD BREAK—
IAN BENSON

The last time Ian and Max talked, Ian bought Intersystems at 106 on Max's recommendation. The stock had then gone up quickly to 115, as the market was seized with dizzy delight after a lowering of the Federal funds rate.

Up to 120

After remaining static for a day or two at about 115, the price rapidly goes to 120. Ian can hardly remember ever feeling so good before. He is extremely pleased with life; he is making money—good money—on his investment in Intersystems, and he is winning the respect and approval of his colleagues—at least those who followed his advice. Ian has noticed that Johnson is less talkative recently and always sits on "the other" sofa during coffee breaks. He avoids talk about Intersystems, except to say that in his opinion, capital gains taxes ought to be higher. The rest of those in the group that haven't invested in Intersystems are generally more good-natured than Johnson. But now that it looks as if all those "speculators" with Ian in the lead will be making another successful trade, jealousy is much more in evidence. Johnson is not the only one critical of making money without "working."

When Intersystems has been at about 120 for a week (Figure

9.1), the discussion in Benson's group about whether it might be best to take the profit gets increasingly animated. The strongest argument from those who want to sell is that they have made more than 10 percent on their investment in less than a month—more than the interest earned on a bank account in a couple of years. It's best not to be too greedy, someone says, because you could lose all of it. Suddenly the proponents of selling within Benson's group are being supported by those who have not invested in Intersystems. "The price could collapse any minute" and "Think about the 1987 stock market crash" are some of the encouraging comments flying round the room.

Ian Benson's eyes darken. He clenches his fists so hard that his nails leave red marks on his palms. He leaps up from the sofa and says loudly in a trembling voice that they can all do as they damned well please, but he is definitely not going to sell—just to make some grudging, envious colleagues happy. He concludes with biting sarcasm that they are just afraid that everyone who

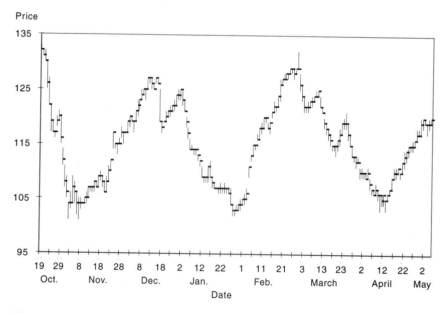

Figure 9.1. After a week's consolidation around 120, some members of Benson's group want to take their profit.

bought Intersystems might make even more money. The talk within Benson's group about possibly selling quickly dies out, and silence settles on the room. Benson's role as leader is obvious to anyone challenging his opinion that Intersystems may well go up another 10 points. Anyone who might still be wondering whether to sell keeps those thoughts to him- or herself.

Up to 129

In the following week, Intersystems goes up to 129, then falls by a point or two. Ian's position as the leader of the group is now absolutely indisputable, and the acid comments from the other sofa are made in a low key. But now, to his surprise, Ian notices that his suggestion to seriously consider selling the stock is not met with much enthusiasm. (See Figure 9.2.) Those who had keenly advocated selling the week before are now saying they should aim higher—for something over 130. Think how morti-

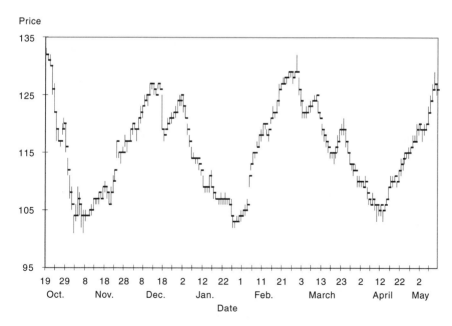

Figure 9.2.   When the price goes to 129, the desire to sell decreases.

fied they would be now if they had sold at 120 a few days earlier, is a common opinion. The price may actually go up to 150 or even as high as 200, is another view. Maybe Intersystems will launch another product, or it might be taken over. Some major investor might push the price up.

When Ian describes his conversation with Max Bork—who strongly recommended selling—and also quotes Bork's opinion that being greedy is fatal, he notices that this has a certain dampening effect on the group.

Ian insists that he really is thinking of selling, but he also feels his conviction beginning to waver. His colleagues are no fools; they are highly skilled engineers. Suppose they are right and he is the one who is wrong? He sees his profit disappear before his eyes after a quick decline, vanishing into a black hole—out of his reach. But his colleagues' greed has infected him, and the thought of how much more he could make if the price really rose to 150 is extraordinarily gratifying. Doubts have set in. In torment, Ian decides to wait at least a day or two before deciding whether to sell.

Fruitless Waiting—Up to 130, Down to 125

Nothing much happens to the Intersystems price over the next few days. The stock moves sideways, both buyers and sellers in the market guarded due to decreasing volume. The people in Benson's group who recently argued heatedly that they should wait to sell are now not so sure. All of them are satisfied with the way the price has been moving since they bought, but they have become accustomed to Intersystems' pattern of not standing still for more than a week before it goes up some more. Now that it has remained static for almost two weeks, impatience and uncertainty spread throughout the group. But when the stock is quoted at 130, these negative feelings disperse like thin clouds on a sunny summer's day. The incipient dejection turns into a mild euphoria. Now comes the next spurt. Now, everyone thinks, it's time for 140. Ian is glad that he decided to wait before selling, in spite of his principles. It would have been very annoying to miss the coming upturn.

By the next day, the euphoria has evaporated. Just before the market closed the day before, the price fell rapidly and mercilessly to close at 127. Now it is down to 125. Benson is annoyed. He has just spoken to Max Bork, who told him he was greedy not to have sold already. To the other group, he complains that he had wanted to sell two weeks ago, and he ought to have known better than to listen to inexperienced amateurs instead of doing what both he and the broker thought best.

Now he has sold his shares. (See Figure 9.3.) His profit is still excellent and he has not the slightest desire to follow his colleagues down to the bottom of the trading range. They can do what they like, but he has made sure that he can buy Intersystems back at a lower price for the fourth time. Confused and slightly shaken by this outburst, no one in the group questions Ian's decision. Still, they think he was unnecessarily rude, calling them amateurs, when he himself has only been active in the market for less than a year.

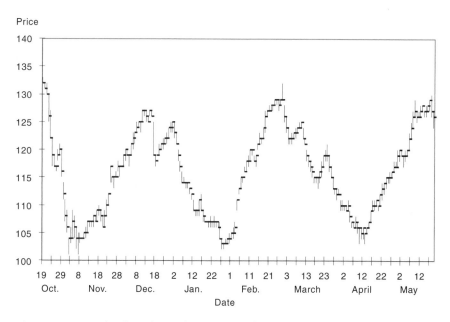

Figure 9.3.   Third trade—After waiting for a further upturn, Ian Benson sells at 125, completing his third profitable trade in Intersystems.

There Is No Downturn

For the next few days, the price remains at about the level at which everyone has sold. Gone is their dejection. It was an excellent trade, even if they did not sell at the high. Now Benson's group feels that it is just a matter of waiting for the next buying opportunity in Intersystems. Benson too has recovered from his earlier doubts. He has actually made a really tidy sum on this last trade, and his eyes gleam as he calculates how rich he will be if he goes on at the same rate.

Intersystems does not go down as expected. After a day or two, it is above their selling price. Still, Ian is confident. He tells the group that he has spoken to Bork, who says Wilson & Partners' pharmaceutical analysts feel that Intersystems stock is fully valued at its present level. It won't be long before the price starts down again, he says confidently and so loudly that Johnson can't help hearing him.

But Intersystems refuses to go down. Johnson, who has been very quiet, begins to perk up. He notices that Benson's armor of self-confidence has developed a small but noticeable chink. When an article in *Business Today* points to Intersystems as a potential winner, Johnson's cheerfulness knows no bounds. Smiling radiantly, he personally hands a copy of the article to everyone on what he calls the "speculator sofa."

Although the members of the Benson group know that they have done good business and behaved in a disciplined and essentially rational manner, most of them still regret selling. The thought that Intersystems might go to 200, as the article suggests, and that then they would have missed a profit of almost 75 points per share makes them grumpy and irritable. But Ian, who feels that their disappointment is directed at him, calms them down by pointing out that they have made money; and if it hadn't been for him, none of them would have bought Intersystems at all. Not only that, he says, but if they believe what the article says, then they are all free to buy back their shares.

When emotions have cooled, a convivial atmosphere returns. The market doesn't seem to have taken the article in *Business*

Today seriously. A one-point uptick compared with the day before is actually nothing to mope about.

There Is an Upturn

The next day, Ian feels as if he had been punched in the solar plexus. He can't breathe. Intersystems goes to 133 in active trading, its highest level since last October. (See Figure 9.4.) But there is no argument within the group. Intuitively, they all feel that Johnson's crowd would be delighted to see evidence of an internal strife, so they keep up appearances, saying that, of course, they sold Intersystems too soon, but they will buy it back when the correction comes. But at the end of the working day, when they meet in Benson's office instead of discussing it in the snack bar, their disappointment does find an outlet. Benson points out

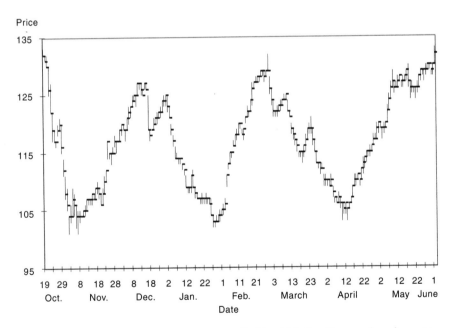

Figure 9.4.   When the price unexpectedly hits 133, Ian Benson breaks out in a cold sweat.

that the situation is under control and they should not be hasty; but the prevailing attitude is that they ought to buy back their shares as soon as possible—preferably first thing in the morning—except that it's so humiliating to buy back at a price higher than where they sold. Most of them feel that if they get a price below 130, it won't be too bad. Maybe it will go down next day, someone says hopefully before they all go home.

There is no downturn, just a continued upturn of a few more points. For Ian Benson, this situation is new, unusual, and unpleasant. The price is now about 10 points higher than where he sold. True, something similar happened with his second investment in Intersystems; but then the stock only went up 5 points after he sold, and it was not all that long before the price began to fall dramatically. Now he thinks this is no fun anymore. By broadcasting his successful investments, he has become both adviser and father figure to his colleagues, who are in the same situation he is in, and a hate object to Johnson, whose face is aglow with malicious delight.

Ian does not know what to do. Max Bork thinks it's unfortunate that Intersystems keeps going up, but things like that do happen, he says. Still, they did three excellent trades with which they should be very satisfied. The firm's pharmaceutical analyst is sticking to her opinion and says she cannot explain the strong buying interest in Intersystems. All we can do is hope for a downturn, says Bork, or put the money in some other stock. After all, Intersystems is only one of many, many stocks on the market. You must see that you can't always be right, he points out. If you fret about money you haven't made instead of being happy with the gains you have made, then you shouldn't have anything to do with trading, Bork says emphatically. Just put your shares in a drawer and forget about them.

After this conversation with Max, Ian feels he has regained his grasp of the situation. After passing Bork's opinion on to the group, they all think the situation is under control in spite of the day's upturn.

For the next few days, Intersystems stays around 136, and calm descends. All they have to do now is wait for the downturn, which is sure to come soon. Then they will act. Who knows? Maybe it was just some inexperienced small investors who drove the price up after that favorable article in *Business Today*. That idea is popular with the group. Ian tells them about the strain when the price soared after he sold for the second time. But he took it calmly, and everything had worked out for the best.

Continued Upturn to 145

There is no downturn. There is a sharp upturn instead. Intersystems has been given a strategically important order based on "the excellent product quality," as the buyer put it. The entire market realizes simultaneously that Intersystems is still a growth company; the large recent order is a clear indication of a brilliant future for the company.

Ian Benson has trouble dealing with his contradictory feelings. What should he tell his colleagues? His self-image has been dealt a tremendous blow. A few weeks ago he was calculating how long it would take him to become a millionaire. Now he is figuring how much money he has missed out on. The colleagues who previously looked on him with admiration now realize that he doesn't actually know all that much about the stock market and that it is only with the help of Max Bork that he succeeded in buying low and selling high three times in a row. Ian realizes he will have to come down from his "high horse." He is not an experienced trader. When it comes to trading, apart from what he has read about the market in the past year and the three profitable trades he has managed to make with the help of Bork, he has neither in-depth knowledge nor experience. Still, the situation isn't too bad, he decides after he has calmed down. Everyone made money, himself not the least. Now he can be one of the gang instead of the leader of the group.

What will they do? Will they rush after Intersystems, or accept the situation and realize that the longed-for downturn is not going to come? They understand that major players are now in on the act; the article in *Business Today* may actually have been right in saying that Intersystems might go to 200. The group is ambivalent. They want to buy Intersystems back, and yet they don't. If the stock keeps going up, it would be right to buy now. But if you rushed to buy and then got an immediate correction,

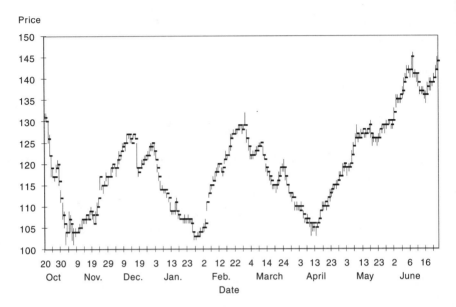

Figure 9.5. With the price up to 145, Ian and his colleagues think it is definitely too late to buy back the shares they sold at 125. History does not record how they exploited the subsequent downturn to buy back Intersystems.

you would feel like an idiot. Everyone else seems to be buying. They actually know very little about the market. Do they think they know best? The accepted view in the group is that if everyone else is buying, they must know what they are doing.

Before they have time to decide, Intersystems soars to 145 on June 7 (Figure 9.5), and the group loses courage. Buying back a stock at 145 that they sold for 125 is entirely too uncertain. Even though it might be the right thing to do, no one wants or dares to make that decision. They will have to be satisfied with the money they made, say a silent prayer for a decent downturn, and start looking for other interesting stocks. On this, they are all agreed. But first, they are going to learn more about the market.

Buying at the right moment, buying low and selling high was not as easy as it sounded. There turned out to be a big difference between having an opinion on what to do and actually making the decisions that involved making or losing money.

Chapter 10

UPWARD BREAK—MAX BORK

When last heard from, Max Bork was energetically calling his clients, recommending that they buy Intersystems. The stock then went up quickly to 115 in market euphoria over the Fed's unexpected lowering of the Federal funds rate.

Upturn to 120

After hovering at about 115 for a few days, the price quickly goes up to 120. Max is very tempted to take his profit at this level. (See Figure 10.1.) He wants to sell at at least 125, but the thought of selling at 120 is appealing. His colleagues and clients ask him what they should do; he desperately wants this—his third trade in Intersystems—to be successful. If he recommends selling now, the trade will be "clinched," and he will escape the mental pressure he is under. Because his two previous trades were successful, some people seem to think he can see into the future, but he has no idea what the price will do tomorrow. Greed is torture, Max thinks. His clients like to remind him how important it is to call them first so that they will have time to sell at a good price before he recommends that his other clients also rake in their profits.

Max is irresolute. Does he recommend selling now, taking it easy, or patiently waiting for a higher price? There is a price to pay for being the center of attention, he thinks. Previously he could buy and sell anything whenever he liked, without anyone paying much attention to his activities. Now he feels he is being

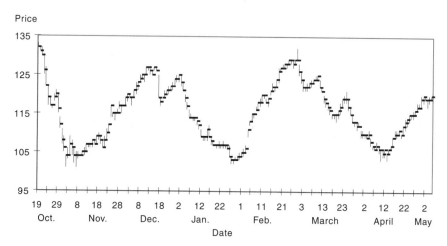

Price

Figure 10.1.   Max is tempted to sell at 120, but he decides to wait for a better price.

watched, and he is not happy about everyone on the trading desk listening to his phone calls to know what he is recommending when it comes to Intersystems. Still, he shouldn't complain, he tells himself. He wanted his colleagues' respect and admiration, and now he has it.

The situation just does not feel as rosy as he had imagined it would. After thinking for a bit, Max makes his decision. He will wait to sell Intersystems, but he certainly will not be greedy. As soon as the price approaches 130, he will recommend selling— forcefully, and with no hesitation. If, despite all expectations, the upturn continues, his clients can hardly complain because they have made a nice profit. He feels relieved. Once he has a clear strategy, being the center of a whole lot of attention suddenly feels good again. Once you have scented the prey, the role of leader of the wolf pack is pretty comfortable, Max thinks philosophically and leans back contentedly, hands behind his head.

Upturn to 129

Max thanks his lucky stars that he waited before selling Intersystems. After barely one week, he has reached his goal; the price is up to 129. To his surprise, he feels some hesitation before beginning to call his clients to suggest that they sell. Suppose Intersystems is being reevaluated, or something is going on in the company—something that he knows nothing about but others do? The volume has actually been unusually heavy this last week. He notices that his colleagues are waiting for his decision and feels he has no choice. After all, he stated, loud and clear, to both clients and colleagues that Intersystems should be sold when the price neared 130. There's no turning back now. He has an intensely unpleasant feeling in his stomach; he feels anxiety creeping back. He must make up his mind. Frantically he tries to think what to do, and suddenly he sees a solution. How simple! Why didn't he think of it before? He will talk to the pharmaceutical analyst. She usually has concrete and definite opinions.

What a relief! No hesitation there. The analyst was very clear about her opinion that Intersystems was expensive at its present price level. Her message is that other companies in the same sector look more interesting right now.

Max loves life again. His anxiety evaporates like water on a hot stove. The wolf is on his way—prey is in sight. He will bring it down with a well-directed attack and then receive the pack's homage.

He relishes picking up the telephone to call his clients, briefly and concisely enunciating five words: "It is time to sell." When most of his colleagues react like a well-drilled troop with orders from a superior officer and make similar calls, his satisfaction mounts. The battle against the market has been won.

Max can afford to feel like a lord. He has no time to call Ian Benson before the market closes, but he looks forward to doing it first thing in the morning. Benson is bound to be triumphant; he has invested every penny in Intersystems. (See Figure 10.2.)

Next day, to his great surprise, Max realizes that Ian is reluctant to sell, saying he wants to talk to his colleagues first. He explains that discussing Intersystems at their coffee break has become a habit; and even though it is really just a formality, it would seem wrong if he sold before he told his colleagues. Although Bork points out that it is risky to have all your money in one stock and dangerous to be greedy, Benson still wants to wait until the next day before putting in his order to sell.

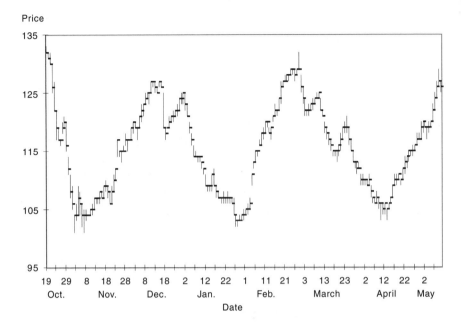

Figure 10.2. When the price goes to 129, Max Bork recommends that his clients take their profits.

Max is slightly offended. He helped Benson make three straight profitable trades, and now he wants to discuss things with his colleagues first. They know even less about the market than Benson does! Oh well, it is Benson's money, and he can do as he pleases. But let's hope he learns his lesson. Nothing blurs a person's judgment so much as greed. Max knows that from bitter experience. Now he has a tormented look in his eye.

 Things turn out just as he had been afraid they would. Benson does not want to sell. Greed has won out. His colleagues want to hang on to their holdings, and, Ian points out, they are pretty clever engineers.

 Do as you like, says Max; just don't say I didn't warn you. Clever engineers, he thinks. We live in different worlds. In theirs, some solutions are right and some solutions are wrong. In my world, you never know whether a decision is going to be right or wrong ahead of time. You can only do your best and behave as rationally as possible. It is hard to be firm when you feel unsure, and there is time pressure—only time will tell whether you were right or wrong. I wonder if good old Benson will ever understand that. He seems to think that profitable trades are normal and that he is smarter than the market. Ian Benson needs a good lesson, Max says to himself, with some annoyance.

Tense Waiting—Up to 130, Down to 125

After Max has recommended that all his clients sell Intersystems, there is a period of tense waiting as he keeps a watchful eye on the stock. He would like the price to drop rapidly and dramatically. Then there would be no doubt that he had been right. The price does not go up, but it does not drop either. Max feels vaguely anxious, but it is not too hard to shake off the feeling. His clients have made a good profit. If the price starts going up in spite of expectations, Max figures he will just have to shrug his shoulders, be content with the money they made, and not brood over profits they missed.

After vacillating for barely two weeks, the price goes to 130, and Max feels uneasy. He thought the danger was past, and now he has been caught napping. At market close, the price is at 127. Relieved, he decides it was a false alarm. When the price keeps dropping the next day (Figure 10.3), it is a pleasure to call Ian Benson to ask whether he doesn't want to sell Intersystems after all. A subdued Benson accepts his suggestion without hesitation. He regrets having listened to his ignorant colleagues instead of Max.

No Downturn

Max Bork is now convinced that Intersystems will keep on dropping. When the price refuses to fall below 125, he is uneasy. A week later it starts to go up instead. When it is back at 130 again, Ian Benson naturally calls to ask what's happening. Max explains as calmly as he can that nothing is happening, that the analyst still thinks Intersystems is fully valued.

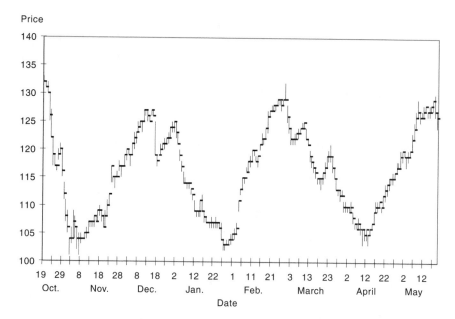

Figure 10.3. Intersystems doesn't manage to break 130, but drops to 125. Max again suggests that Ian sell.

After another week, Max has to start the day by changing his shirt. A column in *Business Today* has "Intersystems May Go to 200" as its headline. He is thrown off balance and spills coffee all over himself. Cursing as the hot coffee soaks through his shirt and stings his chest, he leaps out of his chair. What a way to start the day! Max snarls, extremely agitated. An idiot columnist— and scalding coffee all over his only clean shirt.

All his worries and anxieties now settled just below his ribs, Max waits for the market to open. He tries to prepare himself for what to do if the price opens straight up. But no—Oh wonderful! How absolutely wonderful! Intersystems is up only one miserable point. He knew their pharmaceutical analyst was smart. The market ignores the newspaper column, which "even objectively" Max thinks, is not only bad, but unsubstantiated. When he gets the call from Ian Benson that he had been expecting, he establishes with some satisfaction that the firm's pharmaceutical analyst's assessment is of a higher quality than those scribblings in *Business Today*.

It Becomes an Upturn

The next day, watching to see how Intersystems will open, Bork is calm and relaxed. If yesterday's column really had been correct, then according to his logical and rational analysis the market would have driven up the stock by considerably more than one miserable point. To his dismay, he sees the price go up three points to 133. (See Figure 10.4.) He knows that his colleagues expect some comment from him; he feels an almost desperate need to look cool, calm, and collected. He remembers a cartoon he saw recently in a business paper. A fox is roaming around a pond on which a miserable duck is swimming with apparent calm. In fact, under the surface, the duck is paddling frantically. The caption read: "Be like a duck—calm and unruffled above the surface. Below the surface, paddle like hell."

Max does the only thing he can think of in his agitated state of mind—he talks to the analyst. She is surprised at the upturn but can find no rational reason for it. Intersystems is in the bid-

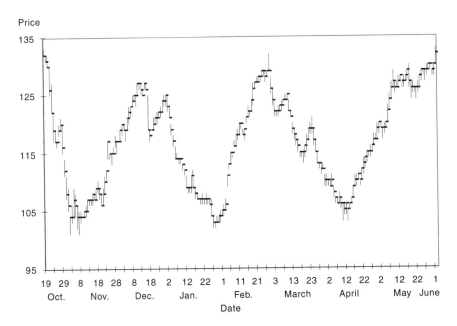

Figure 10.4. When the price unexpectedly goes up to 133, Max Bork comes under pressure.

ding for a major and strategically important order, she says, but it is very unlikely that the company will receive more than a minor share of it because their production problems are still not completely under control.

Max takes a deep breath and calms down. He knows the situation is not really so drastic. He is the one choosing to be upset and frustrated. He knew that just such a situation might well come up. Just because he thinks the price of Intersystems ought to go down—not up—doesn't mean he controls the market. He can't be right every time. Besides, all his clients have made at least one profitable trade with Intersystems. It's just that he had advised them to sell so emphatically.

Max knows that people can be terribly irrational when it comes to money. Instead of being pleased with the profit they did make, some will brood over the profit they missed out on. He will also hear what he hates more than anything else: Why didn't he, sitting there in front of the screen, know that the price would keep going up? Stupid asses, he thinks. They think I have a crystal ball.

Oh well, all he can do is relax and look for a new investment for his clients. He has no desire whatsoever to chase after the stock, and he has no intention of buying it back unless it drops below his clients' selling price. It might be the right thing to do, but pride will prevent that.

Next day, Intersystems is at 135, but now Max is better prepared mentally. When he gets the expected call from Ian Benson, he explains quite calmly, in a voice loud enough so that his colleagues will be sure to hear him, that it is a shame that Intersystems has gone up 10 points since he sold, but the firm's pharmaceutical analyst sticks to her opinion that Intersystems is fully valued. Also, Ian has had three straight profitable trades in Intersystems, thanks to Max's recommendations. If Ian is dissatisfied, he is being really unfair. If he is going to brood over the profit he missed out on instead of being happy about the money he did make, he should definitely not be trading. He might just as well put his stocks in a drawer and forget about them for a year or two, Max says. What is important is that he made money. You can't always be right. Intersystems is only one of many thousands of stocks on the market. Now it is a question of finding another good stock or buying back Intersystems, if the price drops sharply in spite of expectations.

When his colleagues spontaneously applaud, Max gets up and takes a bow, feeling as if he has regained his mental equilibrium along with his colleagues' respect. Even if Intersystems were to keep going up, by having had the strength to make a tough decision under stress, he has lived up to the group's expectations. Of course, his friends wondered how he would handle the situation. No one in the firm had been more successful in exploiting the swings in Intersystems over the past year than Max. His colleagues felt the same pressure he did when the price went up instead of down, as they had expected. It is hard to resist the temptation to chase after a stock that the rest of the market seems to be chasing. That is how Max sums things up.

Now that he has declared openly that he has no intention of doing what the rest of the pack is doing and chasing Intersystems, his colleagues can relax, too. Of course, they are always free to do what they think best, but now that everyone around the trading desk knows that Max has no intention of buying back the stock unless it falls below his clients' selling price, they feel less pressured to "jump on the bandwagon" themselves. It feels good to be doing what everyone else on the desk is doing. Going against Mr. Intersystems—Max and the rest of the group—and the analyst's recommendation, too, would take very high self-esteem and the firm inner conviction of being right.

Continued Upturn to 145

After a day or two around 136, it's time for Max to spill his coffee again. Just before the market opens, he reads on his screen that in the face of tough international competition, Intersystems has won an important strategic order because of the excellent quality of its products. The analyst admits that this was entirely unexpected and now radically changes her view of the company. Obviously, Intersystems solved their problems more quickly than she had anticipated, and the company is much more competitive than she had thought. Although it goes against the grain, she

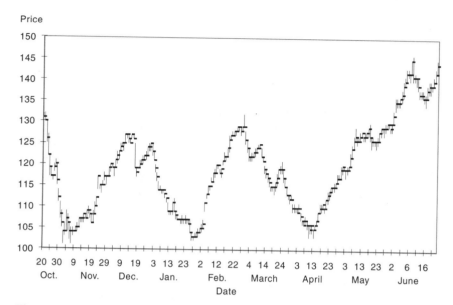

Figure 10.5. When Intersystems is up at 145, Max feels it is out of the question to recommend buying it back. History does not record what he advised his clients to do after the correction that followed.

admits to Max that she had been too pessimistic, and the stock now looks like a buy.

Though Max had been reasonably well prepared mentally for the possibility that Intersystems might go up even further, it's horrible to realize that he recommended selling a possible market winner 16 to 20 points below the day's close. What should he do? What *can* he do? To suggest buying it back at 145 seems out of the question. (See Figure 10.5.) The price has gone up too far since his recommendation to sell. He is depressed and resigned.

He takes a walk in town to sort things out, and the gentle summer breeze on his face begins to make him feel better. The insight that finally clarifies his thinking is that he did not know as much about the market as he thought he did. He ought to have realized that a stock that has moved within a range for months can go up very quickly when that range is broken. Well, he has learned something, and he still has all his clients. Now, he says to himself, the time has come to get out of this melancholy frame of mind and to show the world that this guy is made of the right stuff. The wolf is on the prowl again.

Chapter 11

CROWD PSYCHOLOGY AT AN UPWARD BREAK

Ian Benson, Max Bork, and their colleagues are only a small part of the great crowd that consists of all the Intersystems stockholders—those who have held their shares for a long time, newcomers who bought since the price began to fluctuate, and those who sold or shorted Intersystems, either before or during the period the price fluctuated within its range. It also includes those who showed no interest in Intersystems earlier but who are now thinking of buying or selling short without having taken action yet.

This is the crowd we will be analyzing when Intersystems breaks out of the range on the upside. Initially, with Ian Benson and Max Bork, we studied psychology more in terms of individual behavior. Now, if this book is to give the reader a real insight into market behavior, it is time to explain the vast influence of crowd behavior on price movements in relation to an upward breakout from a long-term price range.

The Vacuum Effect

First, let's go back to what David Fuller calls the vacuum effect. (See Figure 11.1.) The larger part of latent supply above the range has vanished. Many stockholders, that is, presumptive sellers, gradually tire of waiting for an upward trend in Intersystems. At

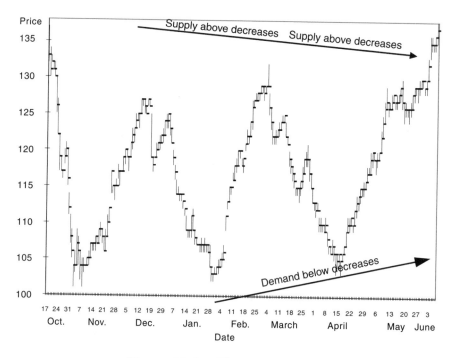

Figure 11.1.   The vacuum effect.

first, only a few sellers lower their selling limits; they are not prepared to accept the price the market is offering, namely a price within the trading range. After lowering their limit once or twice, more of them become impatient at not having sold at the price they wanted. Even the most stubborn of them begin to realize that if they want to dispose of their holdings, they have to "climb down" in the range. Of course, not all of them are keen to sell at the prevailing market price, but the longer the trading range lasts, the more the supply is drawn into the range, since that is where a deal can be done.

As pointed out previously, time is a very important factor. Making the mental adjustment necessary to accepting a price lower than planned takes time. Resistance to selling is ground down only slowly. The longer the stock trades within a range, the stronger the psychological dynamic becomes. After a sufficiently long period in this phase, a psychologically charged situation is built up that may result in a powerful upward price movement. Now because latent supply has been largely drawn away from the market because stockholders tired of waiting for the "right" price have sold within the range, there is a vacuum of sellers above the range.

A clear upward breakout from the range on volume means that there is an obvious imbalance in the market. All those who sold or bought their shares when the price was in the range feel that they have acted either "mistakenly" or "correctly." All buys and sells within the range were executed at a price lower than the present one. As long as Intersystems was ranging, buyers and sellers were equally strong, with roughly the same number right as wrong. Some sold in the upper part of the range and were content, some bought at the lower part of the range and were also satisfied. Of course, the opposite also applies. Some think they sold too low and were dissatisfied, while many others are unhappy, thinking they bought too high.

It is impossible to predict how long a trading range will last, but one thing is certain: it never lasts forever. It is impossible to determine what will trigger an upward breakout from Intersystems' long consolidating phase. It could be a column in *Business Today*, rumors of the big order, positive analyses from major financial houses, buying interest from major players, or a combination of all these factors.

When, after several weeks of gathering strength at the top of the range, Intersystems now breaks sharply upward (Figure 11.2) instead of turning down, as it did previously when it went above 125, many people are distressed, and a study of crowd psychology is appropriate.

Previously, we have defined what makes up the great crowd on the market in connection with the breakout from the range. But a large crowd is itself made up of larger and smaller groups. The two obvious groups in this case are the investors who are disappointed and unhappy when the range breaks on the upside and those who feel it is to their advantage.

Let's first look at the psychology of the negative group and then of the positive group. Then let's study some diagrams of real situations in the market to be sure that the theory is in line

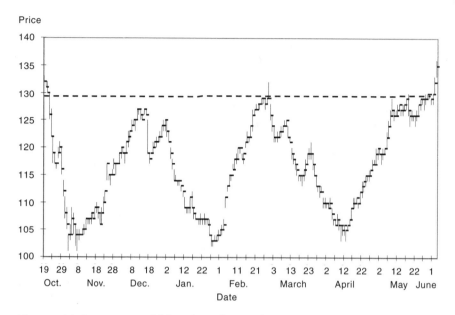

Figure 11.2. A powerful breakout from a long-term range on volume is an excellent catalyst for crowd behavior in the stock market.

with reality. This will give us a look at how this knowledge can serve as the basis for making decisions when trading on the stock market.

Negative Subgroups of Investors

The negative group within the greater crowd can be divided into four subgroups:

I. The Impatient Ones—The largest and most important subgroup, consisting of stockholders who owned Intersystems before it began to range and who have sold all or more than 50 percent of their holdings at a price within the range because they tired of waiting for a big break.

II. The Masters of Timing—This group consists of stockholders who bought once or several times within the range and then also sold at a price within the range.

III. The Wait-and-See Investors—Investors/traders who either bought less than 50 percent of what they planned to buy or who thought about buying but did not have time to make the trade because the share price got away from them.

IV. The Short-Sellers—Investors/traders who sold Intersystems short; that is, they borrowed shares that they then sold, with the intention of buying them back later at the lower price to which they thought the price would drop. When the price breaks upward, they are forced to buy back these shares at a higher level.

Common Characteristics

First, let's establish that those who have sold or shorted Intersystems within the range are mostly dissatisfied and disappointed. Some may be more or less content, but it is extremely unlikely that the majority of those who sold or shorted while Intersystems fluctuated in the range are happy. Most of them are dissatisfied with their lack of gain or possibly even a loss. Even if they sold the stock at a profit, they are unlikely to be pleased. Greed is a torment and tends to turn most people into emotional rather than rational creatures. It is very common for people to fret over money they *didn't* make, rather than to be pleased with the money they actually did make.

Subgroup I—The Impatient Ones

This is probably the largest group in a class of its own, so our analysis is focused on them. For those like Lena Bergwall, who sold at the bottom of the range—just as the share began to range—the mental strain is probably less than for those who, like Ken Erland, waited several months for the price to go up and then, out of sheer impatience and nerves, sold during the two weeks when the share price touched the bottom of the range for the third time, before turning up seriously.

Lena Bergwall and the other stockholders who all sold at about the same time made a marginally better trade in terms of dollars; but for the most part, there was a longer interval between the selling point and the breakout, so the mental torment is ameliorated by the time factor. The memories of the anguish before the decision to sell and of the disappointment when the stock swung upward after they sold have faded. Additionally, the money from the stock they sold is now probably invested in another stock, and the original decision to sell was probably not really wrong, considering how much time elapsed before the stock began to climb again.

But if, after waiting and agonizing for a long time, people get tired of waiting for the upturn that never seems to come and sell at the bottom of the range, only to find that they sold just before the turn finally did come, the strain is very palpable. That kind of sale is not uncommon, but it is one of the most frustrating things that can happen to a trader. It is entirely human to lose patience with a stock that only seems to swing hither and thither—actually just moving sideways. The frustration, the anxiety, and—most significant—the impatience that many investors feel when a share price stubbornly refuses to move in a clear direction is what lies behind many selling decisions on the market. It is not unusual for investors to begin to dislike a stock and to see it as the cause of all their troubles. Instead of taking real responsibility for their decisions, people are inclined to project their negative feelings onto the stock.

Shares in Intersystems are nothing but a legal concept; they have neither feelings nor a will of their own. They do not care in the slightest whether their price goes up, or down, or just marks time. It is human beings who have the feelings. No one forced Intersystems stockholders to buy; they made the decision quite voluntarily. Yet it is much easier to blame the market's incomprehensible pricing and to let the Intersystems stock become the focus of anger than to realize that as a trader one is responsible for one's decisions and reactions. The disappointment is probably due to an insufficiently researched investment decision or to a reluctance to accept the fact that trades do not always produce the expected return. A common and easy decision in such a situation is to sell. That way, the investor avoids the stress, the pressure, and the exhaustion connected with the incomprehensible price swings and may even enjoy some inner satisfaction in taking revenge on the stock for the misery it has caused by refusing to have anything more to do with it in the future.

It is not at all unusual for people to follow price movements of a stock even more attentively after they have sold it than they did when they owned it. The more emotional the selling decision, the more important it is to feel one has done the right thing, otherwise negative feelings have no outlet and tend to have a reinforcing effect. It is very unpleasant for a stockholder to be in anguish for months while the stock fluctuates in its range and then, to top things off, to "be done out of it."

When Intersystems moves up sharply after touching bottom for the third time and it is clear that, with a little more patience, one could have been part of that move, it triggers psychological trauma that can cause people to give up trading. After waiting so long and then missing out by only a few days—sometimes only an hour or two—it is painful to see the price finally move up.

Although the price was at the bottom of the range for the third time when Ken Erland put in his sell order, he was happy with his decision. Gone were the tension and impatience he had been suffering. Still, his satisfaction probably turned quickly to annoyance when Intersystems began going up the day after he sold it. That kind of experience can make even a seasoned trader think about changing professions.

As long as the share price does not go over the top of the range, Ken and other investors in the same situation can hope that the price will go down again, as it did twice before. But once the breakout at the upper end of the range is obvious, living on that hope is no longer possible. One is forced to accept the fact that one has managed to sell Intersystems at the worst possible moment. This can be an almost physically painful realization, bringing on headaches, stomach upset, and insomnia.

At first Sam Rosenberg is very pleased with his decision to recommend that his clients sell their remaining holdings in Intersystems when the share price goes above 125 for the third time. He feels he has acted calmly, rationally, and professionally. When, after a phase of gathering strength, Intersystems shoots right up to 145, neither Sam nor his clients feel that the situation is particularly pleasant. Their stress is certainly considerably less than Ken's. They still sold at a profit, and at a respectable price level. But waiting a month or two for another favorable selling situation and then selling all the remaining holdings just before the much-longed-for upturn finally comes is painful. One week you think you have behaved thoughtfully and wisely, the next you find that you would be better off had you not been so set on selling as soon as the price went above 125. That is really very trying.

When the price breaks upward, Lena, Ken, Sam, and the other stockholders who sold Intersystems within the range all get quite emotional. To varying degrees, they are quite unhappy with the situation, and the psychological dynamic that has built up now results in clear and forceful crowd behavior.

Subgroup II—The Masters of Timing

On three occasions, Ian Benson and Max Bork succeeded in buying Intersystems at a low and selling at a high. Although this kind of excellent timing is not impossible, it is very difficult and quite unusual. Not many investors are likely to have succeeded in pulling off that kind of "hat trick" in Intersystems. It is perfectly possible that some did make one or perhaps two profitable trades during the period the share fluctuated in its range. It is more likely that a great many speculative purchases were made around the third time Intersystems touched the bottom of the range because, at that point, the price fluctuations crystallized into a clear pattern. A number of investors probably observed this: buy when the price falls to about 105, sell at around 125, and make a decent profit. But whether they succeeded in making one, two, or three profitable trades in the stock, it still hurts when the price, instead of falling back, "unexpectedly" abandons its old pattern and breaks out of the range on the upside.

Both Ian and Max, and their colleagues and clients, feel varying degrees of dissatisfaction when things do not go as expected. They would prefer the price to drop quickly and dramatically so as to confirm the correctness of their decision immediately. As we've mentioned several times before, greed can be a torment; it seems to be easier to fret over the money we might have made than to take pleasure in gains we have actually realized.

But this self-induced mental suffering is relatively mild. They have sold at a profit one or more times and escaped months of uncertainty and anxiety over which way the price will move. Still, both Ian and Max wish they had acted differently on the third deal. They are annoyed that they were not more aware of how quickly a share price can rise when a long-term range is broken on the upside.

Now, like many others in the same situation, they feel depressed and ambivalent. Their emotions are in turmoil. They would very much like to own Intersystems again, but it is annoying to have to chase the stock and to buy it back at a price higher than the one at which they just sold it. Suppose it suddenly starts falling sharply? They would look very foolish. On the other hand, if the price were to fall back below the buying price, Ian, Max, and many traders along with them might think of "getting back on the bandwagon." Some are probably finding it hard to resist the temptation to chase after a stock they sold that suddenly turned into the market's darling. All these emotional people contribute to the crowd behavior that develops in this kind of situation.

Subgroup III—The Wait-and-See Investors

John Stennis tried to buy Intersystems twice but was unable to make the trade. Afflicted with decision-making anxiety, he moved his buying limit down as the price neared the bottom of the range. Feeling hesitant and irresolute at seeing a stock price fluctuate dramatically and without warning is very human. One week there seem to be plenty of buyers; the next week, the sellers have taken over. The market is often ambivalent about a stock that has been a market winner and then goes into reverse. Some writers and analysts say the stock is overvalued when growth seems to have stopped; others think the stock is worth buying because the price has retreated from its high, and the problem is most likely temporary.

For this reason, many investors like John hesitate to buy on a correction when there seem to be many sellers. Frequently, people retreat from the buy side and wait to see what develops. Later, when the price suddenly and unexpectedly goes up, people often do not want to rush after it because they were mentally prepared to buy at a lower price.

When a stock like Intersystems has gone up sharply, corrected sharply, and then begins fluctuating in a range, many investors wonder whether they should buy into the company. Those who noted the excellent price development earlier but missed the uptrend now feel that they have another chance to climb aboard. Many who were part of the previous upward trend and sold at a good profit now feel inclined to renew their stake in the earlier winner. Because of spasmodic price development and the wait-and-see attitude of many analysts, however, it is not unusual for buying ideas to remain no more than ideas or to become only strictly limited buy orders. Those who do act may buy a much smaller lot than they might have otherwise.

So when Intersystems finally breaks out on the upside, a large number of people are very likely to react with disappointment and annoyance at not having met their goals. Many of them calculate what their profits would have been if only they had done what they had thought about doing. It may not be too late to buy, but they could already be "sitting pretty" with a handsome profit. To buy now means greater risk and lower potential. Disappointment at missing out on safe and easy money is a considerable factor for many investors. One common explanation for the agony of decision making is that while many investors really "knew" that Intersystems was a good buy, they began to doubt their conviction because so many others were waiting cautiously, and thus they grew uncertain.

When hesitancy toward an upward breakout turns into tangible optimism on the market and when everyone is favorably inclined toward a stock, a decision has to be made. Just as in Subgroup II, when faced with buying above 130, many investors have conflicting emotions. But with the price well below the high, these investors are not as inhibited by pride and prestige as those in Subgroup II about buying at a price higher than where they had sold previously. This probably means that Subgroup III is more inclined than Subgroup II to chase after Intersystems after the breakout. All these emotional people contribute significantly to such a breakout from a long-term range, releasing crowd behavior in the marketplace.

Subgroup IV—Short-Sellers

To sell short means to borrow shares at a certain cost from a stockholder who demands their return at a later time. Believing that the price will go down, the short-seller then sells the shares, intending to buy them back at a lower price and to then return them to the stockholder. The short-seller's profit is the difference between the selling price and the repurchase price. The brokerage conveys the shares lent and takes care of the necessary transactions. Because short-sellers do not actually own the shares they sell, they must post a deposit as collateral for the shares they need to deliver. Those who sold Intersystems short while the price fluctuated in its range and did not buy it back before the upward outbreak find themselves in a precarious situation.

They have to either deposit even more money or securities or buy back the shares they borrowed and sold at a loss. Clearly, short-sellers are exposed to considerable risk. As long as the price does not go over the top of the range, they can hope that the price of Intersystems will turn down again, as it did twice before. But when the upward break is obvious, they can't just observe the fact that they bet wrong. They are not in the same relatively happy situation as Lena, Max, Ian, and John, who may feel dejected and depressed but don't actually have to do anything.

Traders who sold Intersystems short have varying economic powers of resistance in such a situation, and naturally, most investors in Subgroups I, II, and III understand that they have to make some kind of decision, even under stress and time pressure. The investors in Subgroups I, II, and III face the possibility of missing out on a profit. The short sellers definitely lose money for every dollar Intersystems goes up—a considerably greater strain. Will those who sold short buy back the shares and take the loss, or will they count on the stock falling back again?

The unpleasant physical sensations Ken Erland experiences when Intersystems breaks up from the range are easier to deal with than the agony of the investor who has visions of his staked bills growing wings and taking to the air like turbojets. Losing money is not pleasant; the larger the sum and the more quickly and unexpectedly it is lost, the worse the loss feels. More than likely, when the price breaks at above 130, the short-sellers feel great mental strain.

The more emotionally involved in a decision one is, the greater the inclination to do what everyone else is doing. The short-seller in this situation very likely contributes to the crowd behavior that takes shape when Intersystems breaks out on the upside of its long-term range.

Positive Subgroups of Investors

The positive group can be divided into the following subgroups:

I. Long-Term Stockholders—Investors who owned Intersystems before it began to range and kept all or most (50 percent or more) of their holdings.
II. New Stockholders—Newcomer investors who bought all or most (50 percent or more) of the holding they intended to buy within the range and who have held their shares. (This is the most important subgroup.)
III. Non-Short-Sellers—Investors/traders who thought of selling Intersystems short while it was fluctuating in the range but failed to do so.

Common Characteristics

We've established that investors who owned Intersystems previously or who bought within the range are more or less satisfied when the range breaks on the upside. Of course some are dissatisfied when greed takes over, because even if people made money they often wish they had made a little more. After all, they could have bought more shares in Intersystems when they were cheaper. As we've discussed, it is not unusual for people to complain about the profits they *could* have made instead of being content with the money they actually did make. Still, most stockholders probably feel good when the price moves in the desired direction. Making money is good, even if one did not act on the idea of possibly buying more stock.

When Intersystems breaks upward, the positive group has an easier time dealing with the psychological factors than the negative group does. Greed often makes people more emotional than rational, but it is easier to cope with the desire to make money than to deal with the anxiety that creeps in with losses. In the following analysis of the positive subgroups, we will see how emotional behavior can take over when a desire for money seizes hold of otherwise sensible people.

Subgroup I—Long-Term Stockholders

These investors all bought Intersystems before the price began to range. Many have profits on their holdings, despite the fall from the high, because the stock has risen steadily over the year. Some who bought late in the upturn phase have limited losses, and a few stockholders, like Ken Erland, who bought near the high have bigger losses.

When a stock fluctuates within a range for several months, most stockholders are torn between hope and depression. Waiting for an upturn that never seems to come is stressful; and when the stock seems to vacillate for a prolonged period without rhyme or reason, it is easy to lose patience and to sell. Frustration, anxiety, and impatience are strong, troubling emotions that can make even experienced and skilled traders abandon earlier decisions and sell holdings they had intended to hold until the upturn. That way, they can avoid the anguish and uncertainty created by the "irrational fluctuations."

Lena, Ken, and Sam are all stockholders who chose to sell their shares at a price within the range, out of exhaustion, dejection, and fear of a further downturn. When a stockholder feels stuck in a range, it takes considerable patience and confidence to stay put and wait for the upward trend to resume. As long as the price does not soar over the top of the range, the long-term stockholders who chose not to sell must put up with the uncertainty and stick to their belief that, sooner or later, the price will renew its upward trend.

Of course, some stockholders considered selling Intersystems when the price was at the bottom of the range for the third time. Perhaps they talked to an investment adviser or a broker for advice on how to deal with their situation. When an investor feels stressed, the difference between selling and not selling can be a hair's breadth. If there had been a positive article on Intersystems in the morning paper on the day that Ken Erland decided to sell, or if he had talked to a broker who questioned the wisdom of selling, Ken might have changed his mind and watched the upturn that followed with a smile on his lips, instead of feeling every uptick like a drop of molten lead on his bare skin.

Stockholders like Ken who considered selling at the bottom of the range but did not, for various reasons now find that, apart from not selling at the low, they may have not only escaped realizing a loss, but also become owners of a winning stock. The situation has shifted 180 degrees. Owning a stock that was such a burden only recently is now a delight.

When the price finally breaks up out of the range and signals clearly that the period of fluctuation is over, many of Intersystems' "old" stockholders feel relieved and happy. It feels good to be rid of the long-term anxiety. Finally, they are being rewarded with this upturn, which they feel they really deserved. When the break on the upside of the range is obvious, everyone sees that stubbornly clinging to their belief in the company was the right thing to do. Seeing the price forcefully breaking through the "impossible" level at the top of the range is really a delightful experience.

Stockholders who considered buying when the price was at the bottom of the range for the third time but never acted on those ideas are not as happy with the upturn in Intersystems as are those who considered selling at that point. When a stock unexpectedly moves sharply upward, the thinking and the reasoning usually goes something like this:

"I actually thought of buying when the price was down for the third time, but nothing came of it."

"That broker sounded so dubious about buying; he really should have seen that the share was a steal below 110. He should have told me to increase my holding."

"Anyone could see that Intersystems was cheap when the price was just over 100."

"Why didn't I buy at least a few more shares?"

"Actually it was perfectly obvious that the stock of a company with such good products could go only in one direction."

Although the upward break was much anticipated, greed often turns into a fly in the ointment. When the price goes up sharply, when news of the company is good, and Intersystems is the darling of the stock market again, it is very easy to become greedy and overeager for greater profits. Trading with hindsight is a common phenomenon on the market.

When the price breaks up out of the range, all remaining old stockholders get somewhat emotional, feeling varying degrees of satisfaction over the situation. Now, the psychological dynamic that has been built up contributes to crowd behavior. In such a situation, people tend to rush after the share price to buy more shares, simply because the whole market seems to be running in the same direction.

Subgroup II—The New Stockholders

This is the most important of the positive subgroups. The longer the stock has ranged, the more shares have changed hands. This transformation phase usually takes place between old stockholders selling to new stockholders. As we've said before, the time element is very important. The mental process required for the old stockholders to be willing to accept a lower price for their shares than they originally anticipated takes time. Their resistance to selling is ground down very slowly. The longer the range lasts, the more powerful the psychological dynamic becomes. It is appropriate to renew our acquaintance with Peter Ericson and Karen Thurston here because both of them fall into the "new stockholder" category.

Peter Ericson's buy order was set at 100. When the price turned at 101, he missed his chance to buy Intersystems by a very small margin, and he felt very unlucky. It is difficult to deal with missing out on a good trade by a hair. When Intersystems turns down for the second time, he sees a new opportunity to buy cheaply. But he does not want to risk missing out on the trade a second time, watching the price get away from him while he stands on the sidelines. But Peter wants to buy lower than 113. When the price is down to 108, his tactics seem to have succeeded. However, he is wholly prepared for it to go down further and is surprised when the price suddenly bounces up a few points. He is torn between fear of losing money and greed over missing out on a good trade. He asks the manager to buy at the best possible price but only half the number of shares he had intended to buy at 100. Two weeks later, the price is down and turns at 102. Peter has an excellent opportunity to buy the remaining lot at an attractive price, but he declines. He feels doubtful and uneasy; the price might go even lower.

The price movement of a recently purchased stock is studied carefully. People like to have their judgment confirmed and to feel that they have made the right decision. Preferably, the price should go up quickly and dramatically the very next day. If the upturn is delayed or if the price starts going down, doubts about the decision to buy begin to creep in; a downturn is often seen as a threat rather than as an opportunity.

Let's assume from the start that Peter did not buy more stock when Intersystems fell for the third time to a level just above 100. He is cautious and appreciates stability and security in life, so that assumption seems justified. Peter may well have thought about it, but the journey from idea to action may be a long one. Instead, he is probably wondering whether it was wise to buy Intersystems at all, now that he is facing a potential loss on his holding for the second time in a short space of time.

When the price turns up after touching the low for the third time and then, after gathering strength for a while, breaks through the top of the range, Peter thinks that being an Intersystems stockholder is unmitigated happiness. But at the same time, his view of the company changes radically. The article on Intersystems in *Business Today* that he read before he bought had been right after all. The stock was an interesting long-term investment at 120, but you had to be prepared for major price swings. That is precisely what has happened. When he thinks back, he doesn't remember why he was so terribly worried and uninterested in buying more shares when the price was at just above 100. After all, Intersystems is obviously a company for the future.

Now he is torn between conflicting emotions. Should he be satisfied with the money he has actually made or disappointed over the possible profit he has missed out on? If the share price keeps going up, Peter senses that he will be more and more dissatisfied. All the newspapers and analysts are praising Intersystems, remarkably unanimous in their opinion of its bright outlook for the future. The entire market seems to want to own the stock. Peter thinks this ought to be a good time to buy. The temptation to increase his holding is enormous, now that everyone seems so positive. Peter has a strong impulse to do what the majority are doing and increase his holding in Intersystems.

Karen Thurston finds herself in a situation similar to Peter's. For several months she has been wondering whether to buy Intersystems for her clients. When the price falls for the third time and the firm's analyst is more positive, she is tired of the stress and the worry about missing yet another good buying opportunity; so she is willing to risk buying too early as long as she manages to do the trade.

We don't know whether Karen Thurston bought more shares when the price dropped by about 10 percent just after her purchase, but we can assume that she didn't. It is safe to say that she does not find the situation particularly amusing. Having finally bought Intersystems, she is in the wrong after only a week or two. Waiting patiently for the right chance to buy and then acting nervously—out of fear of missing the trade—only to find that her timing was off immediately afterward is very unpleasant. After the agony and the doubt she felt when the stock touched bottom for a third time, she is probably filled with deep inner satisfaction when the price finally turns up. After a brief con- solidation, it even breaks through the supply level between 125 and 130. It is as if an immense burden had been lifted from her shoulders. The air is easier to breathe, the sun shines more brightly, and even the colors of the sky have more beautiful nuances of blue than before.

No matter how skilled and experienced a trader or an inves- tor may be, it is almost impossible not to respond emotionally in a situation like this one. After having "been wrong" on a major holding, there is a wonderful feeling of "being right." Yet people very often wish they had acted even more decisively than they did. Karen had a brilliant opportunity to buy more Intersystems at a price that now seems like a real steal. It would be remark- able if, in the midst of her satisfaction over the Intersystems upturn, she did not feel some irritation, not only over having been in such a hurry to buy, but also over not adding to her holdings at the downturn.

When the mood shifts from bearish to bullish, most people find that despite the higher prices, it is easier to make buying decisions than it was in the bear phase. It is much easier to swim with the current than to go against it. Now that the price is trending up and most of the market feels positive about Inter- systems again, it is likely that Karen is at least considering buy- ing more shares—if only the price corrects enough.

It is not unusual for investors to buy successively when a stock like Intersystems did not have a clear trend before the break. Regardless of whether the philosophy is to buy on weakness— when the price is going down toward the bottom of the range— or on strength—when it seems to be ready to break upward—it is very difficult to keep up with rapid swings. Purchases of a stock that is fluctuating within a range are often spread out over time; and when the price breaks out of the top of the range sooner than expected, a number of newcomer stockholders who began buying Intersystems have not yet had time to become "fully invested."

This group of investors is a very important element in the

crowd behavior that develops at a sharp upward break out of a longer range. If they have been somewhat cautious and restrained when buying their planned holding at a lower price within the range, now that the crowd is running in the same direction, they often rush to buy the remainder at a higher price.

Subgroup III—Non-Short-Sellers

Although not important in our analysis, this group does deserve mention. They contribute neither supply nor demand. Traders who thought of selling Intersystems short but for some reason did not are probably heaving a deep sigh of relief and heading for new hunting grounds.

Some Real Upward Breaks

To truly understand stock market behavior, it is very important that one not rely simply on mechanical knowledge and the search for stereotypical formations of stock charts. That can quickly become merely a search for charts and diagrams that fit into standard templates. It is frustrating enough that reality is seldom as obvious as it seems to be in the technical analysis textbooks. Trading ranges may look alike, but they are never identical. Intersystems is a hypothetical example of how a range can be created, and as we can see from Figures 11.3, 11.4, and 11.5, it is unusual for real trading ranges to be as clear as that of Intersystems. Learning formations by heart limits the ability to interpret the market. What is important to successful analysis is an understanding of the psychological dynamic that builds up in a range, for that is what determines the prerequisites for a forceful price movement when the price range is finally broken. This understanding can also be applied to the analysis of price ranges that may look different.

The aim of this book is not to provide a guide to practical action on the stock market, but rather to convey true insight into the psychology of the market. Because they are intended only to give a general impression, the diagrams in Figures 11.3,

11.4, and 11.5 are not analyzed in detail. The following examples of real market situations are intended to demonstrate the close correlation between the theory presented here and the reality, and that an understanding of crowd psychology in the stock market can make for better decision making in trading.

Microsoft

Microsoft is the world's largest company, developing, manufacturing, licensing, selling, and supporting software products. From 1994 to July 1999, the stock rose from about $5 to almost exactly $100. But during the fall of 1999, when the Nasdaq was having an exceptionally strong run, making new highs almost every day, Microsoft moved sideways in a well-defined range—between $85 and $98. The high of $100 proved to be a very effective lid. From the summer of 1999 to early December, that high was tested seven times, but the stock never broke $98. It seems safe to say that the stockholders, holding the largest technology stock in the world and missing out on a tremendous rally in that sector, were getting more frustrated with every passing day. A strong psychological dynamic is built up during this period; and the rumor that Microsoft is about to settle the government's antitrust case against it sparks crowd behavior. The eighth time that the high side of the range is approached, it finally breaks through and Microsoft reaches over $100. This crowd behavior is reinforced the next day when the company reports that the much-delayed Windows 2000 operating system has been completed. The stock soars almost 10 percent in one day, then going up to 120 in the subsequent two weeks, before a correction (see the far right of Figure 11.3).

Ericsson

Ericsson is also a technology company quoted on the Nasdaq. Ericsson develops and produces advanced systems and products for wired and mobile communications. The company is a global player—among the 50 largest companies in the world. The stock

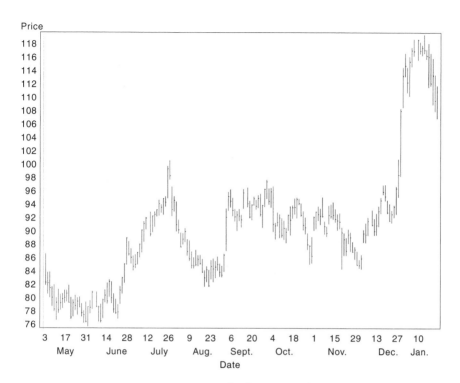

Figure 11.3. Microsoft. (Courtesy of Reuters.)

dropped sharply during the global stock market crisis in the autumn of 1998, losing more than 50 percent of its value. Although it recovered swiftly, rising to around $29 in late November, the upturn came to an abrupt end. A profit warning diluted confidence in Ericsson's management, and the market was acutely worried that the company was losing ground to its competitors. Nasdaq cleared the high of 1998, climbing to a new all-time high, while Ericsson just moved sideways. The $29 level proved to be very hard to penetrate. From November 1998 to late May 1999, that level was tested more than 10 times, but the stock simply did not have the strength to break up through the range (Figure 11.4). Just as with Microsoft, it seems safe to say that stockholders in one of the world's leading telecom companies became increasingly frustrated as they missed out on a rally in that sector. During May, Ericsson's normal pattern changed, not falling back when it reached the top of the range, but staying at that

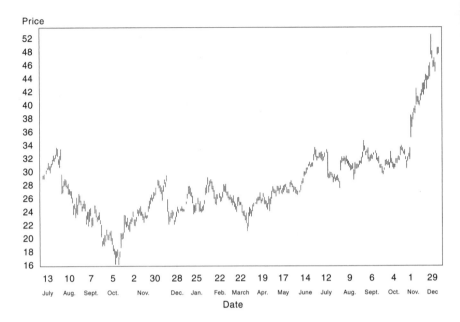

Figure 11.4. Ericsson. (Courtesy of Reuters.)

level. (We will look at this situation in more detail in Chapter 15, in regard to what I call the "balance point.") When leading financial houses published favorable analyses highlighting Ericsson's strength in building systems instead of handsets, crowd behavior is triggered, and the range is clearly broken on the upside. The share soars to an all-time high. Then, in July, when the chief executive officer (CEO) is fired and uncertainty about the future of the company develops, a new range is formed. However, quarterly results published in October are much better than expected, and the stock goes up furiously, gaining more than 100 percent in a three-month period.

Deutsche Bank

Microsoft and Ericsson are both *very* large companies quoted on the Nasdaq. To demonstrate that crowd psychology works, regardless of national boundaries, the third example is Deutsche

Bank, the largest bank in Europe, providing a range of banking services worldwide.

After trending up for more than 16 months, Deutsche Bank, like many European Banks, peaked in the spring of 1998. Bank stocks were among the hardest hit when the global bear market of 1998 struck Europe, and Deutsche Bank was no exception. The stock fell almost 55 percent during the fall, touching 1990 levels. After recovering from the bottom level, the upturn ran into a solid wall of supply at around 57 Euro, and the incipient upward trend became a sideways range between 44 and 57 Euro. (See Figure 11.5.) When it approached 57, it was brutally ham-

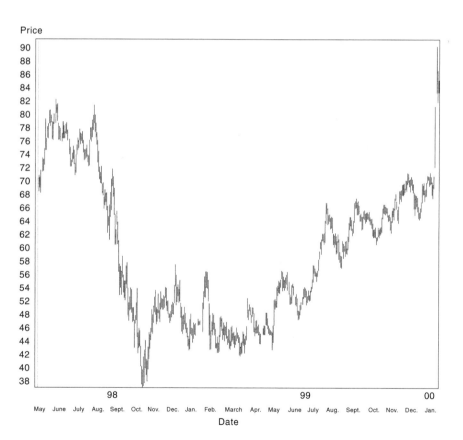

Figure 11.5.   Deutsche Bank. (Courtesy of Reuters.)

mered down toward the lower end of the range. In May 1999, this pattern was significantly altered. After reaching 57 Euro, the price declined as usual, but only to about 50 Euro; then it began to go up sharply. It was obvious that most of the players were behaving differently. Buyers now had the upper hand. When the stock went to 57 Euro for the fourth time, with only a tiny correction, an upward breakout seemed very likely. (We will look at this more carefully when discussing the "balance point" in the last chapter.) After the slight correction, the price went up, through a vacuum of supply, to around 70 Euro. Deutsche Bank then formed a new range that exploded upward on December 23, when Chancellor Gerhard Schroeder announced that the government was eliminating the tax on sales of corporate assets.

Chapter 12

DOWNWARD BREAK— IAN BENSON

In earlier chapters, we examined the thoughts, feelings, and be-havior of Ian Benson and Max Bork, not only when the price of Intersystems was fluctuating in its range, but also during the upward breakout of the range. In this chapter, we will show how they cope—emotionally as well as intellectually, from a decision-making point of view—with something that can be very hard to handle: losing money. Several times while Intersystems was fluc-tuating, they felt anxious and unsure when the price seemed to be marking time or fluctuated longer than expected before start-ing to move in the direction they had hoped. At the upward break, they fretted about having sold too early, even though they had made a good profit. But now things are even more troubling. The psychological impact of losing money in the stock market is considerably more powerful and more intense than that of mak-ing profits.

Recapitulation

When Ian was last on the scene, he had bought Intersystems at 106 on Max's recommendation. When an unexpected rate cut by the Federal Reserve made the market jump for joy, the stock quickly went up to 115.

In the first two weeks after the upturn to 115, the price development is the same for both the upward and the downward breakout, so Ian's behavior at the beginning of the downward break is identical to his behavior at the start of the upward break. During these weeks he feels good and is very pleased with life. The share price goes from 115 to 120. He is making money and his colleagues respect him. Johnson avoids discussing Intersystems except when the conversation slides into politics. Then he takes exception to the "unearned" income through speculation.

All those who, like Johnson, did not buy Intersystems betray a certain amount of envy, now that those speculators seem to have made such a good trade. Though their jealousy is not nearly as obvious as Johnson's, they are clearly irritated that they did not put money into Intersystems, too.

When the price appears to stabilize at about 120, there is a growing body of opinion among those in Benson's group who want to sell that it might be best to just take their profits. Making 10 percent in less than a month should be enough to make anyone happy, they argue, and you never know when it might go down.

Johnson's group soon adds fuel to the fire, and good advice flies around the room. "Greed goeth before a loss," they say, or "When the market crashed in 1998, it all happened very fast." "Better to make a small profit than no profit at all."

All this makes Ian Benson furious. He rises to his feet, eyes dark. His voice tense and quavering, he shouts across the room at Johnson's group, telling them that they're jealous because they are worried that the investors will make even more money. At that, all discussion of any eventual sale quickly dies, and the tense atmosphere calms. No one wants to challenge authority.

Up to 125

A few days after those two weeks, Intersystems goes up to 125. Benson's position as leader of his group is now even clearer. He was right, and most of the others were wrong. Think how they would have fretted if they had sold at 120! Now it seems to be only a matter of time before the price goes to 130. That is the group's main conclusion.

Down to 110

A few days later when the price goes down to 120 instead of up to 130, optimism turns to smoldering uncertainty. The earlier argument in favor of taking the profit is raised once again. Even Ian hesitates, but he feels he has to maintain a self-confident facade so as not to lose authority. However, he tries to think rationally. When Max Bork tells him that a correction is perfectly normal after a sharp uptick of more than 20 points, he feels supported. If you want to make money on the stock market, you can't be the nervous type, he tells his colleagues—a picture of calm and control.

A week later when Intersystems goes down another 5 points to 115, Ian finds the situation extremely uncomfortable. Why had he been so cocky, he wonders, pretending to be a skilled and experienced operator? Now he not only has to cope with his nervous colleagues who are all in the same boat as he is in, but he has to listen to Johnson's taunts, too.

It is amazing how much he dislikes that man. Now that he is under some pressure himself because of the unexpectedly large downturn, he sees how pleased Johnson is. His green eyes are practically aglow with malicious glee. Ian realizes that if he had just kept his trading to himself, the problem would have been much easier to handle. It would have been between him and Max, and no one else. Now half the world knows that he has staked all his capital on Intersystems and persuaded his colleagues to do the same.

Ian Benson actually does not know what to do. He has never experienced such a sharp correction. His limited experience has taught him that the best thing anyone can do is just to wait out the downturn—things usually work out after a day or two. He is quite clear on what he learned from his previous trades in Intersystems: both times he had ended up a few points on the wrong side—either because he had bought or sold too early—and the problem had solved itself when he had stayed calm and followed Max's advice to wait.

When Ian discusses the situation with Bork, he gets exactly the advice he expected to hear, but Max does seem more pressured than usual. Bork may sound quite stressed on the telephone, but Ian knows that the trading desk environment can be hectic, with phones ringing constantly and everybody talking at once.

Max says there's really nothing to worry about. Ian still has a decent profit on his holding, and the firm's pharmaceutical analyst sees no reason to revise her favorable opinion of the company.

"I don't know why the share has corrected by ten points," Bork says, "but I'm advising my clients just to stay calm and not to do anything hasty."

After this conversation, Ian is relieved; now he feels he is on firmer ground. When the Benson group has its daily stock market discussion at the afternoon coffee break, the atmosphere is much more relaxed because Bork's recommendation was so unambiguous. They'll show that Johnson that they can be just as cool as any seasoned professional.

Still, a few days later, May 20, the atmosphere is anything but exhilarated. (See Figure 12.1.) Intersystems has fallen by another 5 points and has stabilized around 110. Ian Benson feels his position as leader of the group is threatened. No one says so straight out, but Benson feels silent reproaches for coming out so fiercely against selling when the price was at 120. Some members of the group are even beginning to wonder whether they should have anything to do with trading at all. The stock market seems totally incomprehensible. Max Bork says that Intersystems is a good stock. The pharmaceutical analyst at Wilson & Partners says Intersystems is a good company. *Business Today*'s stock market column says that Intersystems is conservatively valued, and yet the stock does not go up! They are really just a gang of happy amateurs who would like to make some quick money, but they should have remembered the old saw about the little fish getting eaten by the big fish—or the sharks. At least that is one of the overwrought remarks Ian has to deal with.

Ian Benson definitely does not like the situation and starts worrying seriously. The grandiose plans he had for making the equivalent of a very good annual salary from a single trade now seem very remote. He has quite other thoughts on his mind now. Instead of seeing the risk taking in a positive light, his rashness

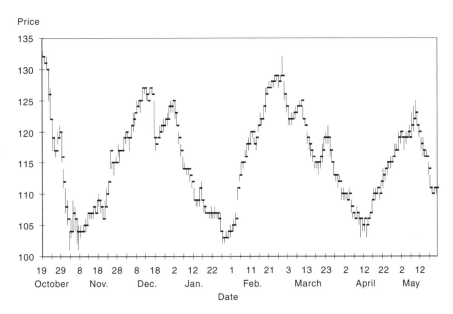

Figure 12.1. When Intersystems falls to 110 and stabilizes there, Benson's group feels very uneasy and uncertain.

in putting all his capital into a single stock is beginning to feel terrifying. Earlier, Ian had never given much thought to how much of his investment he might lose; he was too busy calculating how much he might make. Now when he considers about how big his unrealized loss will be if Intersystems goes down to 90, he feels tremendous anxiety. Breaking out of this negative thinking takes enormous effort. He should remember not only that he still has a profit on the present trade, but also that he already has two substantial profit-making trades under his belt.

When he focuses on this positive rather than the negative, life is a little easier; but the sense of uneasiness simply will not go away. Ian has no experience or skill as a trader, and he has no idea what to do. When he put his last penny into Intersystems, he was simply not prepared mentally for the possibility that the price could go down. He certainly had no plan in the event that it did. Paralyzed and completely unable to act, he is now horribly dependent on Max's advice.

It's just that all my colleagues think I know what to do, he says to himself. The only sensible solution he sees to his present quandary is to do what he did before, as Max suggests: watch the development, and wait for the upturn that is sure to come sooner or later.

When some of the group members criticize him for not coming up with anything better than "wait and see," Ian is angry. Every one of them is free to sell whenever he or she likes, he says, and anyone who sells now will actually make a profit. They are all adults. They can make their own decisions. He did not force anyone to put money into Intersystems.

After this reprimand, the atmosphere calms down. The fellow who had the harshest criticism apologizes, explaining that he is not used to trading and that he hadn't realized how stressful it could be when the price went the wrong way. But wouldn't it be sensible to sell when they have a reasonable profit again? It seems absurd to sell at 110 when just recently the price was up at 125, he tells Ian. But when it goes to 120, wouldn't it be a good idea to get out? He puts this suggestion to the entire group.

Now that there is a plan of action on which everyone in Benson's group can agree, the tension eases, and Ian feels he is in control of the situation again. On his way out of the snack bar, he gives Johnson such a poisonous look that Johnson doesn't dare make any of his customary malicious comments.

Correction to 119

A week after this stormy meeting, Intersystems has begun to go up again after touching bottom at 109. At 113, the atmosphere at the afternoon stock market run-through is noticeably better. The whole group feels a certain pride. They have shown they could handle a negative situation in what they think of as a professional manner. It is Friday; both trading and life are really kind of fun. Now all they have to do is get out with a good profit so that Johnson and his crew will have to eat their words. It feels good to have the upper hand again and to give the hecklers a dose of their own medicine.

When the price has slowly but surely begun to creep up again, greed once again puts in an appearance. Of course they should sell, but there is no point in selling at a bargain price—at least that is the prevailing opinion in the group, an opinion with which Ian Benson wholeheartedly agrees. After all, Intersystems is a good company with good products. Originally they thought of selling between 125 and 130, so when they finally do decide to sell, they definitely should not settle for less than 120. This is announced loudly and clearly so that Johnson cannot help but hear.

When Intersystems is quoted at just a point or two below 120, Ian Benson's self-confidence is back. (See Figure 12.2.) Once again he has handled a difficult situation by thinking as he thinks the professionals do: "If the price goes down, keep calm. It will go up again soon enough."

Ian dusts off his old calculations on how many good trades he needs to make to become a millionaire. Just think how wonderful it will be when he has made so much money that he can

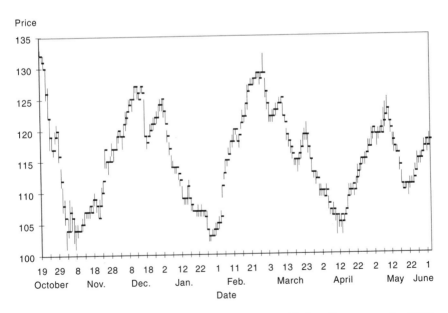

Figure 12.2. When Intersystems corrects to 119, Ian Benson again starts calculating how soon he will be rich.

stop working if he wants and just call himself "Ian Benson—Financier. It feels as if the dream is beginning to be within reach. The day when a single good trade might earn a great annual salary may not necessarily be so far off, he thinks happily to himself.

Fall below 110

Suddenly Ian Benson no longer recognizes Intersystems. The stock had been so reliable. True, the earlier price fluctuations were considerable; and true, he went slightly wrong now and again; but in spite of all that, there was always a clear pattern. The price turned up when it approached 100, and down when it neared 130. Now the present downturn seems completely irrational. He can see no reason why the price should fall again, breaking its previous pattern. He begins to feel like a coiled spring that someone is winding up without rhyme or reason. His mood changes are synchronized with the price fluctuations. Only a week ago he was feeling strong and self-confident. The price was going in the right direction, and he was enjoying the thought of being financially independent; but now all those troublesome, hard-to-handle emotions are coming back. Again, he is reminded that he is no skilled investor and that there is a real risk that he might lose money. When the price goes in the wrong direction, his position as the group's leader is unpleasant. Ian Benson thinks to himself with some anguish that it really would have been much easier if there were someone he could make a scapegoat, instead of being the scapegoat himself.

When he calls Max and blames him for the price dropping from 119 to 111, Max is furious. If Ian is dissatisfied, why doesn't he change brokers? Emphatically, Max reminds him that he helped Ian do two good trades in Intersystems. If Ian would like to sell Intersystems now, Max would be happy to execute the order. He also reminds Ian that he had advised strongly against putting all his capital into Intersystems.

There is a troubling silence on the line. When Ian says nothing, Max asks whether he wants to sell. Ian is ashamed of attacking Max. He apologizes, explaining that he is not used to the stock market and is under stress, not only because of his large holding but also because of his colleagues.

Bork explains that there is no such thing as a "free lunch" on the market and that he, too, is worried. A few minutes later, Ian confesses he does not know what to do if the price falls any further. He doesn't want to lose money. That is not why he bought the stock, he tells Max.

"In that case you have to decide how far down you're willing to let Intersystems go. If the price falls below that level, sell," says Max. "Not below 100, under any circumstances," says Ian immediately, not knowing exactly where he got that figure.

When Max promises to phone immediately if, despite their expectations, Intersystems should fall below 100, Ian finally feels he can relax. Now he has a plan of action to bolster himself.

When Ian and his stockholding colleagues discuss their situation, there is tremendous tension in the air. This time they do not talk openly in the snack bar; no one wants to give Johnson and his crew an opportunity to crow over their troubles.

Ian tells them about his latest conversation with Max Bork and says that he, Ian Benson, still believes that Intersystems could turn into a really good trade, but he is thinking of selling if the price falls below 100.

"It's easy for you to risk a loss," says a colleague. "You already have profits from two good trades."

Ian admits he made money on Intersystems, but in this last trade he has staked more than four times as much money as he did on the first trade. No one else has put in even half as much. He is definitely the one who has risked the most, Ian points out heatedly.

Ian and his colleagues are torn between wanting to make money and fearing the loss of it. Some think that it would be good to sell just to escape the worry; others think that, now, after missing two good chances to sell at a higher price, it would be annoying and unprofessional to sell. The only thing they can all agree on is to wait.

During the next period, the price for Intersystems just seems to be marking time. The stock is parked at just over 110. Ian and his friends begin to feel slightly better. After the last correction, the price had turned up at exactly this level, and they think it's fairly likely to do so this time as well. Taking things calmly and waiting seems like the right thing to do. And when the upturn comes, the group decides that this time, they will not be as greedy as last time. They will be more than happy if they get 120.

But there is no upturn. There is a downturn instead! When the market opens next day, and Intersystems falls by 3 points, Ian's stomach churns. (See Figure 12.3.) Convinced that the time had now come for the price to start going up, he looks on the internet. At least he is alone in his office. He is being eaten up inside. Accusing looks from his colleagues would really have been too much. He tries to calm down. He is still on the plus side, and there is still a comforting distance to his stop level of 100.

When he calls Max, Max tells him exactly what he wants to hear. No, they haven't heard of any unfavorable reports being published. No, the pharmaceutical analyst still thinks the stock is worth buying. Yes, he ought to hold on.

After this conversation, Ian feels better equipped to face his

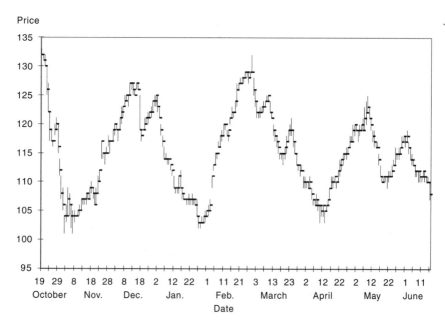

Figure 12.3.   When the price falls below 110, Ian is in torment.

friends. They will be uneasy, but he thinks he has the strength necessary to make them listen to him, not to run off and sell in a panic.

The next week is the worst week Ian has been through in a long time. The Intersystems price keeps dropping, and he does not know how to handle the situation. His position as leader of the group is under serious review. One remark he has to hear is that if he hadn't bragged about his profits like a teenager boasting about his first "conquest," none of them would have bought Intersystems and lost money. His speech on how easy it was to make money was pie in the sky, says another worried and disappointed colleague.

Although they are pressing Ian, he fights back. "You're adults—you make your own decisions. You've had two good chances to sell at a profit, and now you're looking for a scapegoat. I haven't forced anyone to buy, and I'm the one in the worst position."

When Johnson and a few others in the snack bar start applauding and thanking him for the interesting show, all of Benson's group is embarrassed and upset. In their agitated state, they had forgotten that they were quarreling in full view of everyone. As stressed as they are, there is no reason to let the others take such malicious delight in their misery. That same day the price goes down to 101, and Ian feels panic setting in. He had announced that he would sell if the stock fell below 100, but that was a level he had just plucked out of the ether without thinking. He never really thought it could go down that far. He has no desire whatsoever to lose money; executing a "stop" now would be doing violence to himself. Max said he had to be prepared to lose money if he wanted to speculate on the stock market—those are the rules of the game. Easy for him to say that, thinks Ian indignantly. That finance pup from the big city isn't losing any money—only his clients lose money.

The stock market is closing in one hour, and Ian still has not made up his mind. His day is ruined, and he can't concentrate on his work. His thoughts keep going back to Intersystems. Should he sell if the price falls below 100 or not? God, this is so hard, he thinks. Supposing the price goes down to 99 and then turns up sharply? He would be very upset. But if it keeps going down to 80, he will lose a lot of money. He cannot decide. Desperation is creeping up on him. He feels unbearably anxious. He wishes he had never even heard of Intersystems. He would gladly surrender his earlier profits if he could just escape the torment of this moment.

The stock market is closing in 15 minutes, and Ian looks on the Web to let the market pronounce his sentence. Even if the price is as low as 95, he will survive; but he must not forget to stop at the liquor store on the way home.

The price is at 104—at 104! Inwardly, Ian is jubilant. God, what a relief! He can breathe again. The sky is blue, the sun is shining and it is summer. Intersystems went up 3 points from the lowest level of the day, and he does not have to decide whether to execute his "stop" or not. (See Figure 12.4.)

Neither Ian nor any of his colleagues likes having a potential loss on his or her holdings; but they are all gradually beginning

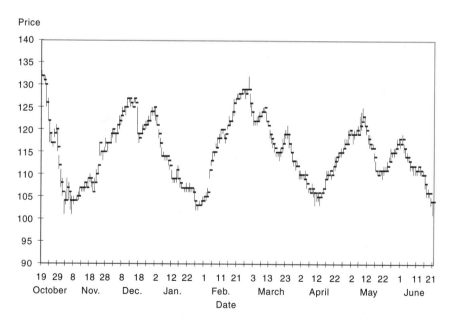

Figure 12.4. When the price turns up from 101, Ian escapes the agony of deciding whether to exercise his "stop."

to get used to the idea. A few points down on a long-term investment is nothing to make a sensible person lose his head, they tell Johnson cockily. No matter how they are feeling inside, they have promised themselves that at least no one is going to laugh at them. And Ian and his group actually do believe that they have the situation under control. The quick killing they thought they were going to make will just have to be a longer term investment instead. By way of encouragement, they tell each other that Intersystems is a good company with a good product; the risk of a downturn to below 100 must be very small.

Under 100

Over the coming weeks, the movements in Intersystems' price reinforce their belief that the decision to hold on to their shares was the right decision. First the price races up to 108, then backs off slowly to 100, only to go up again quickly to 107. The mood among Ian and his colleagues is one of contentment. They tell him that of course things go wrong sometimes. He has to understand that they are inexperienced as traders. The stock market is a new world to them. They are good at calculating mathematical probabilities, but the rules and the logic that prevail on the stock market obviously differ from those that apply in their own sphere. Maybe, they suggest to Ian, once they have sold Intersystems at a profit, they should all learn a little more about how the stock market actually functions.

Things are moving quickly. Two days ago, the price was at 107, but now (July 11) it is down to 100—the low of the year. It is the middle of summer, and half of the group members are on vacation. Those who are left gather in Ian's office for a crisis meeting. Ian is asked whether he is going to execute his stop. Only if the price falls below 100 will he consider it, he answers.

When Ian calls Max, he finds to his consternation that Max is on vacation. When he asks Max's colleague for advice, he is told that the drop in price over the last few days seems exaggerated, and that the present price level should be regarded as a buying opportunity rather than a selling situation. But call back tomorrow, Max will be back. Bork is the one who knows most about the company.

Ian and his group discuss the various alternatives, but they have already decided to regard their holdings as more long term. If they are going to do anything as drastic as selling at a loss, they should at least hear what Max Bork has to say first. So really, there's nothing to do but wait till the next day. Max's colleague also said he had not heard anything negative, so they really do think the price ought to bounce back up when the market opens the next day.

Ian's stomach makes itself felt again, and his head spins. He has visions of hundred dollar bills fluttering to the ground like so many dead birds. He goes to the men's room, turns the light out, and holds his head in his hands, as if to protect himself against the misery washing over him. Why did he ever start trading in stocks? What an idiot he was to think he could become a full-time trader. What is he going to tell everyone? (See Figure 12.5.)

After a while, he starts thinking sensibly again. Intersystems

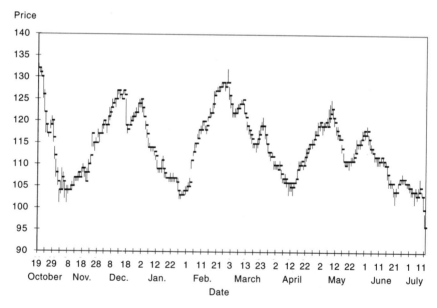

Figure 12.5. Ian Benson's dream of becoming a full-time financier goes up in smoke when Intersystems falls to 96.

has in fact gone down to 96, but Bork explains that another brokerage is dumping shares on the market at this very moment. Because it is a well-known firm with a good reputation, lots of people are following suit. This is pure crowd behavior, says Max. People do not know what to do; so when a major player makes a drastic move, people think that he or she knows something they don't know, and they do what everyone else is doing—sell. But the pharmaceutical analyst at Wilson & Partners thinks that if the price drops further, the stock will just be that much more worth buying.

Ian's previous trades were successful; so even if he sells at a loss now, he will still come out of his stock venture unscathed, though he would lose most of his earlier profits. But it would be horribly embarrassing if the profit he had calculated at something over $100,000 on the deal turned into a loss of more than $40,000. Yet in spite of it all, he would like to sell his entire holding—effective immediately. What do all those who are selling know that he doesn't know? How can he—one lone, small investor—go against the market? Wilson & Partners may well be high on Intersystems, but they are only a quarter the size of the brokerage that is flooding the market with Intersystems stock.

Ian is seriously inclined to sell. At least it would be sensible to reduce his holding. But he cannot bring himself to execute his "stop." Max Bork still believes in the stock and in Intersystems as a good company. What if Intersystems were to go up just as it did before and go all the way to 130? Then he would miss out on about $150,000! The mere thought makes him dizzy. He would be unbelievably embarrassed if he sold at the bottom and lost so much money. The price really can't go down that much further, he says to himself. The bottom must be near. When the price was at 111, his earlier decision on a stop-loss level seemed sensible, but Ian concludes that now it seems quite wrong to sell.

His colleagues listen to him in silence. No one wants to sell at a loss, but the situation is pretty gloomy. Does Max Bork really know that Intersystems is such a good stock? If the stock is worth buying, why are so many other stockholders selling? Because he is in the same boat, Ian escapes what might have been even more severe criticism. They are all aware that they had several opportunities to get out of their positions at higher prices. The group members are torn between greed and fear. They are afraid of losing more money, but at the same time they would very much like to get back the money they put in. Some of them seriously consider selling at a loss, just to get out from under this constant worry that the price could drop even further. How can they, a gang of amateurs, think they know better than the biggest brokerage house on the market?

This is an objection to which Ian has trouble responding. In spite of pressure from several of his colleagues, he does not sell; and no one else really wants to go off and sell on his own. After all, Ian still has a considerably bigger position than anyone else. As soon as the upward correction comes and they can sell without a loss, they will dispose of what they have—quick as flash— and give up trading. This is a decision that the majority can finally accept.

The next day the stock falls slightly again, but Ian thinks that a closing price of 95 is really pretty good, compared with the downturn the day before. He and his colleagues now feel satisfied as long as the price just stays where it is and does not drop further. All they want is for the price to stabilize and liberate them from the anxiety of their situation.

Down below 90

Even Johnson is silent for the next few days. He had an outlet for his envy, and he really doesn't want to kick anyone who is down already. Now that Intersystems is around 90, the daily discussions have subsided. (See Figure 12.6.) Neither Ian nor the rest of the group has the energy to sort out their concerns and to make a concrete decision. Not one of them has any experience in handling anything like this. They bought Intersystems to make easy money in a risk-free trade. Mentally they are completely unprepared and have absolutely no plan of action in the event of a price drop. Ian has resigned from his leadership role, at least temporarily, and is just one of the group. As for Max Bork, he seems to have quite enough problems of his own.

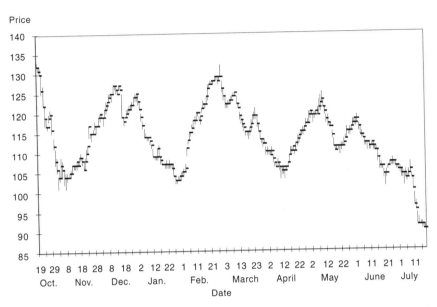

Figure 12.6. When Intersystems falls to 90, Ian and his group feel paralyzed and unable to act.

After a few days of relatively small price fluctuations, Ian's group begins to get a grip on the situation. This simply must be the bottom. After a downturn of almost 30 percent, they figure the stock simply cannot go down any more. Now it really must be worth buying. Of course, they feel it would have been best if they had sold earlier, even if at a loss. But with the unrealized loss they now have on their holdings, they simply cannot sell. More than likely, the price will go up again; and as long as they still own the shares, they will get their money back. By selling now, they would be giving up on that possibility. Then the trade would definitely have failed. That is how most of the group feels about it.

When the share falls yet another 8 points to 82 in spite of all their predictions (July 22), desperation is at hand. They begin to realize that they have been shielding themselves from reality. Their predictions were nothing but wishful thinking, and the talk

about a more long-term view was just something they were telling themselves so they would feel better. If they sell now, the
loss would be severe for all of them and for Ian most of all. Even
though Ian and the others realize that they have based their
previous actions on faulty premises, they can see no alternative
other than holding on to Intersystems.

When the price is down from 125 to 82, they don't want to
sell under any circumstances. (See Figure 12.7.) How would they
get their lost money back? Besides, they are all agreed that the
bottom must have been reached by now.

Max Bork also insists that at the present price level, Intersystems is a bargain. To sell now would be acting out of panic.
If Ian has hung on through the downturn this far, it would be
absolutely crazy to bail out now. Ian did not borrow the money
to buy, Max says. Instead of discussing whether he should sell or
not, Ian ought to be thinking about borrowing to buy more shares.

When Ian tells them that Max has advised him to buy more

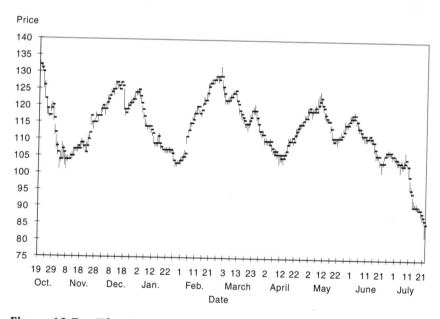

Figure 12.7.   When Intersystems goes down to 82, Ian Benson and his group
definitely do not want to sell.

shares with borrowed money, the group is outraged. Even if they see the logic of Bork's argument, no one wants to invest any more money in Intersystems. They feel cheated. Their attitude toward Intersystems is decidedly prejudiced and skeptical. Instead of the easy money they had counted on, their investment has brought them only misery and problems. To them, Max's suggestion to buy more shares after the drop is a bad joke. They see him as the root cause of their present dilemma. Ian thinks it is wrong to make Max the scapegoat, but he produces only a few lame arguments in defense of Bork because he does not want be on the firing line himself.

When it turns out that 82 seems to be the bottom price for Intersystems, a feeling of well-being spreads among Ian's group. A few weeks ago the very thought that they might be happy at a quote of 90 would have seemed absurd. Now their dream is no longer one of a good profit, but the dream of the possibility of getting their money back and of being free of the mental pres-

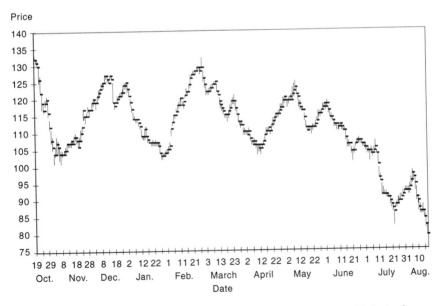

Figure 12.8. The story does not relate whether Ian's group sold their shares at the upward correction or followed the trend.

sure, stress, and anguish their investment brought with it. When the price goes above 95, their earlier nerve begins to come back. Now they only need the price to rise another 10 points before they are on the plus side again. The story does not relate whether Ian and his group use the upward correction to sell or whether they follow the downward trend even further. (See Figure 12.8.)

Chapter 13

DOWNWARD BREAK— MAX BORK

Recapitulation

The last time we saw Max, he had energetically called his clients to recommend that they buy Intersystems. On his advice, Ian Benson bought Intersystems at 106, and the price then went up rapidly to 115 when the market rallied on news of an unexpected rate cut by the Fed.

In the first two weeks after the upturn to 115, the price development was the same for both the upward and the downward break. So at the start of the downward break, Max behaves just as he did at the beginning of the upward break.

After remaining around 115 for a day or two, the price goes up rapidly to 120. Max has been feeling fine and quite satisfied with life these past two weeks, but he is impatient. He very much wants to take his profit here and now. He really wants at least 125, but the thought of selling at 120 is tempting. His colleagues and clients wonder what they should do, and he is very keen that this, his third trade in Intersystems, also be successful. If he recommends selling at the present price level, the trade is a sure thing, and he could get out from under the pressure he is feeling. Because his two previous deals were successful, a number of people seem to think he can see into the future.

Max is undecided—torn between the desire to recommend selling Intersystems now and calmly and patiently waiting for a higher price. He is not happy that everyone on the trading desk is listening to his client calls to hear what he is recommending on Intersystems. But he is satisfied with life. He wanted the respect and admiration of his colleagues, and he has both. It is just that he doesn't feel the situation is as clear as he had thought it would be.

After some thought, Max decides to wait to sell. But as soon as the price approaches 130, he will not hesitate to recommend selling. Then, if the upturn continues, in spite of what everyone expects, his clients can hardly complain when they have made a handsome profit.

Max is relieved. Now that he has a clear strategy to stick to, he suddenly finds he is enjoying all the attention. His role as leader of the wolf pack is actually really fun, as long as the prey has left clear tracks to follow.

Upturn to 125

For a few days after the two-week period just discussed, the price for Intersystems goes up to 125, and Max is very pleased with his decision. How frustrated he would have been if he had strayed from his original plan of action and suggested selling in a moment of impatience and uncertainty, when the price was at 120. Now all he has to do is stick to his plan and wait until the price goes up another 5 points. Then he will start. What a wonderful feeling it will be to finally pull off his hat trick—three good trades in one and the same stock! Of course, he has made two or three good trades in the same stock at other times, but they were just small buys for a few individual clients. Intersystems is quite another matter. With few exceptions, all his clients own Intersystems. For most of them, Intersystems is also their largest holding. There is no question that the boss is beginning to appreciate his abilities, Max says to himself with a smile.

Downturn to 110

A few days later, Max is not quite so self-confident anymore. He had expected the price to be closer to 130, not to have fallen back to 120. Still, he is not too worried. If the price has gone from 103 to 125, a fall of 5 points is extremely reasonable, he says, when Ian Benson asks nervously what has happened. It feels good to be calm and controlled when a caller is rather uneasy and nervous, Max thinks. He notices that when he acts confident and self-assured, his colleagues regard him with increased respect.

A week later, the price has fallen to 115. Max begins to regret his earlier confident attitude. He remembers a song he heard on the radio the day before: "The higher they climb, the harder they fall." That seems to apply to me, says Max with some irony. He really has pushed Intersystems to his clients, more or less guaranteeing that this trade, too, will go right. If he had not been so eager to impress his colleagues, the situation would be easier to deal with. In his eagerness to put his best foot forward, he has painted a picture of the future outlook for Intersystems that he is now regretting. Of course it is a good company with good products and a large market, but he knows you can never, never say that a trade has 80 percent certainty of working out. Now he has gotten himself into a position he does not know how to handle.

He is not mentally prepared for any negative developments. All he has is a plan for exactly when to recommend that his clients take their profits. Investors can cope with a fall of 5 points, but 10 points is another matter. It is very unpleasant. He knows that he has ignored the warning signals of which he was internally aware all along. He was being carried along by his desire to show the boys on the trading desk that he had dared to venture. He wanted so very much to be regarded as one of the best that he forgot humility. There are no free lunches in the market. He really ought to have learned that lesson by now, he says accusingly to himself. Of course he wants his clients to be satisfied and make money, but in his desire to be a "big shot," to be a respected and significant member of the group, he may have acted some-what too rashly. It was so easy to get clients hooked, so he grabbed the opportunity and said nothing to temper their enthusiasm for buying Intersystems. Those who had already done one or two good trades in the stock acted like hungry sharks sensing blood. They attacked their prey in a frenzy. Greedy people who get a whiff of easily made, safe money actually remind him of preda-tors out hunting. Money lust shines in their eyes, and their voices tremble with excitement. The difference is that predatory ani-mals act on instinct and act wisely, even when hungry, whereas human beings act emotionally and irrationally when greed seizes them, or so Max philosophizes.

His profession really is that of stockbroker; he would have been better off if he had talked less about the possibilities, he thinks bitterly. He has been around long enough to know how people can react to losing money, and he is the one who gave them bad advice. When clients make money, they are the ones who are talented and made the right decision.

The scapegoat syndrome, Max calls it—when you happen to land in a bad trade, it is much easier to look around for a scape-goat than to analyze your own behavior. If there is no one like a broker, an analyst, or a journalist to blame, then it is easier to just the blame the market for not functioning properly—that is how Max summarizes the situation. He has noticed how easy it is to fall into that kind of thinking. To him, it would be comfort-ing to blame the pharmaceutical analyst who recommended buying Intersystems and who is now unable to explain why the price is dropping.

With an effort, Max forces himself to think rationally, con-structively. The analyst actually had good reasons for being posi-tive. Even after she contacted the company management, she could find no good reason for the price drop. Her straight mes-sage to Max is that she thinks that for every point it drops, the stock will be that much more worth buying. Max really does appreciate her clear recommendation; he feels calmer now and less vulnerable. With a worked-through analysis behind him, he is now on firmer ground. No one can blame him for acting against his better judgment. His colleagues around the trading desk also pushed Intersystems to their clients, though no one did so as systematically and energetically as Max did. Max is annoyed that they have been studying his behavior as this situation developed, but it makes sense. They all know that he is not the boss, but when it comes to Intersystems in particular, informally at least, he has been given a certain moral responsibility.

When Ian Benson calls, Bork has begun to get a grip on the situation again. He notices that he sounds more forced than usual, though of course it's only human to be somewhat irritated when asked to explain your views on Intersystems for the tenth time in one day. Max tells Ian that the firm's buy recommendation stands, and he has advised his other clients just to take it easy and not do anything hasty. Furthermore, the profit from the holding will still be decent.

A few days later, Max is beginning to find the situation very unpleasant. How far is the price going to drop? This scenario was not at all part of his plan. When he bought or sold Intersystems earlier—a little too high or too low—the situation had soon corrected itself. A 5-point drop was perfectly manageable. A 10-point drop is troubling, but still controllable, but a 15-point drop is both unpleasant and nerve-racking. (See Figure 13.1.) He has no really good answer for his clients when they call to ask what they should do. The only advice he can think of when Ian phones, worried by the downturn, is to take it easy and wait for the upturn which is bound to come soon.

Max feels he has been painted into a corner. The market is down in general, but not to the extent that Intersystems is. His clients are still making a profit on their holdings, but if he advises them to sell now, without giving any reason other than that the price is showing weakness and then it turns up again quickly, he would look like an amateur. He doesn't know what to do. Intersystems had been an excellent stock in which to trade, but now he does not recognize the pattern.

The price should not have dropped from 125 to 110. At the most, it should have fallen to 115. Then, instead of dropping further, it should now be back at 120. He feels a grinding in his stomach, a gnawing worry that the price might fall even further; but he cannot tell his clients that. Grinding uneasiness as a basis

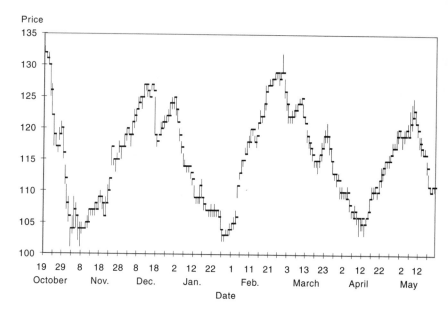

Figure 13.1.   When Intersystems falls to 110, Max Bork feels uneasy and indecisive.

for a recommendation to sell—what would that sound like? Max wonders. When he suggested that they buy Intersystems, he had described how the company was going to expand internationally and grow quickly. To suggest that they sell now just because he has a vague feeling of uneasiness in his stomach that the downturn might continue would sound like a sick joke to his clients.

Max feels that his colleagues expect him to make a decision. No one pressures him, but the strong position he held earlier within the group has been weakened. All his colleagues know they can go wrong in a trade now and again, and he is not being criticized for pushing Intersystems. The price level was clearly attractive, and he had the firm behind him when he acted. Most of his colleagues have recommended Intersystems to their clients, too, and they know that they have to decide what they are going to tell them, but none of them have such large holdings or are as informed about the company as Max is.

Max feels his anxiety beginning to get a stranglehold on him. He does not know what to do next. He is standing there like a donkey between two bales of hay. Never has he experienced such indecision and inability to act. He realizes that he must get control of the situation, but he needs to think in peace and quiet, without pressure or stress. He decides to take a long walk at lunch and not to go back to the office until he has made up his mind.

Just getting away from the trading desk and out into the summer sunshine provides some perspective. Despite his uneasiness and creeping anxiety, the sun is shining in the blue sky. Calm, relaxed people are strolling around the park, and the children near the pool are utterly unmoved by the downturn in Intersystems. People in the outdoor café are enjoying their coffee and the beautiful day. Strange, Max thinks, that only he, and not the rest of the world, seems to worry about the downturn in Intersystems. He draws a few deep breaths to calm himself down and bring some order to his mind.

He is clearly not quite as experienced as he had thought. Otherwise, he thinks, he would never have landed himself in this predicament. It wouldn't even have taken so much to avoid landing in this mess. A little more humility and a little less self-confidence are all that were needed. In regard to Intersystems, he behaved like a rambunctious colt let out to pasture after a long winter. He had only one thing in his head: that as many of his clients as possible buy as many shares of Intersystems as possible. He did not consider the possible consequences if the price went in the wrong direction.

Max stops suddenly. He is not thinking constructively. It's true, he admits to himself, that he has been running too fast, but he really has read up on the company. He timed the purchase very well, and the firm's pharmaceutical analyst verified his favorable opinion of the company. It is pointless to blame himself any more. That just makes things worse, not better. Instead, he should break out of his ostrichlike behavior. The problem will not go away just because he does not want to see it. No, he must pull up his socks, analyze the situation, and make a decision.

After twisting and turning the argument, Max comes to the conclusion that he actually thinks this is an opportunity to buy, not sell, Intersystems. A plan of action begins to crystallize. He will advise his clients, at least those with the largest holdings, to reduce their holdings when the price approaches 120, so that they are not overexposed. He will also tell all his clients that he does not see any reason why the price should go on dropping; but in the unlikely event that it drops further, they should decide ahead of time the level at which they will sell or reduce their holdings to limit their losses.

Max feels his body relax. Now he has control over the situation, instead of the other way around. As he sits down at the trading desk again, his self-confidence has returned. When the first phone call comes from a worried client, Max is in control. He is calm. He sounds confident and reassuring. His colleagues notice his changed state of mind. Max smiles to himself—he has regained his previous strong position within the pack.

Correction to 119

One week later, Max thinks life is wonderful. After falling to 109, the price has begun to go up again. He is very pleased and now has nothing against his clients' large holdings in Intersystems, figuring you have to take risks to win.

When the price approaches 120, Max questions his earlier decision to recommend that his clients with the largest holdings reduce them. (See Figure 13.2.) Everything seems to indicate that Intersystems is on the right track again. In his opinion, if he waits for just a week or two, the price is sure to go to about 130. He tells his clients that one should not be greedy, but there is no reason to just hand money over to others in the market. The agony of reaching a decision and the paralysis that tormented him earlier now seem very far away.

Fall below 110

Max Bork is shaken. A few days ago he was feeling strong, self-confident. At the time, Intersystems was being quoted at 119. He was convinced that the time had come for it to go up further. What happened? The price began to drop again. The anguish of

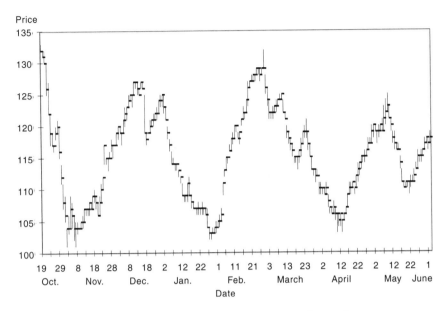

Figure 13.2. When the price corrects to 119, greed puts in an appearance; Max does not carry out his previous plan.

decision making that he had thought was history is back, fiercer than ever. He did not follow through on his plan to suggest that certain clients reduce their large holdings in Intersystems. True, the price never went over 120, but in his phone calls, he never said anything about selling. Instead he recalls guiltily how he had talked about what a good profit would be made when the price hit 130.

Max does not know what to do about this. His earlier plan had included an alternative if the price declined; but the idea of suggesting selling now, when he has already had two good chances, fills him with dread. He has not even decided on a clear stop-loss point; he just tells his clients that if they feel the price is falling below a critical level, they can put in a stop to minimize losses. That was not the main thrust of his advice, just an emergency solution, and not properly thought through.

No, now he does not like his job. He is trying to keep up appearances, to seem calm and unruffled, but he keeps worrying over his predicament. When the telephone rings, he really does not want to answer it and have to talk to yet another anxious or critical client. There really is a price to pay, he thinks anxiously, for being at the center of attention. It is wonderful to feel appreciated and respected, but it is true misery to have to listen to complaints from clients and to get critical looks from colleagues, even though none of them criticize him openly. They know the rules of the game; they also know that they decided to recommend Intersystems to their clients on their own. Still, there is an unspoken but unmistakable demand that Max Bork have the courage to deliver a definite opinion on the present situation, and not stick his head in the sand. After all, he is the one who most emphatically proclaimed Intersystems' excellence.

The day Ian Benson telephones and openly accuses him of giving bad advice, Max is angry. "If there is anyone who ought not to complain, it's you," Max tells Ian. "You've had two good trades in Intersystems, and I expressly warned you against putting all your money into a single stock. If you want to sell, I'll be delighted to execute your order," he adds after his scolding.

There is a painful silence on the phone. He is waiting for Ian to reply, but Ian says nothing. Max's emotions are still running high, and he continues: does Ian want to put in a sell order or not?

When Benson does answer, he is subdued. He apologizes and goes on to say that he is under stress because of his large holding and because of his colleagues.

Max says he understands Ian's troubles. He himself finds the situation trying, but there are never any sure bets on the market. But he still believes in Intersystems, and he still thinks it will be a good trade.

Ian says that he does not know what to do if the price drops even further. After all, he did not buy stock to lose money.

"You have to decide just how far you will let the price drop, and set a stop there," says Max. "You must plan in advance what to do if the price continues to drop. In the unlikely event that it falls below your stop level," he explains carefully, "you must sell." When Max promises to call immediately if the price falls below 100, the stop-level on which Ian decides, the conversation ends on a friendly note.

The price stabilizes for a while at just above 110. Max sighs with relief. He did the right thing after all, he thinks with satisfaction. Now he is just waiting for the price to go up in earnest. His clients have calmed down. His colleagues are talking more about other stocks than about Intersystems. But the next time the price goes to 120, he will definitely recommend that some clients reduce their large holdings, if only because some of them get nervous and are very difficult to deal with whenever the price drops a few points.

When the market opens and Max sees that Intersystems has fallen by 3 points to 107, he hopes that the quote is erroneous. (See Figure 13.3.) This is no fun anymore. Up to now, his clients have had a potential profit on their holdings; now things are beginning to come horribly close to landing on the loss side. Max knows from experience how demanding and unfair people can be

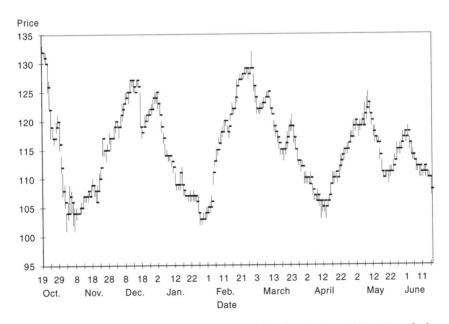

Figure 13.3. When the price unexpectedly falls below 110, Max feels slightly desperate.

if they lose money. It is wonderful to have money, but he thinks it is a pity that money also has a way of bringing out the worst in people.

The selling pressure on Intersystems is obviously more serious than he had thought earlier. The pattern the share price had shown previously has changed. Still, the price just cannot fall below 100, he tells himself without much conviction.

When Ian telephones, Max answers his questions as lucidly as he can. No, as far as he knows, there has been no negative news published about the company. Yes, the analyst still thinks the share is a good buy. Yes, he still thinks Ian should keep his holding.

During the days that follow, Max would have preferred not to have to go to work at all. If he was under pressure before and had hesitated about what to do, things are now considerably worse. His prognoses have been totally wrong. The fact that the analyst is still positive does not encourage him. She seems to have made an obvious misjudgment, Max thinks, with growing frustration. He must do something. But what? He feels a smoldering desperation. His clients start openly questioning whether there is really any basis for his favorable opinion of Intersystems. For several weeks he has argued that the price would go up, and slowly but surely it has gone the other way.

Some of his colleagues have begun to recommend selling Intersystems; they feel that there are more interesting alternatives on the market. It is perfectly clear that Max's positive view of the company is really more wishful thinking than a realistic prognosis.

Max knows that he must decide on the level at which he will recommend that his clients sell or at least reduce their holdings to limit their losses if the price drops even further. The problem is that he thinks it would seem wrong to suggest selling at 99, for instance. He thinks Intersystems is a well-run company. It would be horrible to recommend selling when the stock—God forbid—falls below 100, leaving him there like a fool for having sold at the rock-bottom price. He is torn between greed and fear. He does not want his clients to lose money, but he does not want to miss out on a good trade either if the price has simply had an unexpected, but temporary, downswing.

Oh well, when to recommend to sell is actually not a big problem at the moment, he says to himself. His clients have bought Intersystems at 106, or a few points above, which means any eventual loss will be insignificant because the price has stopped after dropping to 107. But the uneasiness and discomfort are still there. He does not want to deal with his premonition that Intersystems may have established a lasting downward trend. He dismisses the idea as destructive. However, he does realize that he has to plan what to do if his prediction that 100 is the absolute bottom turns out to be wrong.

When his anxiety lets up, Max puts aside his troublesome thoughts by reminding himself not only that it is not he but his clients who bear the responsibility of making a decision, but also that he advised them to decide on a stop level, for safety's sake. Now, finally, he seems to be in control of the situation again. Though he hardly feels satisfied with life, at least he feels less tortured.

What an ostrich he has been, Max thinks, burying his head in the sand like that! Within two days, the price has dropped to 101. Now it is impossible to ignore the reality. He does not feel at all well. He wonders whether he has chosen the right profession. He feels like leaving. He does not want to sit in front of a screen on the trading desk, feeling sick, not knowing whether the decisions he is making are going to turn out to be good or bad. If he had chosen to be an accountant or to work in finance, he would not be living with this wretched anxiety. At least people in those professions can count on certain alternatives, various outcomes, thinks Max, whereas one day he thinks he had been right, only to discover the next day that what he did the day before—convinced he was right—turns out to be wrong.

Why should it be so hard to make decisions? Max wonders. Although he knows full well that Intersystems may drop even further, he still quite automatically believes in the company. Logically, the stock must be worth its price now, if this year's profit does not turn out to be a real disaster. To emphatically recommend selling, now that the price has fallen to 101, seems wrong, though he notices that the selling pressure on the stock is also strong.

Max doesn't know what to do. His clients' losses are still very moderate, so there has been no disaster. But he was the one to go on about a stop-loss level. If he does not recommend that his clients sell now, he cannot in the name of decency go running back later, saying that he had changed his mind and suggesting that they sell at 95 when he did not want them to sell at a price above 100.

He realizes he must make up his mind, but it seems impossible—here in a trading room as chaotic as a henhouse with a fox loose in it. The telephones are ringing even more than usual today, and his colleagues are all talking at the same time—loudly. Meanwhile, he is trying to make what, to him, are important decisions. He has to get away from the trading desk, take a walk, and think clearly.

Despite his change of environment, Max finds it hard to make up his mind. He twists and turns the arguments, trying to be as objective as possible. If only he had not called all his clients, painting such a rosy future for Intersystems and making such a strong recommendation to buy that he seemed to be guaranteeing a price upturn. Then things would be easier, he says to himself with a sigh. Now he is under pressure, stressed out and hounded, and being forced into a decision. He doesn't need to worry about his former strong position on the trading desk; it doesn't exist anymore. He doesn't need to worry about a raise— the dream of "Max Bork, Star Broker" looks about as unattainable as the clouds in the sky. If the price falls any further, he now risks having to have a talk with his firm's lawyer because of his keenness to sell large quantities of Intersystems. There surely will be a number of bothersome sourpusses among his clients who will argue that they were promised "safe money" and ought to be compensated by Wilson & Partners, Max thinks with a heavy heart. He doubts whether he is in the right profession. Still, regardless of the answer to that question, he must find a way out of his dilemma.

After some serious thinking, an alternative finally begins to crystallize. Either he tells his clients that he still believes in Intersystems and that if they want to hang on, they should regard it as a long-term holding and should also be willing to accept some further decline before the stock turns around; or he must suggest that they get out now and limit their losses. The first alternative is his main option, but he decides to use both, depending on the client.

Max is not exactly returning to the office with a spring in his step. It feels to him as if he is heading for a trial with the market as judge and his clients the jury.

"Hallelujah, Intersystems is at 104!" he says aloud after checking the price. He feels his anxiety lifting like the mist on a sunny summer morning. It is good to be alive again. Maybe he was right after all. Intersystems is a good company and 101 was surely the bottom, he thinks, patting himself on the back. (See Figure 13.4.)

"Maybe I'll escape being hauled out into the courtyard for execution," he jokes as the managing director sticks his head around the door of the brokerage room.

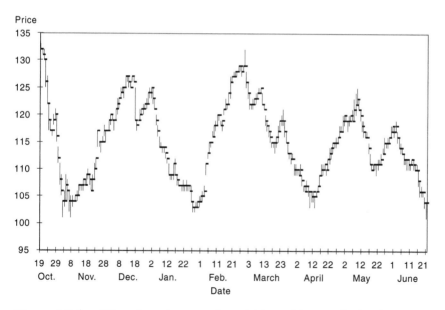

Figure 13.4. When the price goes from 101 to 104, Max thinks that Intersystems has finally bottomed out and that the time for an upturn has come.

Fall below 100

Over the next few weeks, the development of the Intersystems price confirms Max Bork's view that 101 was the low. At first, the price goes up quickly to 108, then slowly falls back down toward 100, only to go back up quickly to 107. It is the middle of summer. Now that the Intersystems crisis is over, Max can take some time off in good conscience. He really needs to get away from the screen and the market for a while. There's actually more to life than stock quotes and commissions, he thinks philosophically, strolling along the beach in warm, soft, white sand, glad that he does not have to worry about Ian Benson and his other clients. His colleagues will just have to answer his phone while he lets body and soul relax.

The very first morning he is back, Intersystems falls below 100. What a lousy day to start back to work, Max thinks. (See Figure 13.5.) All those unpleasant feelings he hoped he had es-

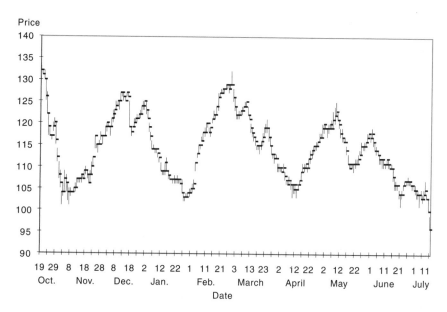

Figure 13.5. When Intersystems falls to 96, Max feels his anxieties returning. His stomach churns.

caped were only dormant, waiting to hurl themselves at him. He is not equipped to deal with this latest development. He has been going along, deciding to stake everything on his profession, not to be merely good at it, but to be really good. Now it feels as if his world is about to collapse. Anxiety is once again poking holes in his confidence. His gut reaction is that he does not want to be part of this anymore. He has a strong aversion to Intersystems; it is causing him these dreadful feelings that he can't escape, as if he were balancing on a plank above a morass, with the hounds closing in from behind. With every step he takes, the plank wobbles, and he doesn't know whether he will fall into the sludge or arrive safely on the other side. He feels trapped. He can't go back and he can't escape. The market shows no mercy, he thinks. He feels sorely tried. Though he does not realize it, deep down he is simply looking for a scapegoat to blame for the predicament in which he has landed himself.

During his vacation, Max came to the conclusion that because of the uncertainty surrounding the company, he would suggest that his clients reduce their holdings in Intersystems. That would not really be admitting that he was wrong. It would simply be a matter of adjusting to reality. He still believes Intersystems is a company with a future, but neither he nor his clients feel good about the great risk involved because Intersystems is the largest holding in their accounts.

A suggestion of that kind means that he is acting, not just reacting to what is happening. He is demonstrating that he is able to make decisions. He is not paralyzed. Naturally, it is a compromise solution, but it is important—both for himself and for his clients—to feel in command and not floating mindlessly like a rudderless boat on the capricious tides of the market.

Now what should I do? Max frets feverishly, his stomach in turmoil. Three days ago Intersystems was at 107, and his clients could have reduced their holdings without losses. Should he call them now and ask them to sell at 96? Unless he believes that there will be a further drop of at least 10 percent, it will be hard to promote selling at this point, he figures. The risk is that the price will simply fall by yet a few percentage points, hit bottom, and then start up again, while he is left off to one side, looking foolish for having recommended selling at the low of the year. It would be terribly embarrassing to hold on through a downturn from 125 to 96 and then to sell in a panic and maybe make a complete fool of himself.

Max begins to feel hopelessly lonely. He is seized with a fierce longing just to do what everyone else seems to be doing, namely recommending that clients sell Intersystems immediately, take a loss, forget it, and look for an alternative stock to buy. Acting differently from the majority is insecure, lonely, and uncomfortable. Most of his colleagues on the desk are tired of the stock. They have already recommended that their clients sell at least part of their Intersystems holdings and reinvest the money. The firm's pharmaceutical analyst still thinks there is no sound reason for the drop in price, but she does not sound as convincing as before. The firm that is really dumping Intersystems is four times as big as Wilson & Partners and has a highly reputable research department. Certainly, his clients will soon be wondering whether he really does know as much about Intersystems as he says he does.

When Ian Benson phones, Max has still not decided what to recommend to his clients. He advises Ian to hold on to his shares, not knowing whether it is wishful thinking or a thought-out recommendation. Maybe he has just chosen the simplest solution to a problematic situation. He knows from experience that people find it easier to accept potential rather than realized losses. As long as they still hold the stock, they can go on living in the hope that the bottom must be near. Max admits that he cannot clearly analyze the reasons for his recommendation, but he simply cannot bring himself to suggest selling at the present price level, regardless of the basis for his decision.

Fall below 90

The downturn from 107 to 90 takes a little more than a week. After that the price stabilizes around that level. (See Figure 13.6.) At first Max is paralyzed. He had considered the possibility that the price might fall below 100, but he had never really taken

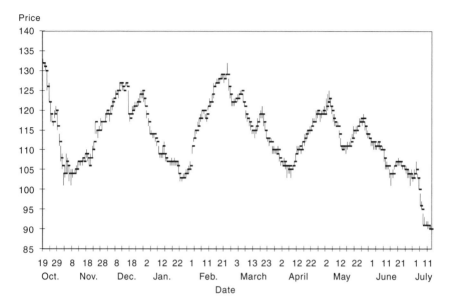

Figure 13.6. When the price falls and stabilizes around 90, Max persuades himself that the bottom *must* have been reached.

such a scenario seriously. He has been in this profession for some time and is well aware that any of the companies quoted can run into problems; but he was not prepared for that to happen to Inter-systems, active in such a growing market. He has never been in a similar situation before, and he has little experience in dealing with it. Of course, in the past, he has made some recommendations on which clients lost money.

On the other hand, all his clients have never been in the position of holding such large potential losses. In all his time as a stockbroker, Max has never been under as much pressure as he is now. He feels powerless. He is fully occupied calming nervous and uneasy clients who call him. He would prefer to escape from it all, but he has to summon up all his energies to sound calm, collected, and reassuring when he talks to them. Being criticized is never fun. It is even less fun when the criticism is justified, Max thinks. He knows he must maintain his calm and not flare up, even if some clients are not only rude but unfair in their comments. Though the situation is extremely difficult, he feels that this is the only way to ride out the storm. He also knows that, somehow or other, he must keep control of the situation. In his present state of mind, he can think of only one solution— to hold onto Intersystems. To sell after a drop of almost 30 percent is inconceivable.

After Intersystems has hovered around 90 for over a week, Max begins to sniff the morning air again. He has heard in a roundabout way that the firm that was so energetically disposing of Intersystems has adjusted downward the rate of growth for the sector in which Intersystems is active. Max calculates that even if this is true, the size of the downturn should be more than enough to make Intersystems well worth buying. He thinks that after a downturn of almost 30 percent, the likelihood that Intersystems has bottomed is pretty high.

A few days later, it turns out that his prediction was totally wrong. After a drop to 86, the price falls another 4 points to 82. Max Bork wishes desperately that he had chosen another profession. (See Figure 13.7.) He wants to do a good job. He did push

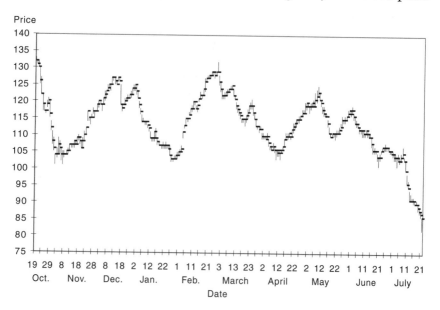

Figure 13.7. When the prices falls to 82, Max once again wishes he had chosen another profession.

Intersystems, he did have ambitions to be at the top of his profession, but he was also totally convinced that Intersystems was worth buying and that all the conditions for a good trade were in place.

Instead, everything had taken a turn he could never have predicted. Instead of climbing in his career, Max appears to be stumbling down some pitch-dark cellar stairs. His anxiety is profound. Will the price never stop going down? Has Intersystems been driven out of business? Could they be going bankrupt? His head whirls with terrifying thoughts, and he agonizes over what the price will do the next day. What does he do if the price falls to 50? Will his clients be so upset that they go to another firm? Will Wilson & Partners be showered with suits for damages because of his fast and loose promises of a "quick and safe" trade? Max wonders whether to put an end to it all and resign. He is under so much pressure that he is prepared to do almost anything just to escape this uncertainty, the doubts, and the almost paralyzing anxiety.

To get away from the trading room and to escape any more critical client phone calls, he tells his colleagues he is going to visit a client. Instead, he sets off toward the harbor. He needs a peaceful environment. The sea has always symbolized freedom for him; and when he is down there, away from clients and the screen, it is much easier for him to put the situation into perspective.

Actually, there has been no disaster. Calculated from his clients' purchase price of about 106, the downturn is only a little over 20 percent. No world war has broken out. His wife has not left him, and his house has not burned down. He has no incurable disease. He is alive and breathing. He has not been in an accident and left paralyzed. His clients have lost money, but he is young and healthy, and Intersystems has not gone bankrupt.

In the end Max Bork feels balanced—in harmony. The situation is no fun, but he can deal with it. The problem is that most clients do not realize that they have only lost the difference between 106 and 82. Instead, they measure the downturn from 125 to 82 and calculate that they are down by almost 35 percent. Max sighs. So often, people are really irrational about money.

On his way back to the office, Max decides to have a long talk with Wilson & Partners' pharmaceutical analyst. Then he will contact Intersystems directly to get real insight into the situation at the company. If he still feels positive about the company after that kind of an analysis, he will recommend strongly that his clients hold on to their shares and even buy more, rather than sell at a bargain basement price. If he comes to the opposite conclusion, he will have to eat humble pie, admit he was wrong, wait for an upturn, and suggest that his clients sell and buy another stock. That is his decision. If the second alternative seems the one to pursue, he hopes he can find a really good stock to buy. It will be much easier to get a client to accept a loss if, rather than explaining what went wrong with Intersystems, he can steer him toward the potential of a new trade.

When Ian Benson calls later that day, Max notices that he has no problem dealing with the situation. Max is puzzled. In the morning he had been thinking about resigning, and now, in the afternoon, he is on the offensive. To his surprise, he sees that nothing has really changed except his state of mind. He realizes that in the future, he must have a plan of action—even for un-expected and unlikely price movements. If he had been mentally prepared for the possibility of Intersystems going in the wrong direction, he would not have been so paralyzed. He would cer-tainly have felt less tortured.

When Max asks Ian Benson whether he ought not to consider buying more shares at the present price level instead of selling, he can almost see Ian leaping up from his chair.

He tells Ian that although he has not completed his analysis, Intersystems is probably a bargain at the present price level. As anticipated, Ian is very skeptical, but Max notices that Ian is surprised that Max seems so calm and relaxed on the phone.

Max knows that he is still in a difficult situation. He cer-tainly cannot blow the danger off, even if the price for Inter-systems turns up from 82, the bottom of the previous day, to 86 just before the market closes. But he is convinced that he has the strength required to handle the situation. There are only two ways to behave, Max says to himself cynically: either he cracks, or he gets stronger. Regardless of whether the downturn with

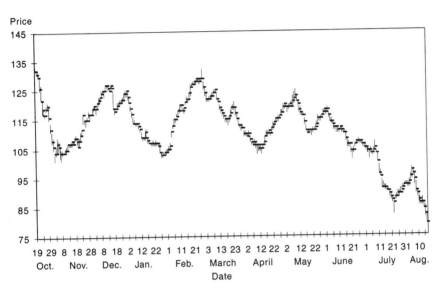

Figure 13.8. History does not record whether Max Bork recommended that his clients sell Intersystems on the upward correction or whether he concluded that the shares were worth holding for the long term.

Intersystems has consequences for him in his role as broker with Wilson & Partners, he knows that he has gained very important experience that will help him build on his efforts to be really good at his profession.

After touching bottom at 82, the price rises to 98 in early August and then falls rapidly again. Whether Max decided to recommend that his clients sell or keep Intersystems is not known. (See Figure 13.8.) If he suggested that his clients hold Intersystems for the long term, it is to be hoped he has a plan of action and is better prepared mentally than earlier when Intersystems hit another bottom. If not, he may soon be feeling more unwell than ever.

Chapter 14

CROWD PSYCHOLOGY AT A DOWNWARD BREAK

As we've already said, Ian Benson and Max Bork are only a small part of the great crowd on the market. Also part of the crowd are all the other stockholders of Intersystems—those who have been stockholders for a longer period, those who only bought stock since it began to range, those who sold and shorted Intersystems, both before and during the ranging period, and those who had no interest in Intersystems earlier but who considered buying or shorting it without executing the trades.

It is the psychology of this crowd that we are going to analyze in conjunction with Intersystems' breakout of its trading range on the downside. People have to behave emotionally for crowd behavior to develop in the market. To give readers a better understanding of crowd psychology, we looked at the more individual reactions of Ian Benson and Max Bork. It is important to understand that in certain situations all active participants get emotional to a greater or a lesser degree. Regardless of how experienced investors may be or how much capital they have at their disposal, they are human beings, and human beings are emotional. It is entirely human to live in hopes, to succumb to wishful thinking, to interpret information to suit one's aims, and to avoid making decisions in a difficult situation. The more emotionally involved one becomes, the easier it is to do what everyone else seems to be doing instead of behaving independently.

Chapters 12 and 13, in describing how Ian and Max, respectively, experienced a situation in which they were losing money demonstrated precisely that. As we have seen, people also become emotional when they make gains. But the pain of losing money is considerably more intense than the pleasure of making it, and when a stock price falls, there are stronger emotions in play than there are when it goes up. So now it is time to explain the large influence of crowd behavior on price development in the case of a downward outbreak from a longer price range.

The Vacuum Effect

David Fuller's vacuum effect comes into play once again. (See Figure 14.1.) Most of the demand below the range has vanished.

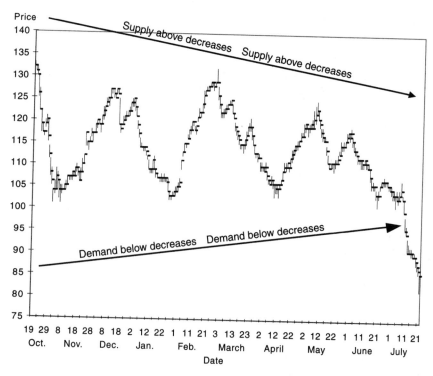

Figure 14.1.   The vacuum effect.

A large number of investors—potential buyers—are tired of waiting for Intersystems to resume its falling trend. At first, many stockholders simply raise their buying limits. They are not prepared to accept the price the market is offering, that is, the price prevailing within the range. After raising their limits once or twice, more and more investors are impatient and stressed at not being able to buy at the price they are willing to pay. Even the most persistent begin to realize that if they really do want to buy, they will have to "climb up" into the range. Naturally, not all investors are keen to buy at the prevailing market price; but the longer the trading range lasts, the more the demand is drawn into the range because that is where a trade can be executed.

As we've already pointed out, the time factor is critical. The mental process necessary to accept a higher buying price than planned is a slow one. Resistance to buying ebbs slowly as time passes. The longer the range lasts, the stronger the psychological dynamic becomes. After a sufficient period in this phase, a psychologically charged situation is built up that may result in a powerful downward price move. Because demand has largely been drawn away from the market by potential buyers who got tired of waiting for the right price and who either bought at a price within the range or turned their interest over to other securities, there is now a vacuum of buyers below the range.

A clear downward break from the range on volume means that there is an obvious imbalance in the market. Everyone who sold or bought Intersystems while the price was fluctuating feel that they have acted "rightly" or "wrongly" at the same time. All buying and selling within the range has been executed at a price higher than the prevailing one. As long as Intersystems fluctuated in its range, the buyers and the sellers were equally strong. Approximately the same numbers were "right" as "wrong." Some sold at the top of the range and were pleased. Some bought at the bottom and were also content. Of course, there are also some who are unhappy because they think they have sold too low and others who feel they have bought too high and are disgruntled.

It is impossible to predict how long a trading range will last, but it never goes on forever. It is impossible to predict with any certainty what will trigger the downward break from Intersystems' long-lasting consolidation. The trigger could be negative analyses from financial houses, an increasingly widespread opinion/rumor of dampened growth in the sector, selling interest from larger investors, or any combination of these factors.

Here is crowd psychology at work when, after a few weeks of gathering strength at the bottom of the range, Intersystems breaks down instead of turning up, as it had done previously when it fell to just above 100. (See Figure 14.2.)

At the beginning of this chapter we defined what constitutes the main crowd on the market in connection with a break from the range. But a large crowd is itself made up of larger and smaller groups. The two obvious groups in this case are (1) those investors who feel that the break on the downside is negative and unpleasant, and (2) those who see this as positive and advantageous.

First, let's look at the crowd psychology in the negative group

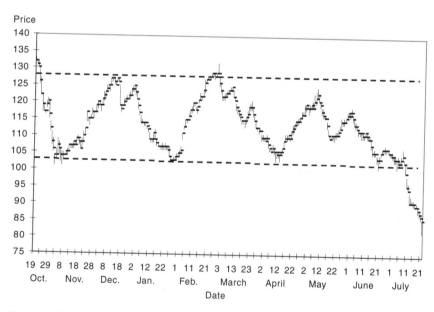

Figure 14.2. An obvious breakout from a longer range on volume is an excellent catalyst for crowd behavior in the stock market.

and then in the positive group. Then we will study some diagrams of real situations on the market to establish how well theory conforms to reality. This will also give us some insight into how what we have learned can serve as the basis for investment decision making.

Negative Subgroups of Investors

The negative group within the crowd can be divided into several negative subgroups:

I.   Long-Term Stockholders—Investors who owned Intersystems before it began to range and kept all or most (50 percent or more) of their holdings.
II. New Stockholders—Newcomer investors who bought all or most (50 percent or more) of their intended holdings within the range and have held their shares.
III. Non-Short-Sellers—Investors/traders who intended to sell Intersystems short while it was fluctuating in the range but failed to do so.

Common Characteristics

It is no fun for an investor to sell in the range only to find soon after that the stock starts going up, to break out on the upside. But this investor still has his money and the freedom of choice to do as he likes. He does not need to make any decision until the situation is clarified. He can try to buy back Intersystems, forget about it and invest in another stock, or simply let it sit in his account. There is no reason to worry about the future destiny of Intersystems unless you are a stockholder. For an investor, the choice is completely voluntary. But once an investor has sold a stock, he tends to follow the price development of that stock intently, very much wanting confirmation of having done the "right" thing and selling at an opportune moment.

Those who already owned Intersystems, who bought in the

range and held on to the shares and then saw the price break out downward, do not have the same agreeable freedom of choice. For every point the price drops, they lose money. They cannot just stand aside and watch the drama being played out in the market.

It is difficult to rank emotional experience. But in general, the larger the holding in relation to total capital, the higher the price paid, the longer the period the shares were held, and the more unexpected and dramatic the downward break is, the worse people feel. Essentially, all Intersystems stockholders are worried, dissatisfied, and frustrated. When the price breaks down out of the range, most of them feel they have to make a decision: sell, hold, or buy more shares. They find themselves in a precarious situation and must decide what to do, even if the decision does not result in any concrete action. When a stock goes up, shareholders can take satisfaction in that fact and just decide to hold on. If the stock goes down, few stockholders look on the situation without some degree of stress, pressure, and dismay.

In the situation that has developed with Intersystems, hardly any shareholders feel they have done the right thing. Most of them look on a loss or on an erosion of gains as something negative. If, like Ian Benson, they bought Intersystems at 106 and the actual loss when the share is at 100 is clearly limited, they may still perceive the loss as considerably greater than it is. It is very common and entirely human to regard even the unrealized gain between 106 and 125 as money lost. Now let's look at one of the three negative subgroups.

Subgroup I—Long-Term Stockholders

Stockbroker Sam Rosenberg's clients bought early in the uptrend and got into Intersystems at a very good price. After riding out the rapid downturn from the high, they sold half their holdings when the price swung up to the upper part of the range for the second time, at Sam's suggestion. At first, Rosenberg was very happy; but when the price crept closer to the earlier bottom again, just above 100, he felt uncertainty come creeping back. He wished he had been bolder and had recommended that his clients sell all not just half of their holdings.

Poor Sam! He was very close to recommending that his clients sell their remaining shares in Intersystems when the price approached the upper part of the range for the third time. He had already decided to suggest that his clients dispose of their remaining shares if the price rose above 125 at a third attempt. But Intersystems is only up and touching his target price for one day, May 9, and Sam hardly had time to think of recommending selling before the price headed south again. (See Figure 14.3.)

How Rosenberg reacted and behaved when Intersystems started its decline is not known, but we assume that he, like Max Bork, did not recommend that his clients sell when the price began to go down. It is very trying to buy a stock at a good price, to watch it go up, and then to be faced with a substantial downturn which transforms into a considerable period of fluctuation before the price finally breaks out on the down side of the range.

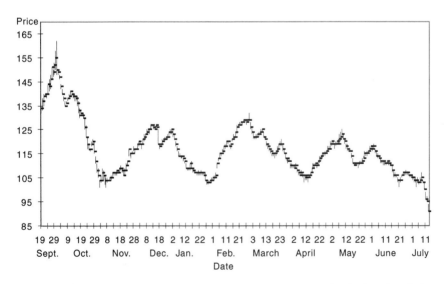

Figure 14.3. When the price of Intersystems swung to the high side of the range for the third time, the stock touched 125 only briefly before beginning to fall again. Sam had no time to recommend that his clients sell their remaining holdings.

Sam cannot get over the fact that he fixed on a price above 125 before making his recommendation to sell. He tells himself accusingly that if only he had been more flexible and efficient, he would have escaped all the agony he is suffering now. But he thanks his lucky stars that at least his clients have sold half their holdings at a good price. If he had not suggested that, he would be under even greater pressure and more worried. He has still not decided what to do, but he very much wants to get out of the hot seat. He will recommend that his clients get out of Intersystems, which he now regards as an unreliable, dangerous stock.

All the stockholders in this subgroup bought Intersystems before it began to range. Some of them reduced their holdings during the trip, but all still have at least half of their original holding. Because the earlier uptrend was very steep, many still have profits. Those investors who sustain losses when the price breaks the range on the downside and falls below 100 feel worse than those who are still on the plus side. But it is no fun to watch a really good profit melt away like butter in the sun. The gains they had thought of as a reality are now very uncertain. If the price continues downward, the gains will disappear completely and even turn into losses at a certain point. There is the unpleasant realization that if this price development continues, it may entail an even worse outcome than today's.

Envisioning many large-denomination bills falling out of the sky and crashing to the ground, one after another, like so many game birds full of lead shot, is hardly conducive to a calm assessment of any situation. It is more likely to cause considerable anguish and to make a stockholder wish desperately that she could extricate herself from the situation she is in. For most long-term stockholders, regardless of whether they realize lower profits or have to take a substantial, real loss, the break out of the range is anxiety producing. The only reward for their patience and endurance is negative feelings—frustration, exhaustion, uncertainty, stress, pressure, and disappointment at seeing their holdings decrease in value.

As long as the price doesn't drop below the bottom of the range, Sam and other investors in the same boat can live in hopes that Intersystems will turn up again, as it has done twice before. But when the price finally breaks out of the range on the downside to fall below 100 and then plummets toward 90, it is clear to most investors in this group that looking at Intersystems as a long-term investment was a mistake. Now they can't live on hope anymore. They have to accept the fact that they were wrong to hold on to their shares instead of selling when they could still have gotten over 100 for them. For many months, these stockholders have waited for Intersystems to resume its upward trend. But now it is doing the exact opposite of what they had hoped.

When the share price finally breaks out from the range on the downside, clearly signaling that the ranging phase is over, many of them feel strong reluctance and anxiety. The long wait has been fruitless. Instead of being rewarded, their patience and endurance are being punished. When the bottom level in the range that earlier had seemed so safe cracks as easily as the most brittle straw, many shareholders are in torment.

An experience like this can be very painful, and it can cause people to act rashly. When they realize that they have done the wrong thing, their anguish can be so acute that they want to escape the emotional pain at almost any cost. Many Intersystems stockholders now actively dislike the stock, seeing it as the real cause of their unpleasant feelings. People usually blame their problems on factors outside themselves. In this situation, blaming the broker for his or her poor advice is the most likely reaction. Blaming the schizophrenic market in general and Intersystems' manic-depressive stock in particular is also fine. This scapegoat syndrome is a defense mechanism used by the investors to protect and preserve their self-esteem; but scapegoating is not constructive behavior when attempting to solve the actual problem. Instead of trying sincerely to make a decision based on facts, the stockholders' aversion to Intersystems may make them behave exactly like everyone else on the market—namely, "rushing for the exit"—selling their shares in that "lousy company" that can't seem to do anything right.

At the downward break from the range, the remaining stockholders all get emotional at the same time, all feeling more or less stress and dismay. In a pressure situation like this one, it is predictably human for people to behave more like members of a herd than as individuals. They do exactly what most of the market seems to be doing: selling while they can still get something for their shares, saving whatever is to be saved, even as they heap scorn and abuse on Intersystems. Finally, when the downward break from the long-term range is obvious to the entire market, the psychological dynamic that has built up is expressed in crowd behavior.

Subgroup II—New Stockholders

In this group we find several old acquaintances. Since Ian Benson and Max Bork did not manage to sell when the price for Intersystems touched 125 on the third upward swing and then started falling again, they have landed in this group involuntarily.

The next acquaintance is Peter Ericson, who only deals in stock very rarely but who became interested in Intersystems. On his first attempt to buy Intersystems, however, he left a buy order that was too low and missed the deal by a hair's breadth. When the price moved toward the bottom of the range for the second time, Peter did not want to miss out again. He was torn between his fear of losing money and his greed. He really did not know what to do. His compromise solution entailed buying half the number of shares he had wanted to buy earlier, but he got nervous and in his eagerness bought at 112. (See Figure 14.4.) Then, to his chagrin, the stock fell to his original "buying level"—just over 100. He was very annoyed, but in spite of the lower price, he did not want to buy the rest of the shares as he had planned. The thought of losing even more money was just too unpleasant.

Remember Karen Thurston, who manages individual portfolios for wealthy private clients? She did not buy any Intersystems for her clients during the uptrend and then felt pressured when the stock turned out to be the winner of the year. So it was with ill-concealed delight that she watched its rapid drop from the high and finally saw an opportunity to buy Intersystems at an attractive level. At first, the firm's analyst for medical companies didn't think the stock was worth buying at anything over

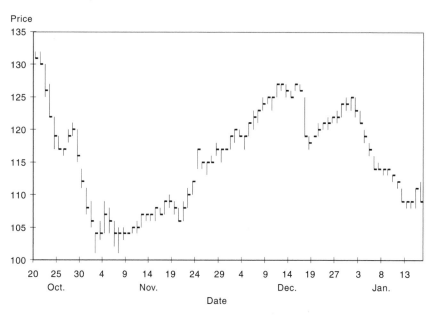

Figure 14.4. Peter Ericson did not want to risk having the price get away from him, so he bought half of what he had wanted at a price considerably higher than he had planned.

100. That was why, with growing impatience, Karen waited for the price to fall below that level. But after a visit to the company, the analyst was more positive, and Karen wondered which would be worse—buying slightly too early and watching the price drop even further, or not buying and risking missing a good opportunity for the third time. She thought it would be stupid to wait just to save a little, so she bought her entire position at 115. (See Figure 14.5.)

Earlier, we saw how Ian Benson and Max Bork reacted to the downward break from the range, so we've already completed a large part of the analysis of this subgroup. But this group is considerably more heterogeneous than the group of long-term stockholders, and that is why the new stockholders must also be considered from other points of view.

The long term stockholders all bought Intersystems before it began to range. They still had at least 50 percent of their hold-

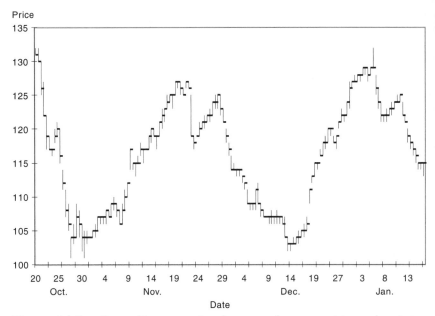

Figure 14.5.   Karen Thurston missed two good opportunities to buy Inter-systems at an attractive price. She does not want to let a third opportunity pass her by.

ings at the downward outbreak. The new stockholders are a considerably more colorful crowd. Among them are those who bought the first time it was down and touched just above 100 and those who bought the stock before the bottom fell out—when the price dropped from 100 to 96.

The latter group, who bought during the weeks when the price was fluctuating between 101 and 108, are neither amused nor encouraged when, a week or a day later, the price falls below 100, only to drop even further quickly. They are unlikely to feel lucky to have escaped the frustration of holding a stock that fluctuated in a lengthy range, only to find that the long wait was fruitless. No, a punch in the stomach sharp enough to take your breath away and double you over in pain is unlikely to make you grateful that you weren't beaten even more severely. Chances are, you will be so busy considering your own bad luck that you won't be thinking about anyone who may have reason to feel even worse. But these stockholders have not had time to build up the same strong aversion, disgruntlement, and impatience with the price of Intersystems while it fluctuated within the range.

They may not be sick of waiting for the price to begin to move in a clear upward direction at long last, but if one of these new stockholders bought a relatively large position and the price dropped like a stone, he or she might still perceive the downward break as a disaster. When your capital is being brutally and mercilessly pummeled by massive selling pressure from a panic-stricken crowd, you can very easily be seized by desperation. In all likelihood, such financial and psychological conditions don't apply to most of these new stockholders. At the risk of simplifying somewhat, it is probably safe to say that the earlier within a range people bought a stock, the more predisposed they are to adopting crowd behavior. The longer investors have agonized over what might happen, the more negative they feel at a downward break. It is also more than likely that they chastise themselves for not having sold early in the range. After all, they had plenty of time and any number of opportunities to sell at a price that was at least above 100.

Among those who bought early in the range, there are sure to be many feeling like a coiled spring under constant and uneven pressure. Karen Thurston did indeed buy relatively late in the range, but she has still been on an emotional roller coaster—her feelings rushing between hope and fear. After waiting for several months, she finally buys at 115. At first, she is very pleased. Just a few days later, the price is at 120. But then, not many weeks go by before the price falls as low as 103. Though Karen was somewhat prepared for a downturn when she bought, there is a real difference between being mentally prepared for a drop in price and actually facing one. She is almost certain to be thinking that it would have been much better if she had bought her holding 12 points lower, instead of using all her resources at 115. Karen is sure to heave a sigh of relief when the price goes up to 125.

Then, unless she disposes of some shares before Intersystems breaks out of the range on the downside, she will clearly see the situation as trying. She has gone wrong again and again. First she missed the entire uptrend. Then, on two occasions, she missed buying at the bottom of the range because the analyst thought the stock was overpriced at 100. When he eventually changed his mind and became positive, Karen bought at 115, out of fear of missing a third time, and ended up on an express elevator going up and down several times before finally crashing through the floor on its way to some unknown fate.

Peter Ericson bought even earlier in the range than Karen, but there are some important differences. He bought only half as many shares as he had initially intended. He has a very clear philosophy of long-term investment and feels no need to explain or to defend his actions to anyone except himself. No one will criticize him if his portfolio does not perform as well as the market as a whole. He is also in the happy situation of not needing the capital he has invested, so he has the luxury of being able to forget about Intersystems.

Peter finds himself in a more comfortable position than Karen, but he still doesn't like ending up with a loss. He would prefer to ignore the price developments in Intersystems, but that is easier said than done. He is barely able to resist the temptation to study the stock market quotations. At first, he is very happy when he finds that the share has recovered and is climbing up to the top of the range again. But after having fallen for the fourth time, to just above 100, the price does not turn up as it had before. Instead, it plummets.

Peter is very disappointed. Maybe it would be just as well to sell that wretched stock. The analyst in *Business Today* seems to have seriously misjudged the company's potential, and he was stupid enough to break his own most important rule: only invest in old, large, and safe companies that cannot go bankrupt. Feeling unsure and down is understandable when you have bought a stock that the rest of the market seems to be rejecting. Is he really some lone, small investor, hanging on to Intersystems when everyone else seems to be doing exactly the opposite? He would feel easier in his mind if he knew that he could safely forget about Intersystems, instead of being forced to live with his present anxiety.

Still, Peter's predicament is easier to deal with than Karen's. Karen is more ambivalent. She is torn between contradictory feelings of fear and greed, prestige and anxiety, independence and crowd behavior.

Suppose she doesn't sell and the bottom falls out of the price? Suppose she sells and the price turns up sharply? Can she really sell at a loss now that the firm's analyst is finally positive and she has just recently taken Intersystems into her portfolios? Karen's clients pay her to make sure that their money produces a satisfactory return. How will she be able to explain and justify her behavior if Intersystems just keeps going down? Should she try to disregard the Intersytems downward break and explain to her clients that the investment will be a good one as long as they are patient and look at their holdings as definitely long-term? Wouldn't it be wonderful to sell, as everyone else seems to be doing, and to escape the pressure she is under, simply admitting that her decision to buy Intersystems was misguided? She could lick her wounds for a while and then come back with batteries recharged, her strength renewed.

When the price breaks forcefully downward on volume, Ian, Max, Peter, Karen, and all the others who bought Intersystems within the range are all in a situation that is hard to handle emotionally. To some degree, they all feel disappointed and discouraged. Making decisions based on emotions when we are feeling uncertain and hesitant about what to do next is very human. Under stress, we tend to act more like a member of the crowd, making the same decisions as the majority rather than as an independent individual. When the range breaks on the downside, the psychological dynamic that built up in a lengthy range shows itself in crowd behavior, with a resulting pressure to sell.

Subgroup III—Non-Short-Sellers

This group has little importance in this analysis, and it is mentioned only for formality's sake. While contributing neither to supply nor demand, investors who thought of shorting Intersystems but for some reason did not do so are probably either disappointed at not having followed through and looked for more promising hunting grounds or wondering whether to act on the upward correction that so often follows a rapid and forceful downturn.

Positive Subgroups of Investors

This positive group within the great crowd can be divided into several subgroups:

I.   The Impatient Ones—Stockholders who owned Intersystems before it began ranging and who sold all or more than 50 percent of their holdings at a price within the range because they tired of waiting for a big break.

II. The Wait-and-See Investors—Investors/traders who either bought less than 50 percent of what they planned to buy or who thought about buying but did not have time to carry through because the share price got away from them.

III. The Short-Sellers—Investors/traders who sold Intersystems short, that is, they speculated on a downturn, borrowing shares that they then sold, intending to buy them back at a lower price. Now that the price is breaking downward, they can carry out their intentions.

IV. The Masters of Timing—Stockholders who bought one or more times within the range and then also sold within the range. (Depending on their behavior, this group can fit either into the positive or negative group within the larger crowd.)

Common Characteristics

Investors who owned Intersystems previously but sold all or most of their holdings within the range are more or less content when the range breaks on the downside. As we've pointed out, it is difficult to rate people's emotional experience, but the larger the holding was in relation to capital, the higher the price they received, the earlier they sold in the range, and the more force apparent in the downturn, the more satisfaction they will feel.

Most stockholders are likely to be content with having sold

as much as they did, now that the price is moving in the direction they had feared. However, some are sure to wish they had sold everything, instead of hanging on to part of their position. With varying degrees of relief, they can maintain that they avoided losses when the price broke down from the range. The psychological situation for those who sold short and made money on the downturn is the same as it is for those who bought shares with borrowed money when the range was broken on the upside. Because they face greater risk in selling short, the short-sellers' satisfaction and sense of well-being is probably even greater than it would have been if they had simply made a profit on an ordinary stock purchase.

When Intersystems breaks downward, the psychology in the positive group is considerably easier to handle than that in the negative group. Clearly, the anxiety people experience when they lose money is much more potent than whatever satisfaction is derived from not losing money or from actually making it. But as we will see in the analysis of the positive subgroups, emotion can easily take over rational thinking.

Subgroup I—The Impatient Ones

These stockholders owned Intersystems before it began to range; but when the price fluctuated within the range for a while, they no longer wanted to hold it and sold all or most of their holding before the downward outbreak occurred. Let's go back to Lena Bergwall and Ken Erland, last seen in connection with the upward break. There, they represented the stockholders who had grown tired, meaning that when Intersystems broke on the upside, they perceived it negatively. They are now in what seems to them a more agreeable situation.

Lena Bergwall sold at a good profit at the bottom of the range, just as the stock began to fluctuate. (See Figure 14.6.) Ken Erland waited many months for the price to go up. Then, out of impatience and nervousness, sold at a big loss during the two weeks the stock was hitting the bottom of the range for the third time. (See Figure 14.7.)

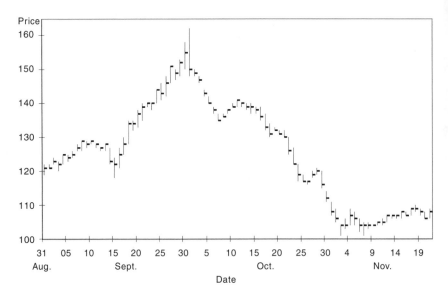

Figure 14.6.   Lena was anxious and afraid that the price would fall below 100. Tired of waiting for it to go up to its earlier high, she sold at a price lower than she had intended.

Now that the price is on a downturn instead of moving up out of the range, there is no question that Lena sees this as a positive development. Clearly, in spite of everything, she did the right thing, and she should actually be quite pleased at having got 108. But she does not follow the stock market with much interest. She simply put her savings into the IPO (initial public offering) of Intersystems, thinking it ought to be as good as risk free, so maybe she doesn't even notice Intersystems' strong downturn. She also sold just before the price went up quickly to 127, and it is primarily the timing of this bad sale that influences her attitude to the ongoing developments in Intersystems' stock. Presumably, Lena was irritated when she realized that she could have sold at a considerably better price if she had not been so worried that the price might fall below 100. If she notices the development now, she would most likely experience the sharp downturn as a satisfying revenge for her previous ignominious retreat.

Price

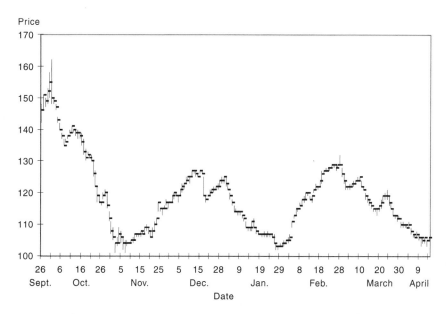

Figure 14.7. Down 50 points for the third time, Ken Erland (out of overwhelming anxiety) decided to sell, even though the price was at the bottom of the range.

Ken bought his shares near the high. He has agonized over the sharp price fluctuations. Although he has lost a third of his capital, he still feels as if a burden had been lifted from his shoulders when he sold, and he has escaped that constant grinding worry about losing any more money. Still, just as with the stockholders who have grown tired, it was horribly frustrating for Ken to wait for several months and then to sell at the worst possible moment, just before Intersystems started on its upward trend again.

Initially the price development for Intersystems is the same when the price breaks up or down out of the range. So at first, Ken is just as troubled mentally as in the earlier scenario, when the price moved upward. He waited so long for the upturn, and now it seems he has missed it by a single day. But as long as the price does not go over the top of the range, Ken and other investors in the same situation can hope for it to turn down again, as it has twice before. That is precisely what happens in the present scenario, where we will look at crowd psychology in a downward break.

After the third upturn toward the top of the range, the price starts its downward trend. Now stockholders like Ken, who sold after considerable anguish and pressure when the price touched the bottom of the range for the third time, no longer feel every price rise like a whiplash. As it moves downward, their frustration with their "mistake" slowly but surely diminishes, and their disappointment at not owning Intersystems is replaced by satisfaction at having sold.

These ex-stockholders are pleased and relieved when the price finally breaks down from the range, clearly signaling the beginning of a downturn. It feels good to know that, despite everything, they were right to sell. Liberated from their long-term anxiety, they can now smile as the previously stable, apparently immovable price level at the bottom of the range cracks with force.

However, once their joy has subsided, it is not at all unusual for a fly to appear in the ointment, even though the downward break had been wished for. The price has dropped sharply, rumors about the company are negative, and Intersystems has become the market's punching bag. Obviously, selling was the only thing to do. Those who sold at a good price early on in the range now look upon the remaining stockholders' obstinacy and vain hopes with mild superiority. They got a good price for their shares, and are they out from under all the nasty feelings that those who held on are still having to endure.

The stockholders who waited a long time before selling are naturally pleased that they sold before the price fell below 100. Still, that first liberating flush fades when they realize, with mortification, what should have been obvious before: they should have sold long ago. Trading with hindsight—all previously difficult questions now answered—is a very common phenomenon on the market.

With the downward break, stockholders who still have some of their holdings in Intersystems become quite emotional and ambivalent. Are they happy to have sold *some* of their shares, or are they mortified that they are still holding some? Though they are thought to be more positive than negative, there is no question that they wish they had sold all earlier. Having already sold more than half, their resistance to selling the remainder is considerably less than it would be had they not sold at all. They have already made a decision in the right direction; even if they wish they had acted more decisively before, if they sell the rest of their stock at a lower price, they will still be considerably better off than they would be had they done nothing.

It is very likely that these stockholders, not knowing whether to sell or to hold, are swept along by the herd mentality that develops when a large number of people all get emotional at the same time. As we have seen on numerous occasions, when people are under stress and do not know what to do, they commonly act in accordance with the majority and sell precisely at the moment when everyone else on the market seems to be selling.

Subgroup II—The Wait-and-See Investors

In this group we will find one of the previous types—John Stennis. On two occasions John Stennis had tried to buy Intersystems below 100, but he was seized by decision-making anxiety. As the price neared the bottom of the range, he moved his buying limit down; and because his limit was a few points too low, he missed the trade both times.

He was obviously annoyed by this. Tired of trying to buy at an attractive price, he began looking for alternatives. (See Figure14.8.) When Intersystems eventually falls below 100, he is very pleased that he had been cautious and severely limited his buy orders.

The market's attitude toward a stock that has been a market winner and then reverses sharply is often divided. Some writers and analysts maintain that the stock is overvalued, as growth seems to have stagnated. Others feel it is worth buying because the price is off from the high and the price is probably temporary.

So, like John Stennis, many investors hesitate to act on their intention to buy on a correction when there seems to be a large

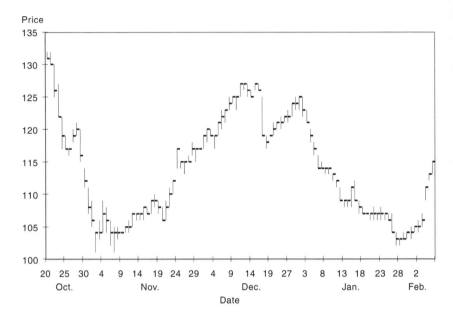

Figure 14.8. Twice, John was unable to buy Intersystems because he had set his limit too low. Frustrated, he turned his attention to other investments.

number of sellers. In a situation like this, people often retreat from the buy side and simply await developments instead. If the price then suddenly and unexpectedly goes up, they seldom race after it because they had wanted to buy at a lower price.

Because of the spasmodic price movements and the wait-and-see attitude of many analysts, it is not uncommon for buying interest to remain nothing more than interest or buy orders priced too low. Nor is it unusual for those who actually do buy to buy less than planned.

When Intersystems finally breaks out on the downside, many investors are probably grateful that they did not act on their intentions. Whether they set their buying limits too low, whether they judged the situation as too uncertain to warrant acting on their earlier intentions, whether they were unable to decide, or whether they simply never got around to buying because of the rapid and unexpected drop in price, these investors are glad that they did not put any more money into Intersystems. Many think luck was on their side. If they were afraid of a downturn, naturally they would not have bought at all. But even if they wish they did not own any Intersystems stock at all, most are likely to feel they got off lightly.

But people are only people. When the first rush of relief at not owning more Intersystems stock than they do has worn off, some investors are usually upset and irritated that they still own *any* stock in the company. Some surely blame themselves because they bought without being sure that it was the right thing to do.

"I was dubious about the company's future," they say to themselves, or "Why couldn't I just keep my hands off it? I should have been more careful; losing money is no fun."

Even though most investors are probably fairly pleased that they don't own more than they do, when the price breaks downward, everyone who owns shares in this group has to make a decision. Just as in Subgroup I, when faced with selling, many investors feel contradictory emotions. It is never easy to sell at a loss, but the reluctance to sell is significantly less than it would be if the holding were larger. When the market's earlier wait-and-see attitude toward a downward break turns into palpable pessimism and when everyone seems to be down on the stock, resistance to selling decreases. When everyone else is dubious about Intersystems and seems to be selling and you find yourself feeling stressed about your situation and uncertain about what to do, it is not only common but also very human to do what the crowd is doing—sell.

Subgroup III—Short-Sellers

Of course, those who shorted Intersystems before the downward break are more or less content. As was shown under Common Characteristics, the psychological experience of those who sold short and made money on the downturn is the same as that of investors who hold stock bought with borrowed money when the range is broken on the upside. Because they face higher risk with short-selling and borrowing, they feel more gratified than they would if they had simply executed an ordinary stock purchase. The greater the risk, the greater the strain, and the more satisfaction the investor is likely to feel once it is clear that he has been proven right. But risk is a two-edged sword. Those who have sold short and have hit an upturn rather than a downturn are surely in the group that experiences the upward break in the most negative possible way.

Investors who make money on a downturn naturally do not all look at the situation in the same way, but their basic attitude is positive. As always, for many of them greed puts a damper on their satisfaction. Now that it is obvious that they were right to sell short, it may also seem obvious that they ought to have taken an even greater risk and made even more money. The uneasiness and uncertainty that they may have felt before the break fades quickly when the new situation looks so obviously advantageous, and they can find it difficult to handle the thought of all the easy money they missed. The profit on capital is good in a successful short-selling trade. It is not surprising that it is very common for people to want to make an even larger profit than by buying back shares at the prevailing price.

People like to make a profit feel tangible by imagining what they would buy with it. If investors imagine a European vacation or a new car, for instance, they probably will turn up the emotional volume. When the majority of Intersystems stockholders seem to be clearly running in the same direction, it is easy for an individual investor to get carried away, to adopt the crowd's behavior and to short even more shares. When Intersystems breaks out on the downside after its long-term range, investors in this subgroup very probably reinforce crowd behavior.

Subgroup IV—The Masters of Timing

Suppose Ian Benson had sold his entire Intersystems holding when the price approached the top of the range for the third time. And suppose that at the same time, Max had recommended that all his clients sell all their shares in the company. How happy these two gentlemen would have been to see soon after that they had sold Intersystems at the right moment for the third time. Ian Benson would have held onto his dream of being a financier. Max's position at Wilson & Partners would have been strengthened even further, and he would be negotiating from strength in his anticipated bonus negotiations.

After their successes, they could have calmly waited for the fourth downward swing, or they would have shifted their attention to other investment opportunities. However, it seems safe to assume that they would certainly have continued to study the price development of Intersystems because they had experienced the swings in the price of this stock so intensely. First they would confirm that they had sold at the right moment; then they would want to see if it might be possible to buy the stock successfully in a fourth trade. The downturn in Intersystems' stock—from top to bottom within the range—takes time. It is very likely that the money does not stay in the account while the two of them look around for other interesting trading opportunities. Even if they use the gains from Intersystems to buy other stock, there is nothing to say they will not dispose of those shares later or borrow against them to generate capital to buy Intersystems back eventually.

Attitudes toward a stock in which so many successive and profitable deals have been made are very positive. As discussed earlier, shares are not living creatures. They have no emotions, and they do not care in the slightest what Ian, Max, or anyone else thinks of them. It is people who have the feelings and who choose stock on emotional and/or rational grounds, depending on whether they like, dislike, or feel neutral toward a stock.

In this case, Ian Benson and Max Bork are clearly almost in love with Intersystems. To them, the name is a symbol of satisfaction and success. Their learning pattern after their trades in the stock is also very clear: if you buy as much as you can at the bottom of the range and sell when the stock goes up, you make a lot of money with low risk.

Considering Ian's and Max's positive experiences in their previous deals, however, there is a considerable possibility that they have gravely underestimated the risk in an eventual fourth investment. As we've seen so many times before, a price range exists only for a limited time, and when a long fluctuating phase breaks—either up or down—the price movement is often powerful because of the psychological dynamic that has built up.

We don't know whether Ian invests all his disposable capital again or whether Max calls around and pushes Intersystems as energetically as before when the share price approaches 100 for the fourth time. But as we've said earlier, assuming that no directly negative information on the company clouds the issue and that the mood of the market is not gloomy enough to make the stock not seem worth buying at around 100, it is very likely that they will buy and/or recommend Intersystems again. (See Figure 14.9.)

Though few investors are as successful in their timing as Ian and Max, they are naturally not the only ones to have completed three good trades. Certainly, many more have succeeded in two or at least in one good trade in Intersystems by buying at the bottom of the range and selling during the upturn.

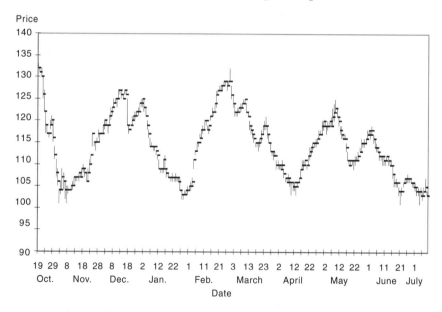

Figure 14.9. If Max Bork and Ian Benson had succeeded in selling when the price was above 120 for the third time, it is very likely they would have bought Intersystems back the fourth time it touched bottom.

The speculators embarking on this game yet again, including Ian and Max, will experience a downward break very negatively, feeling intense mental pressure. When we studied the new stockholders, we analyzed how those people who bought during the weeks when the price fluctuated between 101 and 108 experienced the downward break. It should also be noted that these investors are definitely not to be found in that group of the great herd that perceives a downward break as a positive thing.

Investors who did not buy Intersystems at this stage but kept their money in cash or invested in another stock feel quite content. Peacefully and quietly, they can follow Intersystems' rapid slide from 100 to 82 and ponder at what level they might consider the stock worth buying.

If the majority of this subgroup had repurchased or even increased their earlier holding the fourth time Intersystems touched bottom, the group would reinforce crowd behavior at a downward break. On the other hand, if most did not buy back Intersystems, their role in the crowd behavior that develops when the range breaks on the downside would be less significant.

Some Real Downward Breaks

IBM

IBM is one of the 10 largest companies in the world, providing customers with advanced information technology, systems, products, services, software, and financing. After breaking out from a range in April 1999, the stock had a bullish run until it hit a ceiling just below 140 in early July. After a correction of about 15 percent, it tried to resume its upward trend, but it lacked the strength. Instead the price began to drift downward toward 120, at the lower end of the range. When a major brokerage firm downgraded IBM out of concern over third-quarter profits, the price dropped below 120 but then bounced up quickly. However, the relief was short-lived. Pessimism about IBM's mainframe sales sparked another sell-off, which turned into crowd behavior when the range was clearly broken and the stock dropped sharply to about 105. After pausing briefly at this level, the company actually issued a profit warning because customers had delayed mainframe purchases. The stock tumbled more than 19 percent, the worst drop since the 1987 crash. (See Figure 14.10.)

Deutsche Bank

Deutsche Bank was used in Chapter 11 as an example of an upward break, but it serves equally well as an example of a downward break. After trending up since early 1997, Deutsche Bank, like many European banks, began to lose momentum in the spring of 1998. The German stock market continued to soar, but Deutsche Bank settled into a range. In May, the stock actually hit an all-time high at just over 80 Euros; but this was unsustainable, and it continued to drift sideways. When the German market

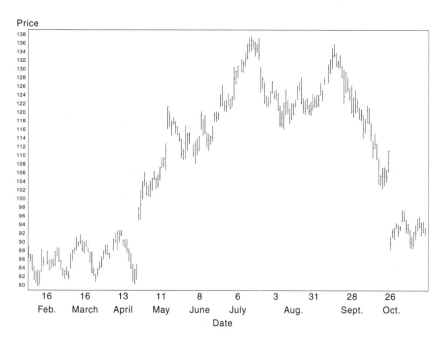

Figure 14.10.   IBM. (Courtesy of Reuters.)

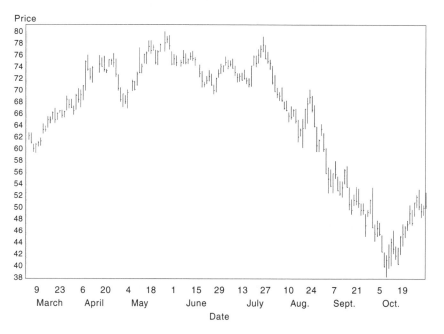

Figure 14.11.   Deutsche Bank. (Courtesy of Reuters.)

peaked in July, Deutsche Bank made a final attempt to break through 80 Euros to break the range on the upside, but this failed when the entire market began a swift decline. The stock hesitated for a few days at the lower end of the range, just over 70 Euros; but when the global bear market hit Germany, crowd psychology won out. The price smashed through this level and plummeted to about 60. When the market as a whole tried to recover, the lower end of this range was tested from below, but the bear market continued. During a climax of selling in the autumn, the stock fell almost 55 percent, back to its 1990 levels. (See Figure 14.11.)

K-Mart

Through its more than two thousand stores, mainly in the United States, K-Mart offers products ranging from food and clothes to

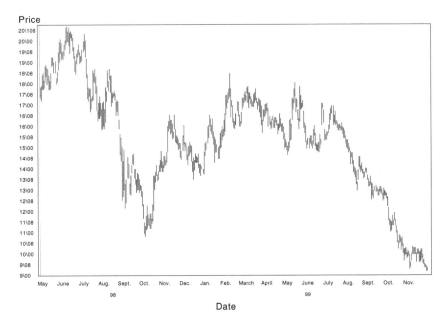

Figure 14.12.   K-Mart. (Courtesy of Reuters.)

home improvement and beauty care. Its stock had peaked in 1992 at about 28, but then dropped to below 6 in early 1996. In the summer of 1998 it went up to about 20 and fell back to just over 10 in the fall. In early 1999, it spiked to over 18 and then began drifting sideways. After testing the lower end of the range at around 15 in April, it ticked up sharply, hitting 18 in May and then falling back again. A final attempt to break through 18 only managed to reach 17 before falling back, to linger at just over 15 again. The following week, the retail sector was deemed among the market's worst performers, and crowd psychology made itself felt. K-Mart broke out on the downside, falling to 13. Joy over second-quarter profits brought a three-day bounce before the share price continued on its route south. (See Figure 14.12.)

Chapter 15

CONCLUSIONS

Under certain market conditions, individual investors of varying backgrounds, experience, values, and capital begin to behave similarly, even though they do not know each other. A specific market situation like the long-term range, for instance, creates growing frustration, impatience, and anxiety. These in turn influence people's behavior, which gradually becomes increasingly similar and thus more predictable. This psychological dynamic creates conditions for the crowd behavior that develops when there is a forceful break—a rapid and steep rise or fall in price on volume—from a range that has held for a lengthy period.

We have defined what constitutes the great crowd on the market in connection with a break from the range previously, establishing that it is made up of two main groups:

I. Investors who find a price break upward a negative experience (the negative group at an upward outbreak) and those who find a price break downward a positive experience (the positive group at a downward break).
II. Investors who feel that an upward price break is a positive experience (the positive group at an upward outbreak), and those who find a downward break a negative experience (the negative group at a downward break).

These main groups were then divided into various subgroups, and their reactions at break up and down from the range were studied to gain deeper insight into how they and their behaviors evolve. As long as Intersystems fluctuated within its range, the two main groups were equally strong, though this changed depending on whether the price was nearer the top or the bottom of the range.

When a clear break from a lengthy range takes place, one group has a clear advantage over the other. At a downward break, Group I, now called the bear crowd, has an advantage over Group II, the bull crowd. At an upward break, Group II, the bull crowd, has the advantage over the bear crowd.

Although the subgroups forming their respective crowds are not identical, their common characteristics are so obvious and unified that in the future, the bears and the bulls will be considered as two distinct units.

Pivotal Point or Balance Point

In his book *Jesse Livermore, Speculator King*, Paul Sarnoff describes Livermore, one of the most famous stock market speculators ever. One of the most colorful and talked-about investors of all time in the United States, Livermore began his financial career in 1891 at the age of 14 and was active in the market until his tragic death in 1940. Jesse Livermore made and lost four fortunes in his day; he was known by such sobriquets as the Boy Plunger, the Cotton King, the Wall Street Wonder, and the Great bear. He was also thought to be one of the forces behind the great 1929 crash. In his own book, *How to Trade in Stocks: The Livermore Formula for Combining Time, Element, and Price*, Livermore described what he calls "the pivotal point." Perhaps "balance point" might be more apt. My use of this term is not identical to Livermore's interpretation, but "pivotal point" or "balance point" are both excellent ways of describing the balance between the bear crowd and the bull crowd. At a given point, the pendulum swings to give the advantage to one of the groups, which then dominates the market's view of future price development.

When Intersystems falls from the top of the range for the third time after fluctuating for many months and then deviates from the norm by staying at that level rather than going up again after reaching the bottom of the range, a clear and obvious balance point is created. The bear crowd and the bull crowd now fight a dubious but important battle. What if the bull crowd wins, with the result that the price begins to go up as before, or suppose the bear crowd gathers enough strength for a massive attack on their opponents' most important and heavily fortified positions—the clear demand level between 101 and 108? (See Figure 15.1.)

When the price of Intersystems swings up from the bottom of the range for the third time after fluctuating for several months, then breaks its normal pattern by not falling back when it reaches the top of the range, but sticks at that level, a very significant balance point is created. The bear crowd and the bull crowd are now fighting a tough and decisive battle. What if the bear crowd wins, and the price falls back as before, or suppose the bull crowd gathers strength for a decisive attack on the enemy's

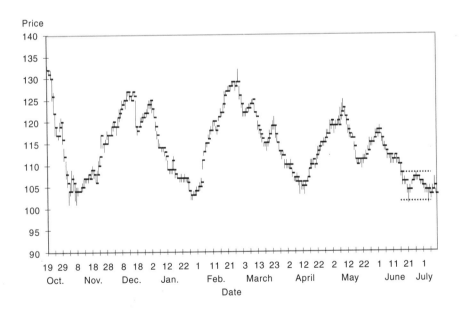

Figure 15.1.   After the price has fallen from the top of the range for the third time, it stays between 101 and 108 for a few weeks before the downward break occurs. This is an easily definable "balance point."

well fortified lines—the clear supply level between 124 and 129? (See Figure 15.2.)

In the case of Intersystems, there are two very clear balance points that, unfortunately, are not at all obvious when a share price breaks down or up out of a range. Often it is not at all clear whether a stock will break up or down from a range. However, identifying the balance point will greatly improve the chances of predicting the direction of a breakout accurately. We'll talk more about this concept and its practical applications later in the chapter.

Downward Break—The Bear Crowd Triumphs

It is true that every stockholder is an individual, but a large majority of stockholders who have either held onto most of their

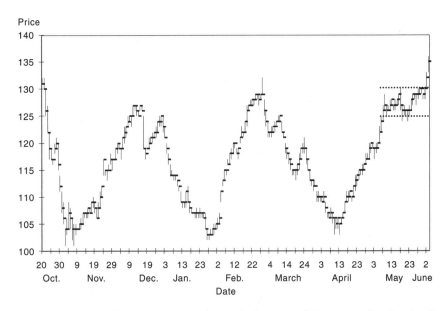

Figure 15.2. After swinging up from the bottom of the range for the third time, the price "sticks" between 124 and 129 for a few weeks before the upward break occurs. This is a very clear "balance point."

holdings since before Intersystems began to range or who have recently bought the stock clearly perceive a downward break from the range as a negative event. Those who considered selling the stock short are annoyed that they did not act on their intentions, but they do not experience the situation as negatively as the stockholders do. They have missed only one of many opportunities to make money and to avoid the bitterness that losing money may entail. The more carefully the investors considered the decision to buy or to hold the stock and the greater the mental preparation for the possibility of being wrong, the less anguish and unpleasantness they experience, and vice versa. However, no one likes owning a stock that has been exposed to massive selling by some of the larger market players, or one around which there are rumors of unfavorable reports of diminished growth in the market in which the company operates, or one that goes down a great deal quickly and, in the eyes of most participants, also unexpectedly. It becomes a question of how frustrating and troubling the situation feels to stockholders.

As we have said, it is not easy to rank human emotional experiences in any kind of order. But the greater the holding in relation to capital, the higher the price paid, the longer the stock was owned, and the more unexpected and forceful the downward break is, the greater the strain on the stockholder is going to be. When people are worried, pressured, and under stress, they are inclined to participate in crowd behavior, which means chucking those wretched shares in that lousy company that does nothing but incur losses and evoke unpleasant, hard-to-deal-with feelings. Farsighted stockholders armed with the necessary patience to await the eventual upturn of Intersystems are exposed to the greatest mental strain of all. After several months of fluctuating, the price finally breaks—down rather then up from the range. Their only reward for their faith and patience is a lot of bad feeling and watching their capital being eroded. They have the best reason for disliking the downturn, and they would be the first to abandon the bull crowd and join the bear crowd.

When the price breaks *downward*, the *sellers* obviously have the advantage. When the downward break is clear to the entire market, hesitation about future share price evaporates. The market has announced its verdict. Stockholders who sold all or most of their holdings are pleased, and the short-sellers are rubbing their hands in glee, though some wish they had sold all their shares or shorted a larger position. Those who have bought fewer shares than they intended thank their lucky stars, but they regret having bought any shares at all. Investors who meant to sell short, but didn't, fret over lost profits. Those who held all or most of their shares are truly sorry that they didn't do something else. The sellers—the bear crowd—are strengthened in their conviction that they did the right thing, whereas the buyers/shareholders—the bull crowd—fret over their misbegotten decision.

Upward Break—The Bull Crowd Triumphs

All investors are unique, but it is very likely that nearly everyone who sold, sold short, or bought fewer shares than they had planned or who failed to buy while Intersystems was ranging, experience an upward breakout as more or less negative. The more carefully thought out and rational their decision was, the less mental pain they are said to experience, and vice versa. But no one is particularly pleased at having sold or failed to buy Intersystems after the stock is described as a potential market winner. The company has won a large strategic order, and the stock quickly climbs sharply and, in the opinion of these investors, unexpectedly.

Those exposed to the greatest mental strain in this situation are the short-sellers—they have the most to lose in an upturn. This group sees its capital being rapidly eroded and has the most motivation to act in this new situation. They would be the first to abandon the bear crowd and take the lead among the bull crowd instead. Stockholders who waited a long time to sell and have a large holding in relation to their capital and who dispose of their holdings at a low price just before the price unexpectedly and forcefully breaks out of the range on the upside are exposed to the next-greatest mental strain. In their emotional state, they are apt to adopt crowd behavior and do what everyone else appears to be doing, namely chasing the share price to buy back at a higher level. They want to hold a ticket on that express train speeding away toward continually escalating prices again.

When the price breaks upward, there is no doubt that the *buyers* have the advantage. Once a breakout on the upside is apparent, uncertainty disappears. The market has announced its verdict. Both those who owned Intersystems previously and those who bought within the range make money. They are pleased and happy, though many of them wish they had bought even more. Those who did not get around to buying at all or who bought less than planned regret not acting more forcefully. They fret over lost or reduced profits. Those who sold or shorted the stock and miss out on profits or lose money desperately wish they had behaved differently. The buyers—the bull crowd—are reinforced in their conviction that they did the right thing, whereas the sellers—the bear crowd—are pained by their wrong decision.

The Strongest Crowd Shows the Way

Crowd behavior develops in emotionally charged situations. A powerful break from a long-term range is an efficient catalyst for crowd behavior in the marketplace. People become emotional—either frightened and anxious, or greedy and euphoric—and move easily from individual to member-of-the-herd status. Overcome by their emotions and not knowing what to do, investors clearly tend to do what everyone else is doing and follow the strongest crowd. At a downward breakout, the most plausible conclusion is that the bear crowd easily recruits new members from their weakened opponents, the bull crowd. At an upward break, the opposite happens: the bull crowd rapidly acquires new members from the weaker bear crowd. The more emotional and uncertain people become, the more likely they are to do what the crowd is doing and accept the view of the majority—whether the bear crowd or the bull crowd—when they sell or buy Intersystems, depending on whether the price has signaled a continued downturn or an upturn.

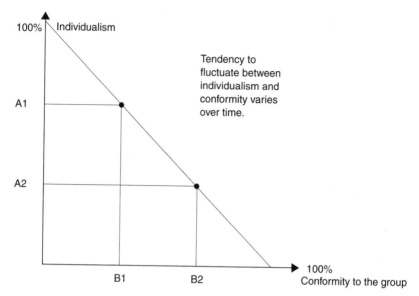

Figure 15.3.   At (A1, B1), the individual is more independent and less a member of a crowd than at (A2, B2). *Source:* Tony Plummer, *Forecasting Financial Markets* (London: Kogan Page, 1993), p. 22.

The Criteria for Crowd Behavior Are Met

To refer again to Tony Plummer's ideas mentioned in Chapter 7, people in the situation we've described act less as individuals and more like members of the herd. (See Figure 15.3.)

When crowd behavior influences people's actions, their individuality is reduced in favor of adaptation to the group. In situations in which crowd behavior is apparent, the individual has moved far down to the right in this figure. The intersection of A2 and B2 illustrates this.

When a clear and forceful break from a price range that has prevailed for a longer time frame takes place, the three fundamental criteria for crowd behavior in the stock market are in place:

1. All investors who bought or sold Intersystems have a very simple common aim. They easily feel a certain fellowship

and identify with other participants in the market. They want to make money or they want to avoid losing money.

2. The breakout from the range is the catalyst that releases an emotional reaction, primarily fear or greed, and that makes investors feel inclined to accept the views of the ruling groups, whether the bear crowd or the bull crowd, on the coming price development.

3. The share price that is clearly moving down or up after the break fulfills the function of the leader of the pack, either driving its members over the precipice or urging them on to greater heights.

Not a Textbook

As I stated in the Introduction, this book is not a representation of economic theory, economic history, investment analysis, or psychology. Nor does it lay claim to scholarly exactitude. It was inspired by David Fuller's behavioral approach to the stock market, but essentially it describes my personal opinions on the critical importance of crowd psychology to behavior in the market.

As early as 1918, John Maurice Clark wrote in an article entitled "Economics and Modern Psychology," published in the *Journal of Political Economy**: "The economist may attempt to ignore psychology, but it is sheer impossibility for him to ignore human nature. . . . If the economist borrows his conception of man from the psychologist, his constructive work may have some chance of remaining purely economic in character. But if he does not, he will not thereby avoid psychology. Rather, he will force himself to make his own, and it will be bad psychology."

---

*Quoted in Richard H. Taylor, "Managing and Investing Rationally in an Irrational World" (presented at seminar titled *Program on Investment Decisions and Behavioral Finance*, Harvard University, Cambridge, Mass., November 1997).

But instead of borrowing good psychology, economists continued inventing bad psychology. Sixty years later, the prevailing opinion in academia was quite obvious. Michael Jensen, a financial economist at the Harvard Business School,* wrote in 1978 that "the efficient markets hypothesis is the best established fact in all of social science."

Most economic models and theories constructed to explain how different markets function are still based on the assumption that human beings make decisions on strictly rational grounds and that the markets are efficient. But it is with some satisfaction that I feel new winds beginning to blow through the academic world. Behavioral finance came a long way in the twentieth century. It is now breaking upward, becoming more and more accepted and respected in the academic community. What Henry O. Pruden of Golden Gate University in San Francisco points out in "Behavioral Finance: What Is It?" (an article in the *June 1996 Newsletter of the Technical Securities Analysts' Association of San Francisco* [TSAA], page 2) shows the new direction. He writes that a dramatic change is taking place in traditional economic thinking. He maintains that "what is taking place in finance is apparently an ideal example of the paradigm shift model." This means that when the prevailing theory exhibits too many anomalies, a change in thinking will gradually take place and lead to a radically different model for explaining reality. Pruden expects that behavioral finance will lead economists to begin to study the markets from the point of view of how people really respond, instead of basing their assumptions on how a rational human being ought to react in various market situations.

The aim of this book is to provide fundamental insight into

---

*Quoted in Nicholas Barbieris, "Mispricing or Risk? A Closer Look at Some Stock Market Puzzles (presented at seminar titled *The Fourth Major European Programme on Behavioural Finance*, London, England, November 1999).

and an understanding of crowd psychology in the market. It is my hope that this work will contribute to a greater interest in the psychological mechanisms active in the stock market.

Crowd Psychology in Trends

As this book progressed, however, I gradually came to realize that there were more psychological factors to illustrate than I had originally anticipated. Herd behavior makes itself felt primarily in two situations in the market: in connection with a powerful breakout from a long-term range and at the strong acceleration phase that often takes places at the end of a long-term trend. My original intention was to illuminate and explain both these occurrences. However, the subject turned out to be far too comprehensive for one single book on psychology in the stock market.

A study of the forceful crowd psychology that may develop with trends is essential to painting the whole picture. Market hysteria, or a financial bubble, for instance, which is very often preceded by a sharply accelerating upward price movement with conspicuous elements of euphoria, occurs during the final phase of a long upward trend. A stock market crash or financial meltdown usually occurs through a sharply accelerated downward price movement at the end of a negative trend, with obvious features of panic. But a trend usually goes through several psychological phases before these phenomena actually take place. For instance, it often takes time for many of the people making money in an upward trend to realize that this trend, which seemed so invincible earlier, has actually changed direction. It can be a very long road from tentative pessimism to full-scale panic. Having gained some understanding of these different phases, it is then important to study what David Fuller calls trend-ending characteristics, that is, the actual signals that a trend is nearing its end. The sharp acceleration phase mentioned earlier is only one of three trend-ending characteristics that Fuller has identified.

A Better Basis for Decisions

Apart from the crowd psychology in the market, psychology on an individual level has also been examined to demonstrate how emotional people can become when they make or lose money. Crowd psychology would not arise in the market if people were soulless, rational robots rather than the sensitive individuals they are. So it is very important to understand that no market participant, regardless of experience and access to capital, can avoid occasionally making decisions based more on emotions than on rational thinking.

Whether the reader is a novice in the stock market or a seasoned market player, it is my hope that he or she will recognize his or her own behavior in some of the situations in which the characters find themselves. The more trades and investments readers have made, the greater the likelihood that they will recognize their own thoughts, experiences, and behavior.

Understanding crowd psychology on the stock market establishes a better foundation for decision making in regard to trading and investing. It is a far better way of examining a market situation than poring over a textbook to find examples of technical analysis that seem relevant to the reality the investor faces. Lessons learned by rote from reading charts severely limit an investor's ability to analyze the market. Charts must be studied to the extent that one develops an intuitive feeling for market psychology. Rather than presenting a number of stereotyped price patterns that readers learn by heart and are then asked to locate in different charts, the in-depth study of crowd behavior in this book brings the hope of a deeper understanding of market behavior. Most patterns found in charts are just variations of trading ranges. It is important that an investor be able to observe the basic structure of ranges and to understand the psychological dynamic that has built up within a specific stock and also to have a full picture of the market. In what kind of trend are the market and the sector? Are the market and the sector on their way up or down, or are they just marching in place? What is the mood of the market and the sector—euphoria, panic, resignation, or hesitancy? What do such influential factors as bonds, currencies, and foreign stocks look like?

Practical Applications

In this book, rather than focusing on practical applications, my aim has been to convey an understanding of market behavior. The task of explaining and describing crowd psychology in trends ought to be complete before we undertake an in-depth study of how to use what we have learned to carry out profitable trades. Using an understanding of crowd psychology to enhance trading is actually the subject for a whole new book, but let's look at some real situations to be sure that my message about the balance point has come across.

You can never be *sure* when a range will be broken or what direction a breakout will take. But trading with an understanding of crowd psychology and the ability to identify balance points certainly increases your odds. The important message you need to able to read in a chart is when a clear change of the psychology in the stock is taking place. You must understand that the creation of a balance point is a powerful indication that the behavior of the market majority has shifted. In the case of Intersystems, the range is well defined, and the balance points are distinct and easy to spot; ranges and balance points are not usually that obvious. To have validity, the balance point must be located at the top or the bottom of the range, but as you will see in the following cases, a balance point does not need to fit between two parallel lines.

Observing the basic structure of a trading range, understanding the psychological dynamic that develops in a range, and identifying the balance point are the *key* concepts when trading with crowd psychology, but this knowledge is not a "golden key" that will generate successful trades without any difficulties.

It is important to recognize in what kind of trend the range is found and to understand that breakouts sometimes take a direction different from what is forecast. When the price does not continue to rise or to fall after a breakout but retreats into the range, the situation is what David Fuller calls a "false break." In these cases, he uses a rule he calls the "midpoint danger line." Victor Sperandeo, in his book *Trader Vic—Methods of a Wall Street Master*, calls such an event "2B."

We will study trends, psychology in combination with false

breaks from a range, and practical cases based on real trades at another occasion. We will see that buying and selling in connection with a balance point works very well when the decisions are made by a calm, logically thinking, independent person and not by an emotional creature who rushes in the same direction as the crowd without analyzing the situation.

Examples of Balance Points

Ericsson

Let me refer again to Ericsson, described when presenting examples of real upward breakouts in Chapter 11. During May 1999, Ericsson alters its normal pattern in a distinctive manner. Earlier, when the stock reached the top of the range at around $29, it did not have the strength to stay there for more than a few days. Too much supply was unleashed at this level, and it was obvious that the bear crowd was calling the shots. The sellers did not have much of a problem in defending their lines. This time, however, Ericsson does not fall back when reaching the top of the range but instead stays there for five weeks. This is critical; it tells us that the psychology in regard to Ericsson has changed. A majority of the participants are behaving differently. The bull crowd is acquiring new members from their weaker rivals, the bear crowd.

Every balance point has more or less unique features. It can last for only about a week, as in the case of our next example, Deutsche Bank, or it can last for over a month, as it did with Ericsson. Sometimes it can be neatly fitted between two exact parallel lines, or it can be somewhat irregular, as with Ericsson. But the balance point is always located at the bottom or at the top of the range. Unfortunately it is not always obvious when a share price is going to break down or up out of a range. If, for example, the market is in a strong up or down trend, ranges can very well be broken without the creation of a balance point. In the case of Ericsson, though, the balance point is as distinct and obvious as anyone could wish for.

Jesse Livermore, in his book *How to Trade in Stocks*, wrote that whenever he had the patience to wait for the market to arrive at a pivotal point before making the trade, he always made money. He argued that he then commenced the trade just at the right psychological time, at the beginning of the move.

Well, I don't dare argue that you will always make money if you are able to identify the balance point, but Jesse Livermore's observation is very important. If you begin your trade when the market has reached a balance point, you are beginning at the moment when the psychological dynamic is at its peak. There is a vacuum of sellers and buyers, both above and below the range, and only a small spark is needed to ignite crowd behavior, which—as in the case of Ericsson—can result in forceful movements both up and down. (See Figure 15.4.)

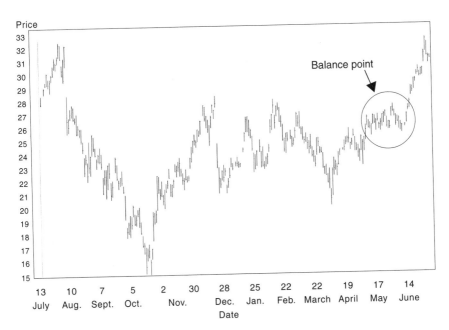

Figure 15.4. Ericsson. (Courtesy of Reuters.)

Deutsche Bank

For Deutsche Banke, another of the examples of a real upward breakout in Chapter 11, the balance point is not as obvious. The range of Deutsche Bank is almost perfectly fitted between 44 and 57 Euro. The first attempt to break out on the upside is made in November 1998 and the second in January 1999. It is not until May 1999 that the next attempt occurs. The move starts explosively from the very bottom of the range in mid-April but loses energy when it reaches the upper side of the range in early May. The price falls back, but only to around 50 Euro at the end of May, and then quickly recovers. By June, a fourth breakout attempt is made. It is now evident that the behavioral pattern among the majority of the participants has changed. The bull crowd has gotten the upper hand; and when the stock rises to 57 Euro this fourth time and just gets a tiny correction, a balance point is created. In the case of Ericsson, it takes only a quick glance at the chart to identify the obvious balance point. Spotting this point in the chart of Deutsche Bank requires an understanding of the psychological dynamic that is built up in the range. The balance point is simply the last logical moment in a psychologically explosive situation that has been building for more than six months. It is there, even if it is hardly advertising itself. This modesty, however, does not stand in the way of a forceful movement. When the breakout finally takes place, Deutsche Bank goes up 20 percent in 10 days. (See Figure 15.5.)

The Psychology of the Individual Investor

You have spent time learning to understand crowd psychology in the stock market, but you still face an even greater challenge: gaining insight into your own individual psychology. As an investor, you must avoid numerous psychological pitfalls on the stock market. Here are a few:

If you buy a stock that is fluctuating in a range, with the intention of making money in an upward breakout, it is very human to be impatient if the expected price movement is de-

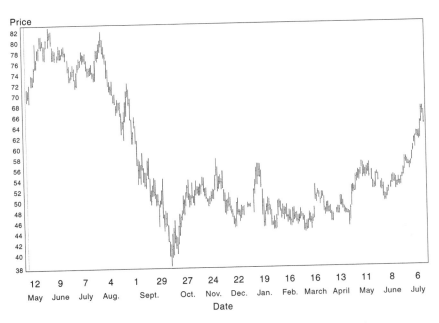

Figure 15.5. Deutsche Bank. (Courtesy of Reuters.)

layed. It is easy to lose patience and to sell your shares just before the long-awaited break comes. Many traders/investors are very reluctant to sell at a loss, and letting losses become long term while realizing gains early on is a very common practice. Selling at a profit is a much more agreeable experience than the one of selling at a loss. Many investors break the most familiar of all the rules of the stock market: "Cut your losses, and let your profits run." The rule is clear and simple, but it is hard to put into practice. There is a big difference between expressing an opinion on a stock and actually "pulling the trigger" and making the trade you are recommending to others. The desire for hefty profits—to make a killing—easily leads investors to take far too much risk, exposing them to great stress and reducing their ability to make carefully considered decisions if their investments begin to go wrong.

So how should you handle the problems entailed in making trading decisions in periods of uncertainty and time pressure? The American psychologist Ronald Barach has done research on the psychological aspects of economic decisions and investments and has some remarkable insights into people's relations to money and how people behave in various market contexts. In his book, *Mindtraps*, he gives 88 different examples of psychological pitfalls of trading. Simply and clearly, he identifies and explains the problems connected with stock investments. He also describes how to deal with them and how to avoid repeating the same mistakes.

Van K. Tharp is one of the leading United States authorities on the psychological aspects of trading. He has carried out more than four thousand psychological profile studies on individual investors, conducting hundreds of interviews with the most successful people in the profession to discover what qualities they have that are critical to success. He has worked as a "coach" to reputable Wall Street investors and has published five volumes of *The Investment Psychology Guides*, as well as *Trade Your Way to Financial Freedom*, which is designed to help readers work through the psychological questions important to master when trading and to learn how to create a trading system that really works.

Another leading authority in the United States is Adrienne Laris Toghraie, a trading coach internationally recognized in the field of human development. She helps her clients push through their self-imposed limits to new levels of success. Over the past 10 years, Adrienne Toghraie has interviewed and coached many successful people around the world and has written and cowritten several books, such as *The Winning Edge I* and *II*, and *Trader's Secrets*, which teach efficient trading psychology and explore the minds and emotions of successful traders.

Mental training is natural for athletes. Working on the stock market can be like taking part in a sports competition every day, which is why insight and knowledge of one's own psychology is an extremely important piece of the puzzle when striving to be a good trader/investor.

Constance Brown, a former Olympic swimmer, has good insight into what it takes to become a top athlete. She has written an excellent book, *Aerodynamic Trading*, about what it takes to become a successful trader. She offers considerable insights into the dynamic interplay between trading psychology and performance and teaches the trader how to stay calm, remove emotional blocks, and visualize success.

An in-depth study of the psychology of the individual investor would fill at least an entire book, which is why that will have to wait for another time. However, for anyone wishing to increase his or her understanding of the subject now, the aforementioned books by Victor Sperandeo, Ronald Barach, Van K.Tharp, Adrienne Laris Toghraie, and Constance Brown can be recommended warmly.

Using crowd psychology while trading can be very rewarding, but it is critical to study crowd psychology in the markets without becoming emotionally involved. Study what is happening in the market with your eyes wide open and with a calm, clear mind. Otherwise, you can easily be carried away by your emotions and become part of the crowd instead of a serene observer of the phenomena playing out before you.

The stock market is a fascinating world. Nobody in the stock market ever knows everything, and everyone must work constantly to improve and to learn more. But there are always challenges to be met and difficulties to be overcome.

I hope you have found this book useful and enjoyable.

GLOSSARY

annual meeting A meeting held once a year at which company management reports the year's financial results to stockholders and at which the board of directors, the highest decision-making body of a corporation, stands for election.

annual report A report issued once a year to stockholders stating a corporation's financial condition.

bar chart A chart commonly used in technical analysis, based on daily, weekly, or monthly data. The vertical axis represents price, the horizontal axis represents time. For each new unit of time, for example, one day, a vertical bar is plotted from the day's high to the day's low. On the right side of the bar, a small tic is plotted to identify the closing price. Sometimes a small tic is also plotted on the left side of the bar to identify the opening price. For every new unit of time, you move one bar to the right. Volume is usually plotted by a vertical bar under the price at the bottom of the chart. All charts in this book are price bar and volume charts. (See Figure G.1.)

bear A market participant who believes the market or prices will fall.

bear market A long-term trend of falling market prices; can last from several months to years.

bid The highest price a prospective buyer is willing to pay for a security at a given moment.

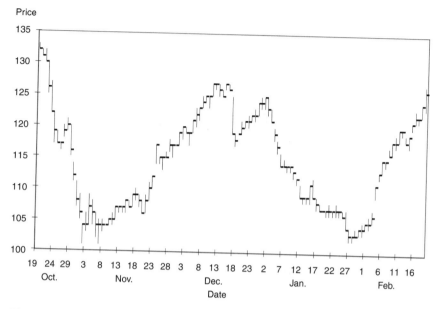

Figure G.1. This is an example of a *bar chart*. Observe that volume is not plotted in the chart.

bid/offer　The lowest price at which anyone is willing to buy (bid) a security at a given moment versus the highest price at which someone else is willing sell (offer) that security.

breakout　A distinct and forceful price movement out of a range that goes above or below previous levels of resistance or support at the top or the bottom of the range. Usually, these movements are accompanied by rising volume.

broker, brokerage　A person or firm that acts as an intermediary between buyers and sellers of securities and charges a commission for each transaction.

bull　A market participant who believes the market or prices will rise.

bull market　A long-term trend of rising market prices; can last from many months to years.

buy signal In technical analysis, a recognizable chart pattern thought to be indicative of an upward future price development.

commission The fee charged by a broker or a brokerage firm for buying and selling securities for the accounts of customers.

consolidation phase A period in which prices stay in a relatively narrow range and do not break out either up or down.

consumer price index (CPI) The most common index used to measure change in consumer prices and, thus, inflation.

corporation A legal entity separate and distinct from its owners, with only limited liability, whose ownership is easily transferred through the sale of stock.

dividend That portion of a company's earnings that is distributed to the stockholders.

Federal funds rate (Fed funds rate) The rate banks charge each other for overnight loans to meet overnight reserve requirements. The Fed funds rate is a highly sensitive indicator for interest rates.

Federal Open Market Committee (FOMC) Committee comprised of members of the Federal Reserve Board and others that sets short-term monetary policy and interest rates.

Federal Reserve Board Governing body of the Federal Reserve System; consists of a group of seven members appointed by the U.S. president and is responsible for setting the monetary policy of the United States and for regulating interest rates, banking requirements, and margins applied to the purchase of securities.

Federal Reserve System (the Fed) The central bank system of the United States; consists of 12 regional Federal Reserve banks that regulate U.S. monetary policy and the U.S. banking system.

gross national product (GNP) The total value of all goods and services produced in a country.

growth company   A company in which both profit and turnover are expected to grow at a fast pace. These companies are often found in the high-technology sector and in information technology, biotechnology, medical technology, and other sectors such as the pharmaceutical industry and Internet media.

irrational   Illogical, unreasonable, or ill-considered; lacking normal cohesiveness and clarity of thought.

latent   A term usually used in regard to dormant but real buying interest or selling pressure characterized by buyers and sellers waiting for the "right" price before taking action.

limit order   An instruction to buy or to sell securities at a specific price level or better.

market order   An instruction to buy or to sell at the best current market price.

point and figure (P&F) charts   Charts used in technical analysis, ignoring small price fluctuations, that more easily identify price patterns. Volume is not plotted in P&F charts. A rise in price is recorded with *X*s, and a fall in price is recorded with *O*s. These changes are recorded only if the price has changed a certain number of units or percentage points. In the computer-drawn Ericsson chart (Figure G.2), a white box indicates the beginning of a new month, and a black box indicates the beginning of a new year.

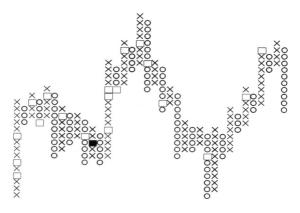

Figure G.2.   Point and figure chart—Ericsson Chart.

portfolio manager   A manager designated to handle investments on behalf of individuals or institutions; usually has full authority to make investment decisions.

quarterly report   A report on a company's financial condition that is issued four times a year.

range   Period of time during which a stock price swings between two obvious high and low price levels (i.e., a price moving sideways).

rational   Characterized by reason, logic, and the application of common sense.

realized gain or loss   A profit or a loss resulting from the sale of a security.

securities and Exchange Commission (SEC)   A federal agency charged with supervising U.S. stock markets.

sell signal   In technical analysis, a recognizable chart pattern thought to be indicative of downward future price development.

selling short   Sale of a security that the seller borrows at the time of sale to deliver to the buyer with the intention of buying the security back at a lower price in order to take advantage of an anticipated decline in price. The person having a short position is liable for delivery of the security sold until the position is bought back.

share   Unit of ownership in a company represented by a certificate entitling the owner to a share of the company's profits and to a vote at the corporation's annual general meeting.

solar plexus   An important nerve center located in the abdomen just in front of the diaphragm.

stock   A symbol of part ownership in a corporation; represents the right to receive a share in the profits of that corporation.

stockholder   A person who owns stock.

stock market   An electronic-based auction market or a trading floor where the members of the stock exchange meet to buy and sell securities.

stock register   A record of stockholders in a corporation.

technical analysis   Theories and methods or models for studying price, volume, and time factors for the purpose of predicting the most probable direction of certain markets or securities without regard to fundamental data such as quality of management or products or services the company produces.

trading range   *See* range.

traditional technical analysis   The study and analysis of patterns identifiable through bar and point and figure charts as an aid to predicting future price trends. These charts were first plotted by hand, but the advent of computers has enhanced the capabilities of technical analysis dramatically, allowing for the combination of variables such as price, volume, and time to create an almost infinite number of charts. Though they are excellent tools, computers are not essential to the study of bar or point and figure charts, which is why the term "traditional technical analysis" is used in this book to refer to these methods.

BIBLIOGRAPHY

Barach, Roland. *Mindtraps:Unlocking the Key to Investment Success*, Raleigh, NC: Van K. Tharp Associates, 1996.

Beckman, Robert. *Crashes*. London: Sidgwick & Jackson, 1988.

Barberis, Nicholas. "Mispricing or Risk? A Closer Look at Some Stock Market Puzzles." Presented at seminar titled *The Fourth Major European Programme on Behavioural Finance*. London, England: November 1999.

Bernhardsson, Jonas, *Tradingguiden*. Stockholm: Ficher and Co., 1996.

Brown, Constance. *Aerodynamic Trading*. N.p.: New Classics, 1995.

Fuller, David. *The Chart Seminar Workbook*. London: Chart Analysis Ltd., Suite 1.23, Plaza, 535 Kings Road, London SW 10 0SZ, United Kingdom.

Kindleberger, Charles P. *Manias, Panics, and Crashes*. New York: John Wiley & Sons, 1996.

Le Bon, Gustave. *The Crowd*. Marietta, GA: Cherokee Publishing, 1982.

Livermore, Jesse L. *How to Trade in Stocks: The Livermore Formula for Combining Time, Element, and Price*. Reprint, Greenville, SC: Traders Press, 1991.

Mackay, Charles. *Extraordinary Popular Delusions and the Madness of Crowds*. Reprint, New York: Harmony Books, Crown Publishers, 1980.

Plummer, Tony. *Forecasting Financial Markets*. London: Kogan Page, 1993.

Sarnoff, Paul. *Jesse Livermore—Speculator King*. Greenville, SC: Traders Press, 1985.

Sperandeo, Victor. *Trader Vic—Methods of a Wall Street Master.* New York: John Wiley & Sons, 1991.

Taylor, Richard H. "Managing and Investing Rationally in an Irrational World." Presented at seminar titled *Program on Investment Decisions and Behavioral Finance,* Harvard University, Cambridge, Massachusetts, November 1997.

Tharp, Van K. *Investment Psychology Guides.* Cary, N.C.: International Institute of Trading Mastery Inc., 1992. 8308 Belgium Street, Raleigh, NC 27606.

Tharp, Van K. *Trade Your Way to Financial Freedom.* New York: McGraw-Hill, 1998.

Toghraie, Adrienne Laris, and Murray A. Ruggiero Jr. *Traders' Secrets: Psychological and Technical Analyses.* Cary, NC/East Haven, CT: On Target Press/Ruggiero Press, 1999. Trading on Target, 100 Lavewood Lane, Cary, NC 27511.

INDEX